IMAGES
of America

NEWPORT

AND THE NORTHEAST KINGDOM

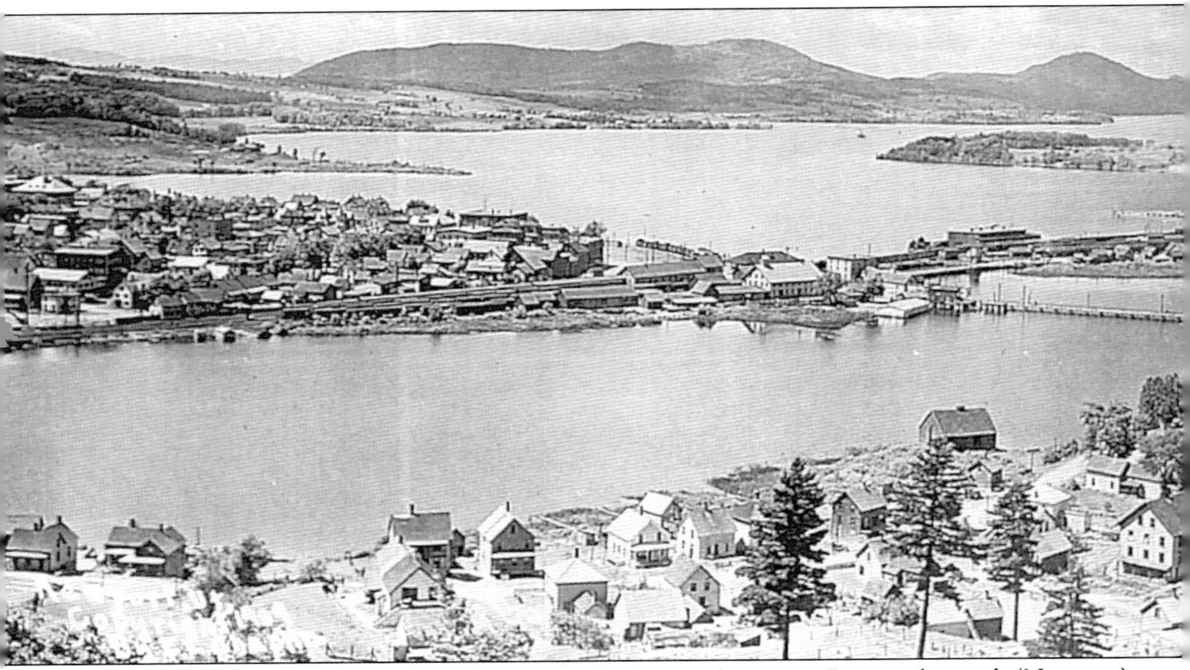

Here in the Northeast Kingdom of Vermont, the first settlement in Duncansborough (Newport) began on the Lake Road, on the west shore of Lake Memphremagog in 1793. Other scattered settlements surrounding the lake followed. In 1820, the Village of Newport was a dense wilderness of large pine trees. Log canoes were used to ferry local Indians and early settlers across the international waters of the lake, where the imaginary boundary line between Vermont and Canada can be found only six miles north of the village.

Dedication

Dedicated to my husband and children, Kelly Shawn, Timothy, and Heather, and to grandchildren who will carry on our love for our adopted city of Newport on Lake Memphremagog and for the Green Mountain State of Vermont.

IMAGES
of America

NEWPORT
AND THE NORTHEAST KINGDOM

Barbara Kaiser Malloy

ARCADIA
PUBLISHING

ISBN 978-0-7385-0298-1

Published by Arcadia Publishing
Charleston, South Carolina

Printed in the United States of America

Library of Congress Catalog Card Number: Applied for.

For all general information contact Arcadia Publishing at:
Telephone 843-853-2070
Fax 843-853-0044
E-mail sales@arcadiapublishing.com
For customer service and orders:
Toll-Free 1-888-313-8665

Visit us on the Internet at www.arcadiapublishing.com

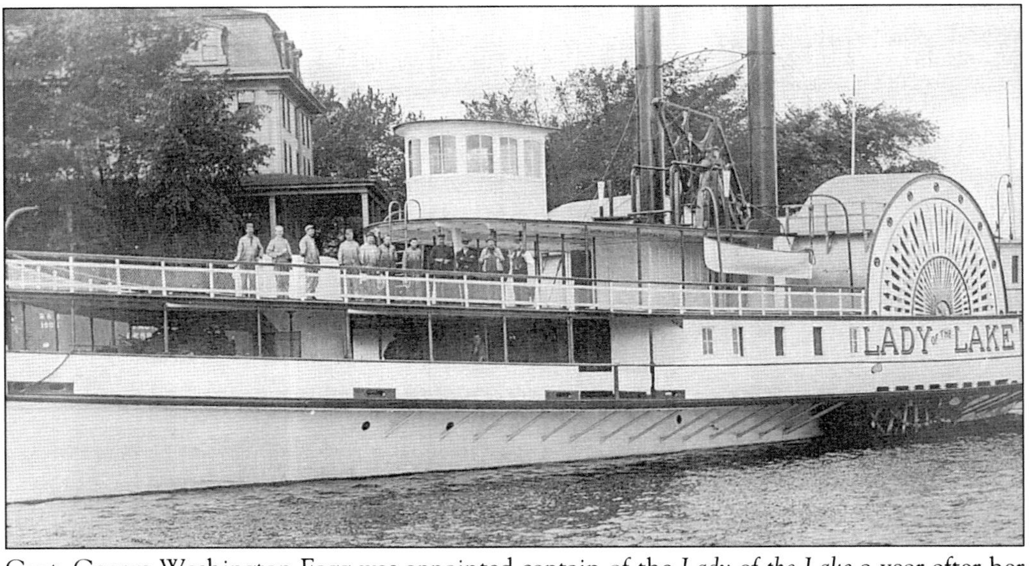

Capt. George Washington Fogg was appointed captain of the *Lady of the Lake* a year after her maiden voyage in 1868. This famous steamer was the largest paddlewheel steamer on the lake and could carry 500 to 800 passengers; it made two trips a day from Newport to Magog, Quebec. The *Lady of the Lake* is docked at Newport's Steamboat Wharf to accommodate the guests at the famous Memphremagog Hotel as shown in this old photograph.

Contents

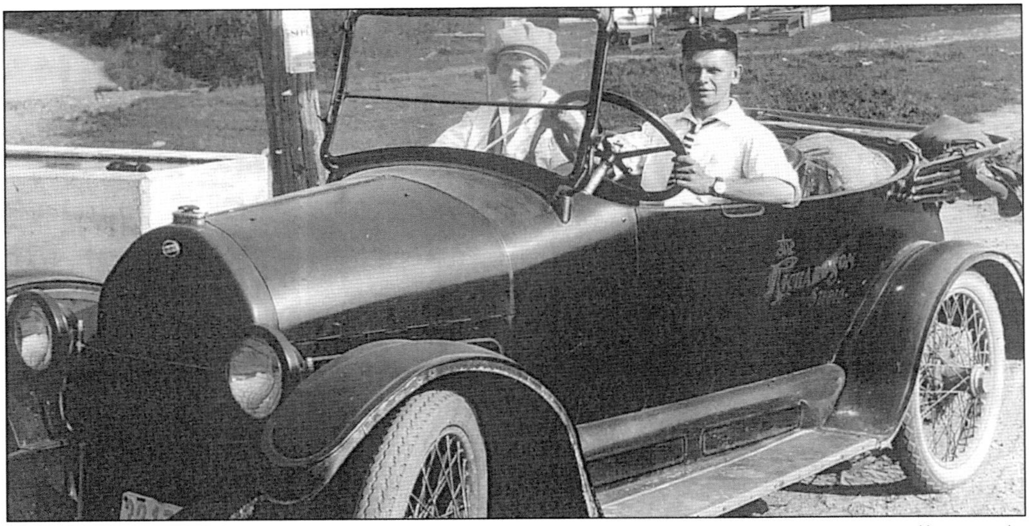

Pictured are Mr. and Mrs. Harry W. Richardson. (Courtesy of Richardson Cartee Collection.)

ACKNOWLEDGMENTS

My sincere appreciation is extended to my friends, my new friends, and those who shared in my enthusiasm with their entrusted photographs or with historical or harmonious story elements.

Thank you Ranson (Bill) Adams; Reginald Alexander; Dana Blanchard; Robert Bigelow; Beautiful Waters; City of Newport; Chet Carpenter; Joan Carpenter; Joan Scott Curtis; Curtis-Britch Funeral Homes; Richard Davis, M.D., Ph.D.; Derby Historical Society; Michael Dunn; Hazel Blake Fountaine; Frontier Crossroads; Goodrich Memorial Library; Cynthia and Richard Hall; Jessie Hamblett; Haskell Free Library and Opera House; Loretta Hilliker; History of Derby; History of Orleans County; Cora Johnson; Judy Kavanagh; David Kelly; late Mildred Kendall; Memphremagog Historical Society of Newport; Lorraine Maloney; Lucille Gardner Mooney; Monsic Lodge #65, Newport; Anne Taylor Moore; Delores Moore; John and Lois Moore;, Mary Ann Mulkin; Marvin and Carol Needleman; Emily Nelson; Emily Newcomb; Newport Daily Express; Orleans County Historical Society, Richardson-Cartee Collection; Robert and Janet Orr; Evelyn Palin; Mr. and Mrs. Philip Prangley; David Provencher; June Quigley; Pat Rumery; Edith Selby; Successful Vermonters; Richard Scott; St. Mary Star of the Sea Church; Stanstead Historical Society, Quebec; Don Whipple Studio; Gilbert Whipple; and Dale Woods.

Last, but by no means least, special thanks to Harriet Fletcher Fisher of Lyndonville, who encouraged me to follow my dream of bringing the Northeast Kingdom of Vermont's history alive for all to enjoy today, and for future generations.

The Richardson-Cartee Collection of photographer's original glass and celluloid negatives was presented by Roger Cartee of Newport and made available to the Orleans County Historical Society. With the support of the Orleans County Historical Society, credited photographs have been entrusted to be used in the publication of this book.

Harry Wendall Richardson, son of James and Myrtle (Rockwell) Richardson, was born March 9, 1894, in Newport. In 1915, Harry married Alice Whitter of Massachusetts. Upon his return with his bride, he had his first photography studio and art supply shop in 1918 on East Main Street. With his wife, Alice, as a lifetime associate and specialist in studio portraits of children, their business was known as the Photo Craft Shop and Richardson Studio.

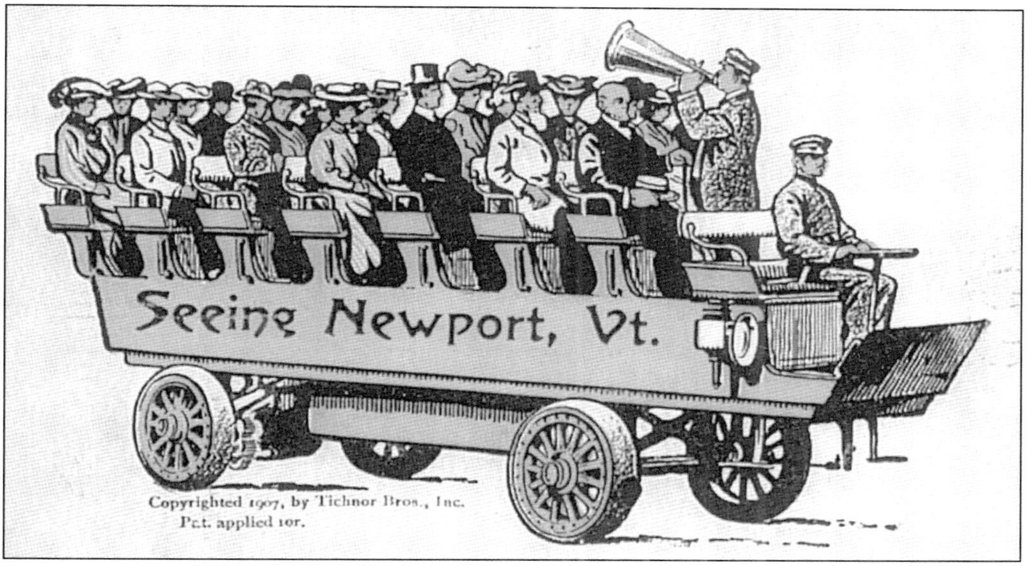

Introduction

Welcome . . . to a pictorial nostalgia portfolio of photographs and captions that capture our wistful yearning to go back and take a "peek" at an era gone by.

Come and join us as we "hobnob" with folks from olden days in the villages of Newport City and Newport Center Town on Lake Memphremagog; West Derby and Derby Center; and Derby Line, Beebe, and North Derby. We will go back in time and re-visit their homes, farms, businesses, hotels, summer resorts, historic landmarks, or go aboard the old steam boats and railroad trains as we reminisce here on the Vermont/Canadian border in the Northeast Kingdom of Vermont.

Come travel north across the international border up Lake Memphremagog where the earliest inhabitants were the Abenaki Indians, one of the many Algonquiam nations who lived and hunted along the lake and fished in its waters. Re-visit the famous summer resort of the Mountain House Hotel that once stood at Owl's Head Mountain, Province of Quebec, in the late 1800s where both Vermonters and Canadians enjoyed a Gilded Age.

The Village of Newport's Main Street was the same type as pictured in any small village of the late 1800s, with businesses, houses, fenced in yards, shade trees, dirt roads, and the customary hitching rails and posts. The town's charter was signed in 1801; on October 30, 1816, Vermont legislators changed the name to Newport.

Batesville was a hamlet west of Newport Village, which boarded on Prouty Bay and was annexed to Newport in 1895. On March 5, 1918, Newport and West Derby joined in forming the new City of Newport. The first city council members were Mayor Curtis S. Emery, W.R. Prouty, Ernest W. Savage, James T. Gardner, and Harry A. Black.

TIDBITS OF THE TOWNS

The Village of Newport Center Town was chartered on October 30, 1802. Brothers Abail and Hallet Adams made the first clearing at the crossroads where Vance Hill and Bridge Street once met on Main Street.

George Little Sleeper, Esq., was known as the "Father of Newport Center." Sleeper, Esq., ran a hotel on the corner of Bridge Street where the Newport Creek once ran under the covered bridge. The first shingle and sawmills stood here before the first railroad station was built.

Formerly a part of the Town of Salem, West Derby grew from a barely settled area in 1800 into a forceful industrial and residential area.

Among the earliest settlers in West Derby, the Dane Brothers arrived in 1815 and built mills on the Clyde River. In 1820, Capt. John Sias of West Derby purchased the point of land where Newport City now stands for $250.

The causeway was once called Sawdust Avenue, due to the fact that swampland near the Clyde River had been filled in with shavings and saw dust from the International Mill near the lake.

The Town of Derby consisted of Derby Center, Derby Line, Beebe, and North Derby and was chartered on October 20, 1779.

Derby Center was established when Capt. Timothy Hinman made the first permanent settlement near Mills and Kilborn Hills. The earliest industries and mills were built and centered around the wooden covered bridge over the Clyde River.

The Town of Beebe, bordered on the north by Beebe, Quebec, Canada, is a small village named after its first settler Zebulon Beebe in 1796.

"Can-USA" Street, known as the friendliest "unguarded border in the world," runs in the center of the street. The houses on the south side are in Beebe, Vermont, and those on the north side are in Beebe, Quebec, Canada.

The Village of Derby Line, located four miles north of Derby Center, is one of the largest ports of entry and is closely associated with life across the Tomifolia River in Canada. Derby Line, Rock Island, and Stanstead, Quebec, are known as the Three Villages.

In 1879, a Derby Line businessman, Lewis Young, invented the Axle Cutter, patented in the United States and Canada, and formed a partnership with Colonel F.D. Butterfield. The first foundry factory was located atop of Foundry Hill, in Rock Island, Quebec.

North Derby, on Lake Memphremagog, known as Lake Park, Pine Bluff, and Eagle Point, saw summer cottages in the 1880s, when farm land was leased; it soon became a social center for the region.

One

Newport City-Newport Center on Lake Memphremagog

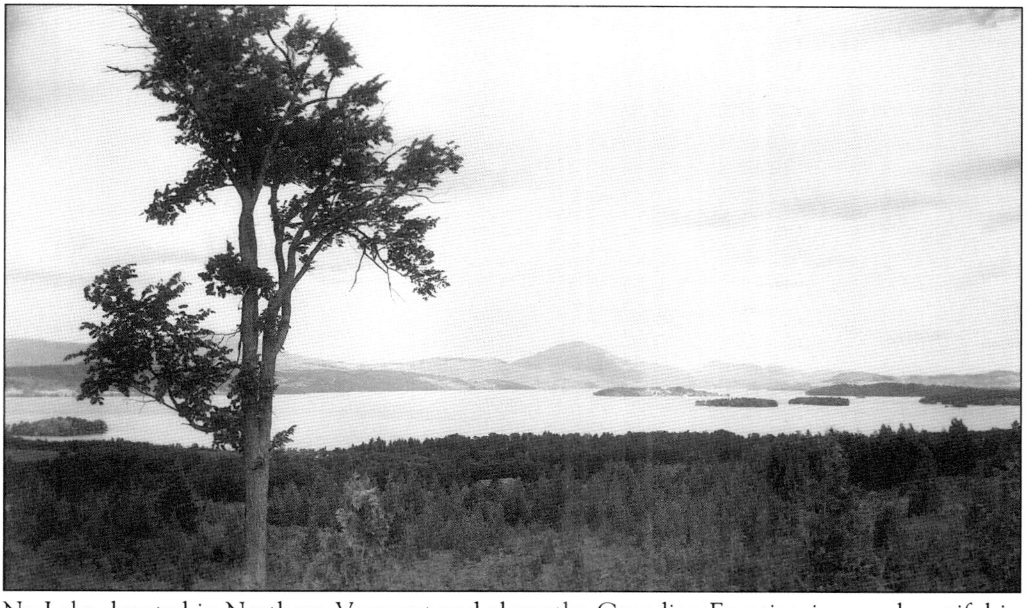

No Lake, located in Northern Vermont and along the Canadian Frontier, is more beautiful in appearance than Lake Memphremagog or the "Geneva of Canada." Vermont's North Country is the crown jewel of the Northeast Kingdom, where Newport lies at the head of the lake, nestled here on the U.S. and Canadian border. This area has a "legend" of a sea serpent, which inhabits the international waters. (Courtesy of Richardson Cartee Collection.)

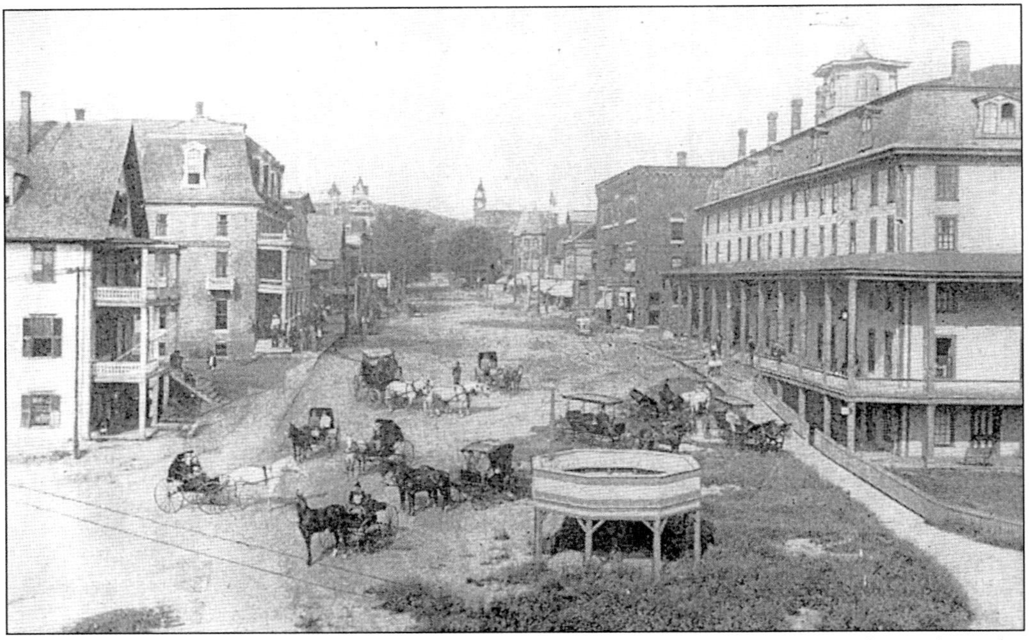

All the teams seen at Railroad Square on Main Street in this 1890s photograph are from the stables of Pratt and McQueen, proprietors of the Memphremagog Stables, once located behind the hotel near the lake. They also owned the Newport Hotel livery sale and feed stables. These teams could be furnished to parties or individuals at short notice, with or without drivers.

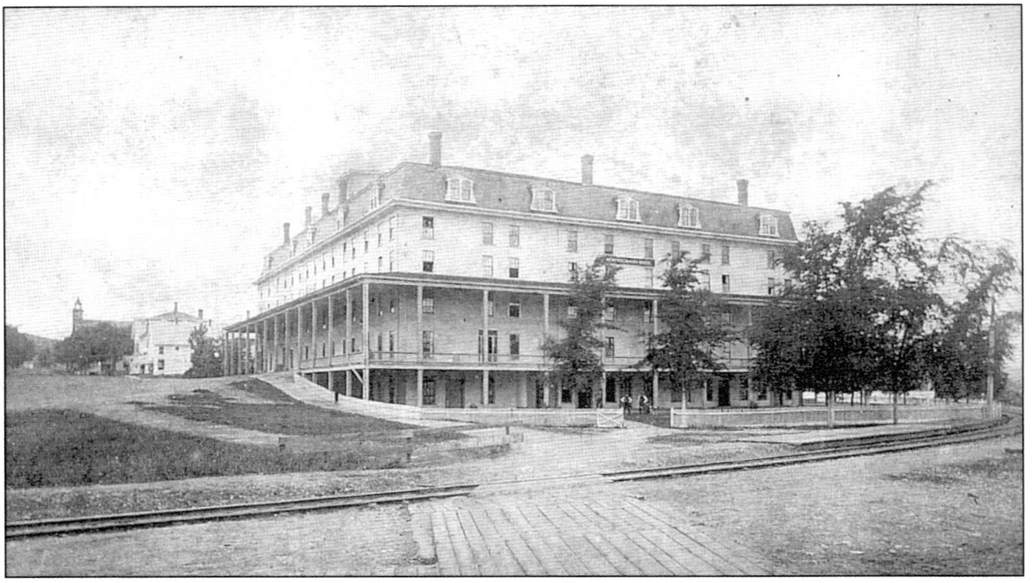

Three famous hotels once stood near the lake at Railroad Square, including the Memphremagog Hotel built in 1838; the Hurt's Hotel, located across the street and built in 1871 near the tracks; and the Bellevue Hotel, built in 1873, and known as the Newport Hotel after 1878.

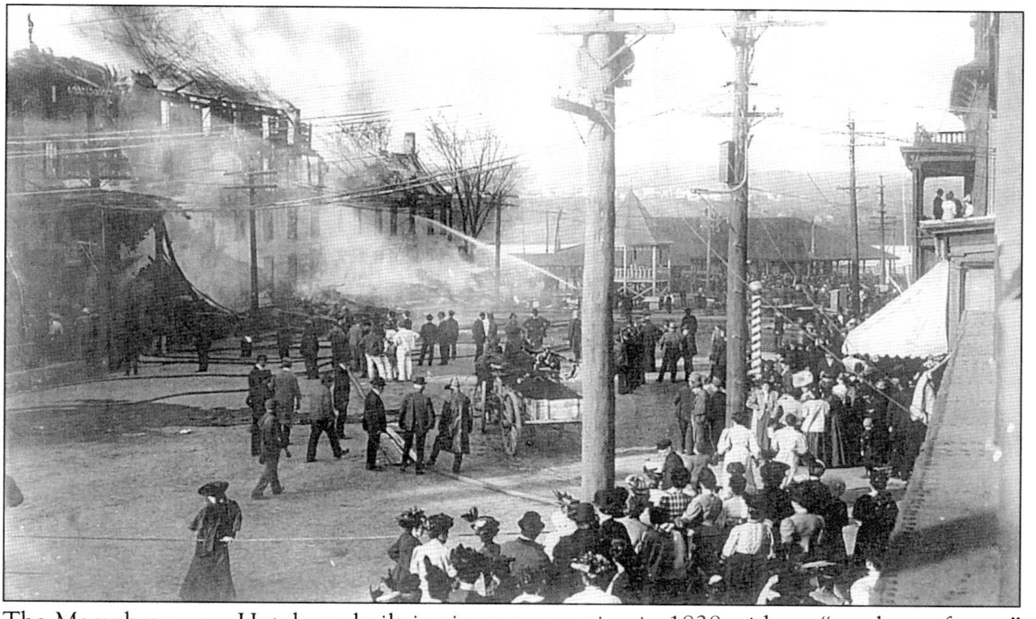

The Memphremagog Hotel was built in six stages starting in 1838 with an "axe hewn frame." By the 1890s, the hotel contained rooms for 400 guests and spacious piazzas that overlooked the lake and the Green Mountains of Vermont, providing quality that surpassed most hotels. The hotel, where the *Lady of the Lake* once docked at her wharf, was destroyed, as seen in this photograph, when a fire left nothing but a smoldering heap of ashes on May 15, 1907.

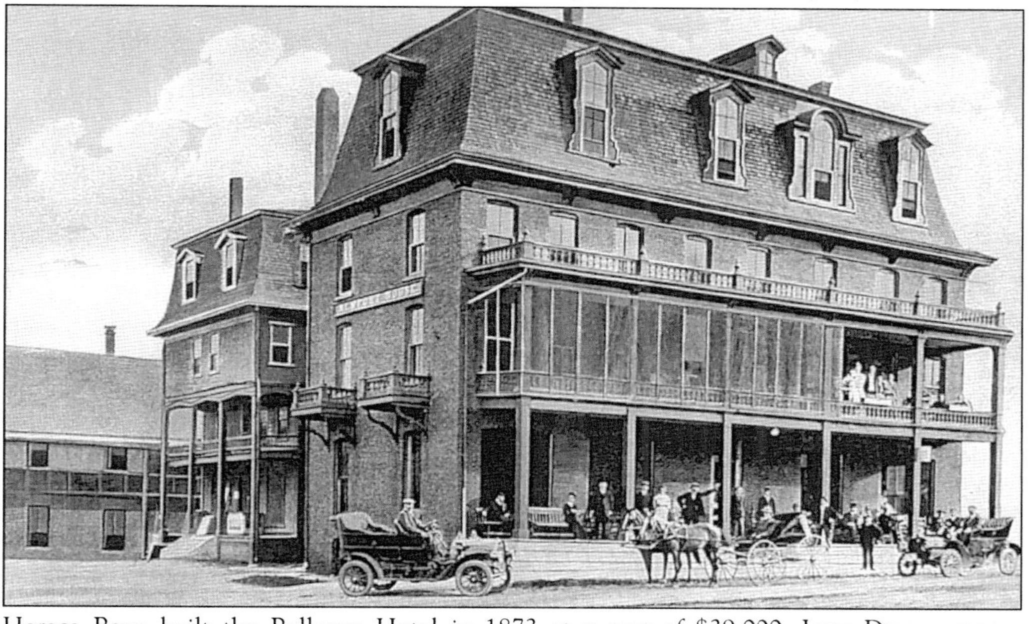

Horace Bean built the Bellevue Hotel in 1873 at a cost of $39,000. Jerry Drew, veteran hotelkeeper and stagecoach driver, purchased the hotel in 1878 and renamed it the Newport Hotel. Drew made the best repairs, along with new "hair mattresses" in each guestroom. On May 15, 1973, when the sun set, the famous Newport Hotel closed its doors and was torn down, leaving a heritage of memories.

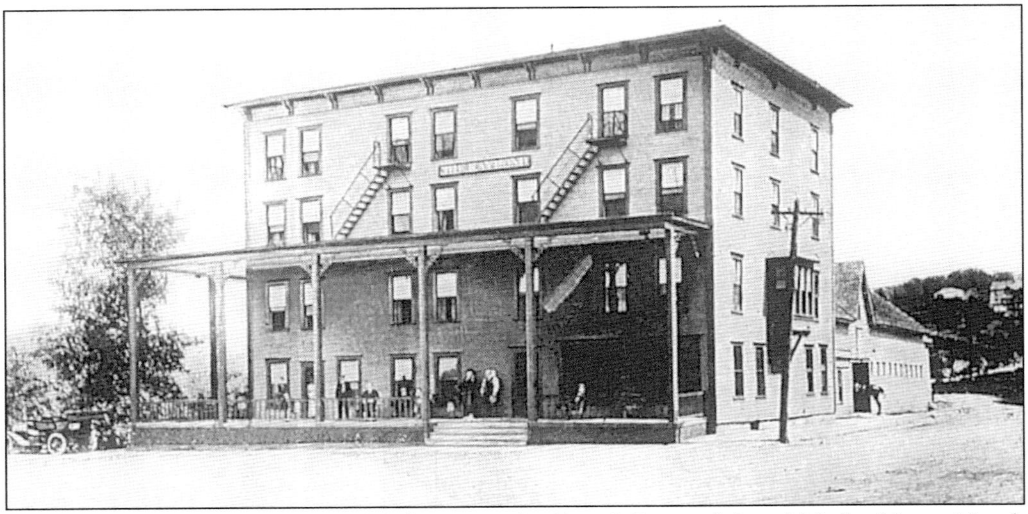

The Raymond House was remodeled in 1893 by David Sisco of the old Lake House Hotel, located near the wooden bridge at Railroad Square. Before the 1890s, there was the "villages first car-wash," or "buggy-wash," on this site. A platform was built to extend out over the lake and was used by the town's residents as a place to wash their wagons or buggies.

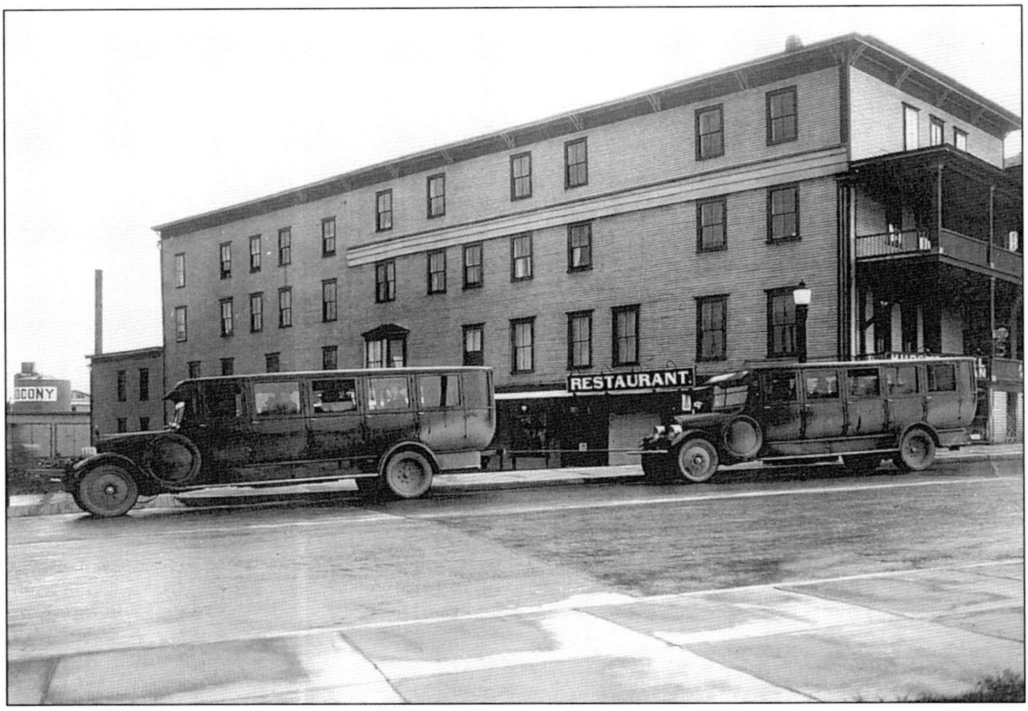

The Hurt's Hotel and Restaurant, built in 1871, stood near the railroad tracks, allowing easy access for railroad men and travelers to eat and sleep. The old hotel, once known as the Drew Block, headed for destruction in 1943; razing was delayed by the owners until after World War II.

At the Lane Opera House, the "Kake Walk" was won by Newport dancers, seen here from left to right, Beatrice Skinner Black and Mildred Pomeroy Kendall, who performed in the Young People's Minstrels on April 15, 1919.

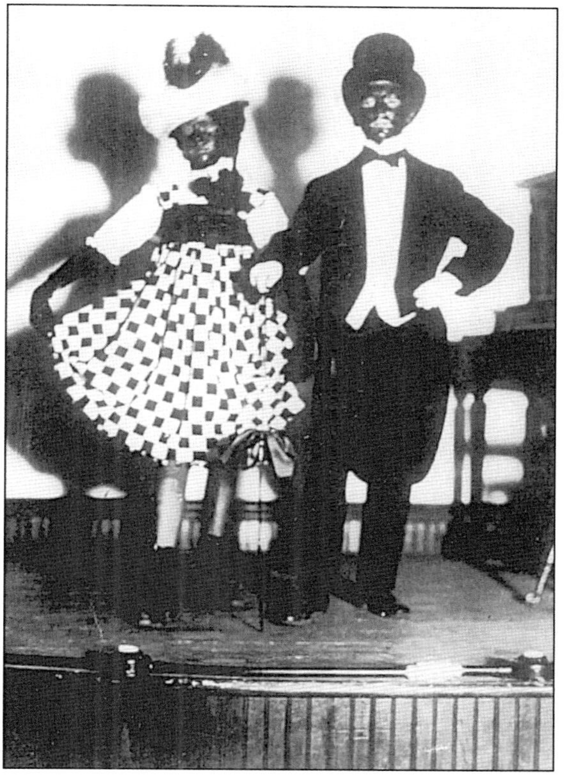

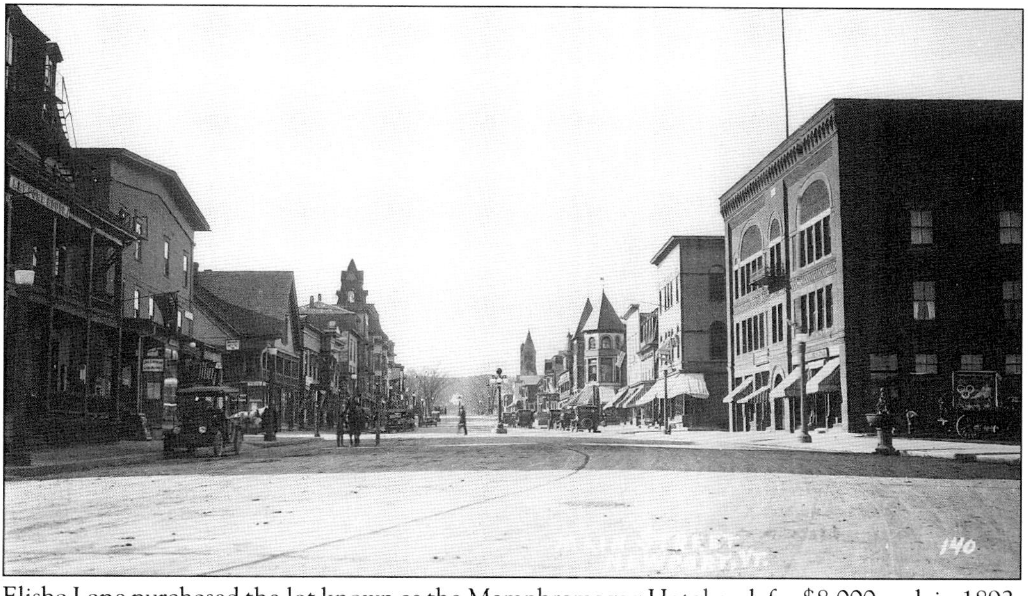

Elisha Lane purchased the lot known as the Memphremagog Hotel park for $8,000 and, in 1892, erected the Lane and Son Block, shown in this photograph on the right with Lane's dry good business on the first floor. On the third floor was the famous Opera House, designed to seat 800 people with folding chairs, balcony, elegant electric chandeliers, and foot lights. (Courtesy of Richardson Cartee Collection.)

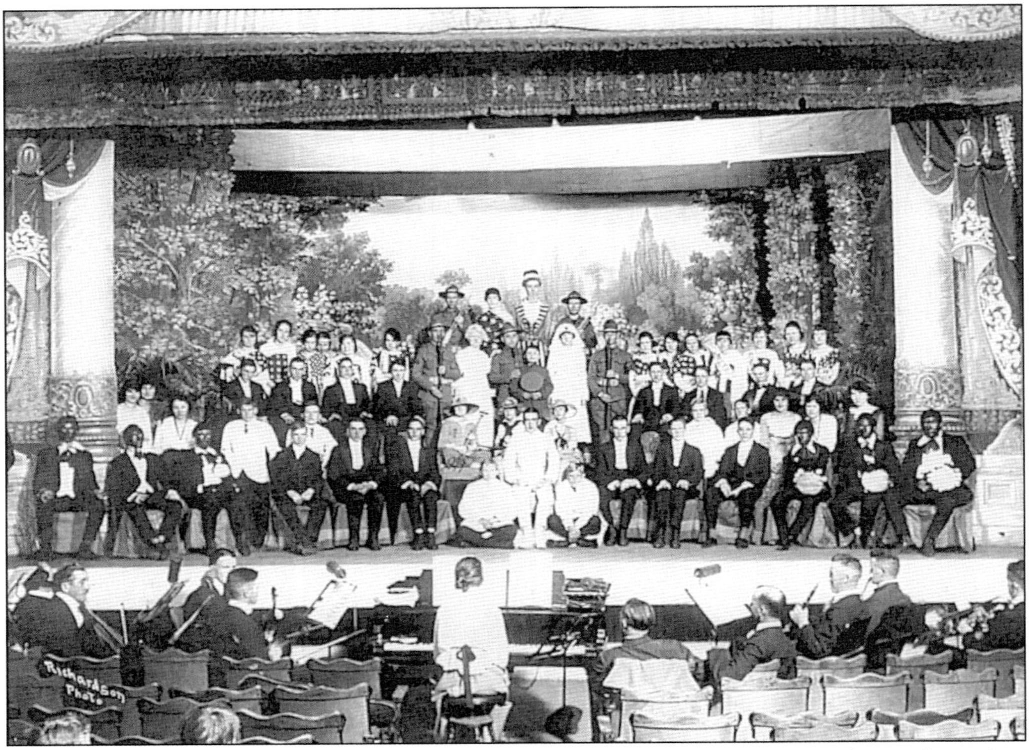

At the Lane Opera House on April 15, 1919, the "Young People's Minstrels" performed to benefit the Newport City Hospital Fund. The minstrel's show people, black face comedians (white actors), singers, and dancers arrived at the Newport Railroad station, then paraded up Main Street with great "fanfare," which was their way of advertising.

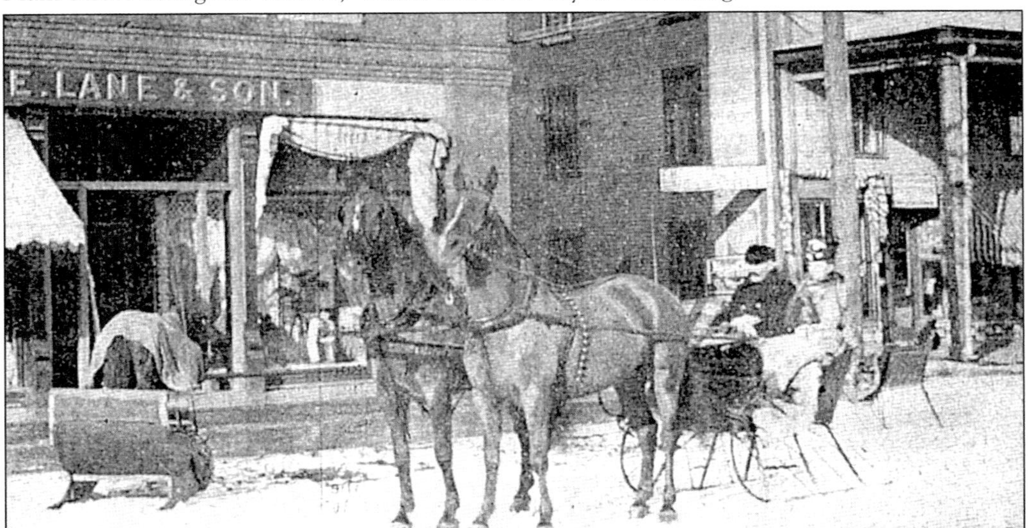

Herbert E. Lane, son of Elisha, and wife Charlotte pose in front of his E. Lane and Son store, in 1907, along with their two horses named Floradora and Buttermilk. A fire broke out on December 6, 1923, and destroyed this historical landmark on Main Street.

Fifty-year country merchant Judah E. Foster took his bride Sarah Weeks, whom he married in 1878, to Vermont where he opened an up-to-date men's retail store on Main Street. Foster's real pastime was boating on the lake with his rowboat the Cape Cod Cat; his rabbit dog would come along for the ride.

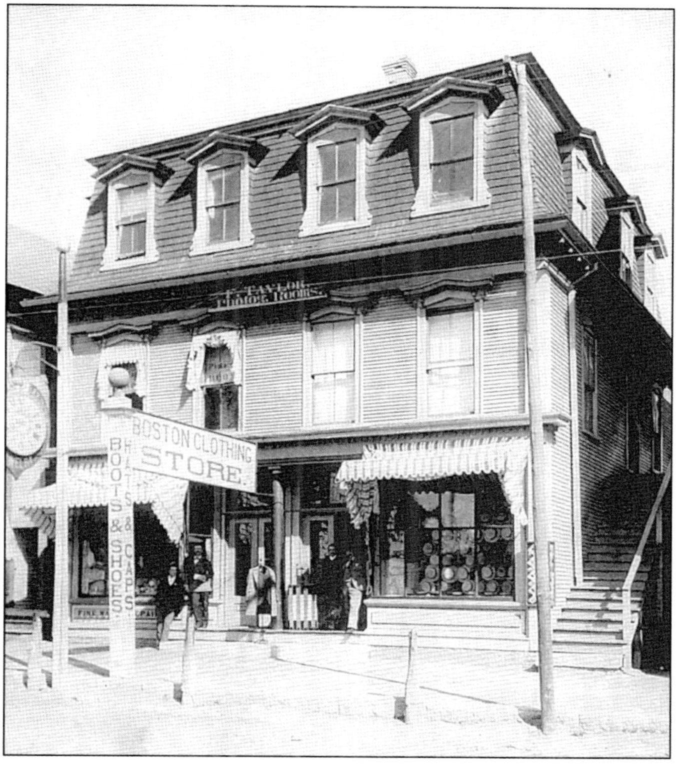

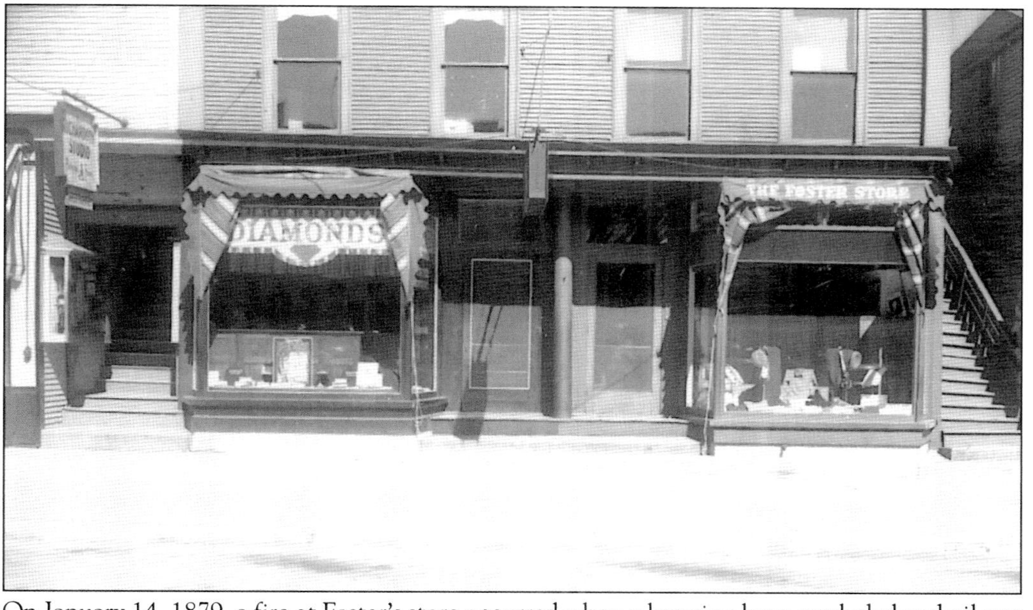

On January 14, 1879, a fire at Foster's store occurred when a hanging lamp exploded and oil was spilled over clothing in a corner window. Parties passing by outside broke open the window and extinguished the flames with plenty of snow. "Never a grudging word abcut the place you live in but something in praise of it" was the motto Foster felt should represent the attitude of any local townsmen. (Courtesy of Richardson Cartee Collection.)

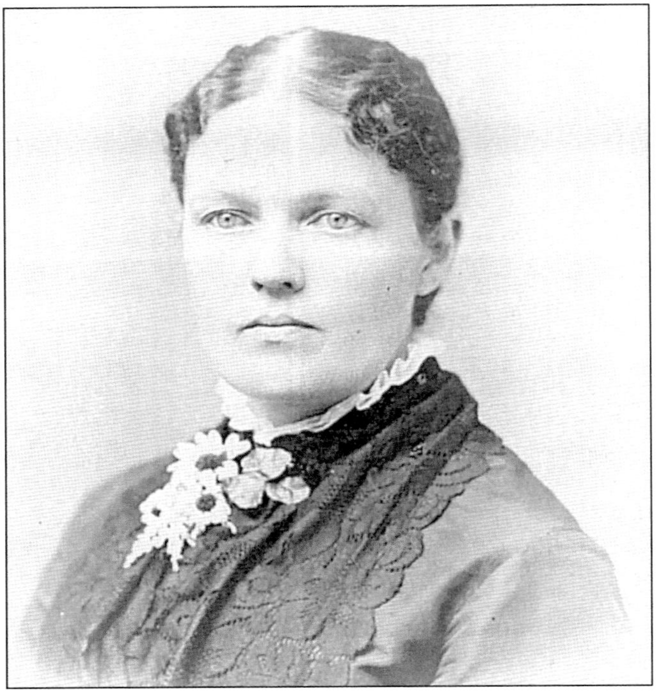

Ellen Jane Wells Green, born in 1847, was daughter of Thomas and Jane Wells and the oldest of nine children. Ellen tended to the family farm in Coventry while her father was away during the Civil War. The wife of Herza Green, Ellen passed away in 1934 leaving behind a daughter, Hattie.

Herza S. Green, born in 1843, was known in musical circles as a member of the first Newport Band in 1860. They played for the *Lady of the Lake* moonlight excursions. Green learned the jewelers trade and bought the business from W.W. Hutchins, closing out his business stock in 1898. Green passed away in 1905.

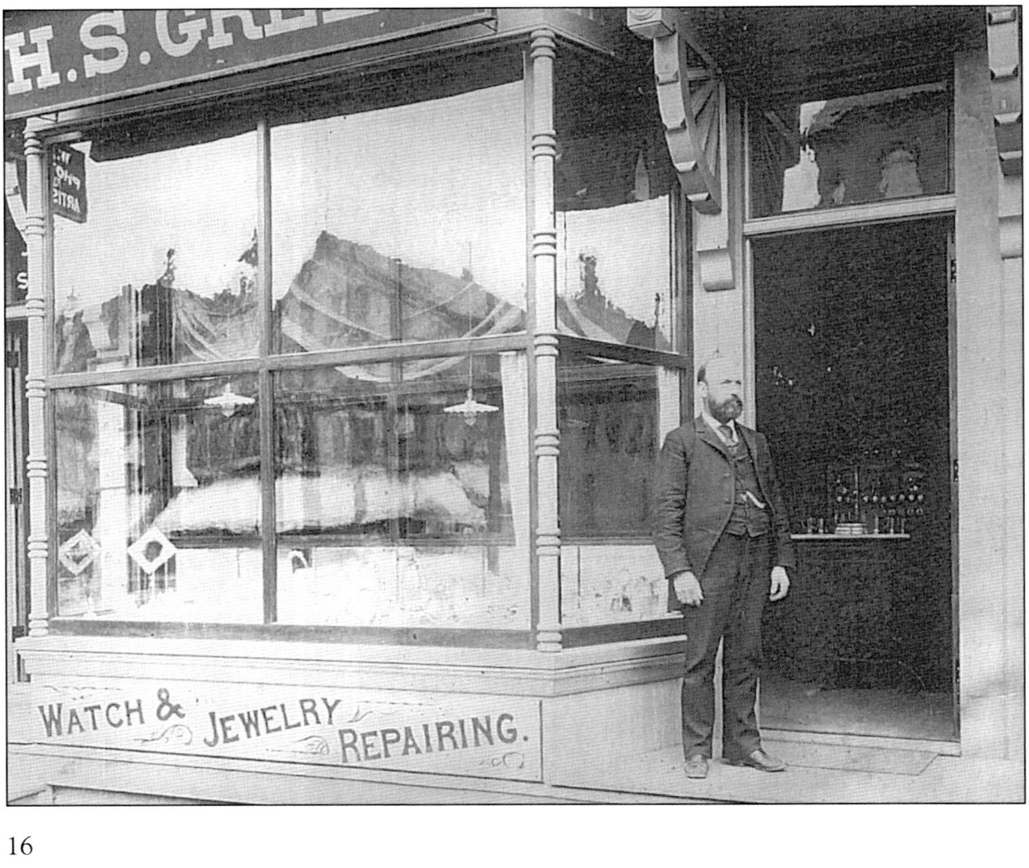

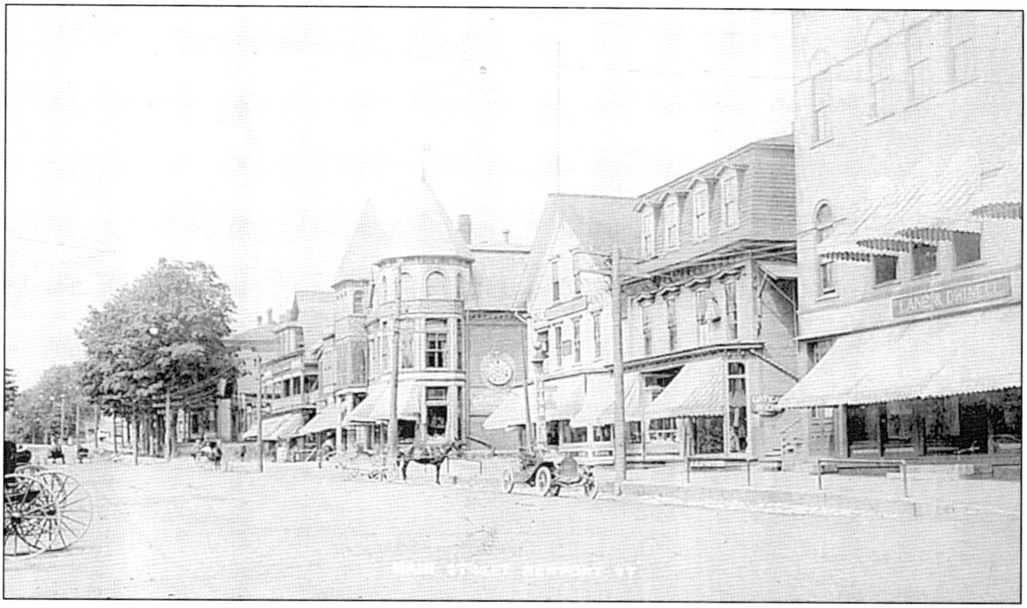

Wilbur W. Hutchins, born 1860 in Newport, was a jeweler, watchmaker, and watch repairer. He was a natural mechanic; by the age of 14, he had repaired his father's watch and made tools for the profession.

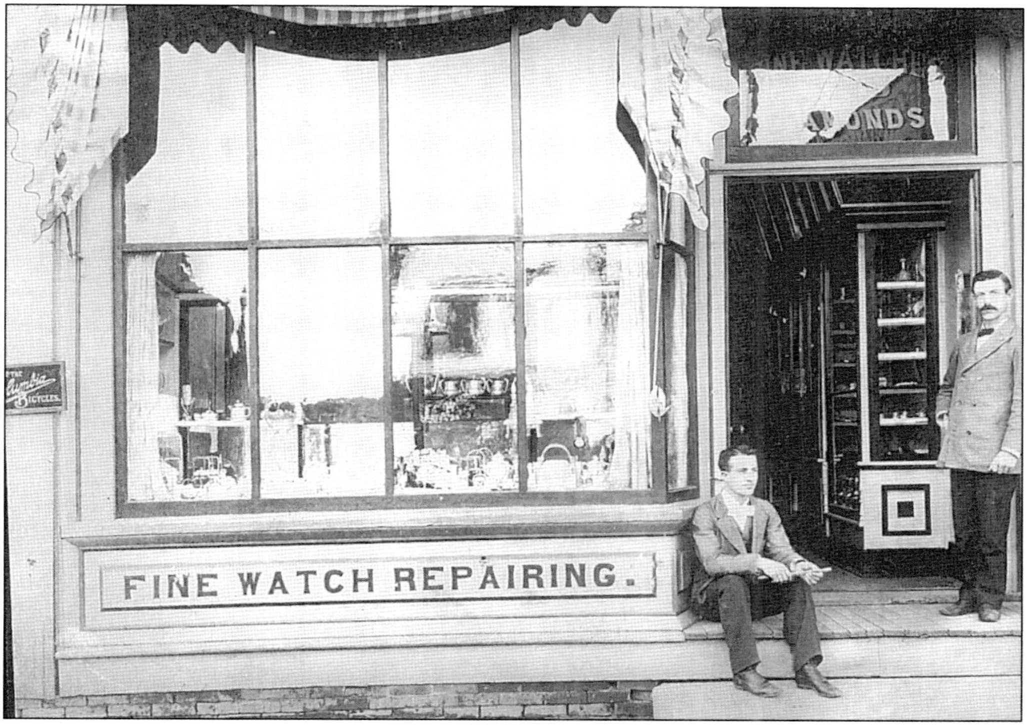

In 1892, Hutchins, seen standing in the doorway of his store, put out an attractive novelty sign in the shape of a watch in front of his store window in the Foster Block. The oversized watch had transparent dials and an electric light that furnished the correct time 24 hours a day.

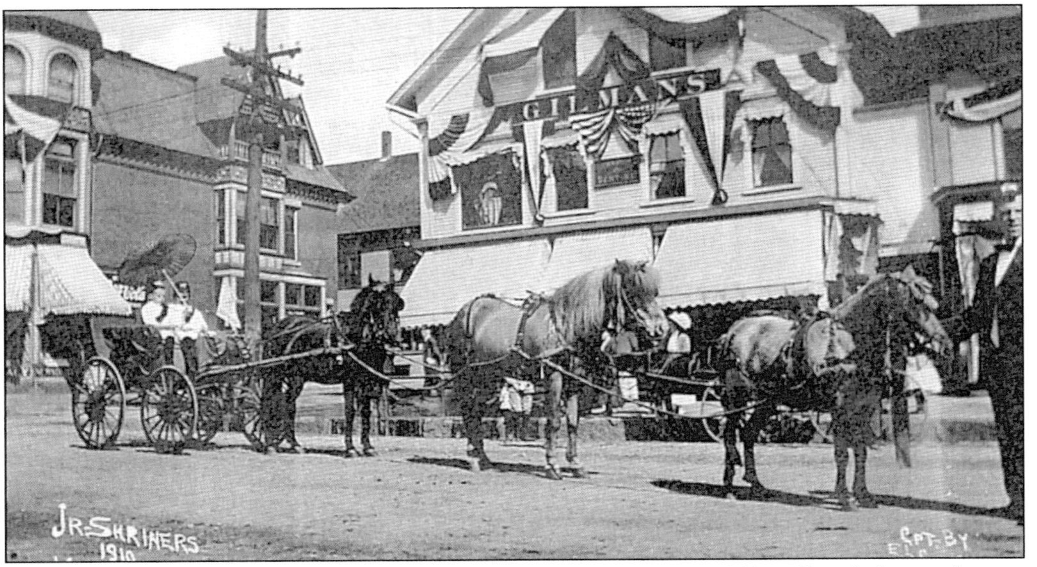

William C. Gilman & Son established a store on Main Street in 1863, selling ladies and mens clothing, millinery, and home furnishings.

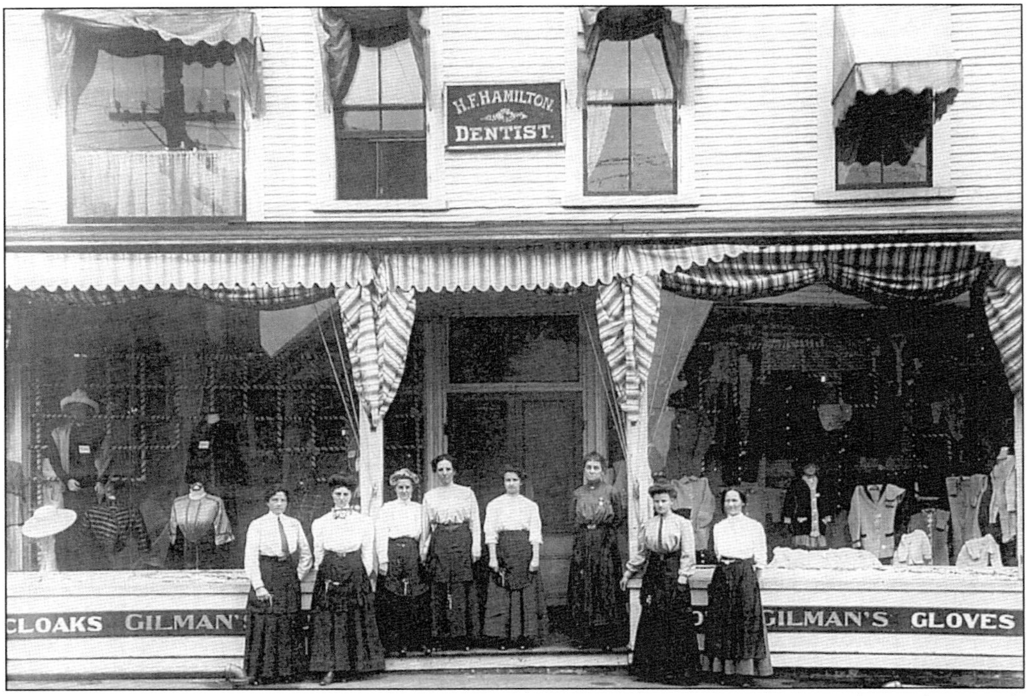

A representative of Gilman's dressmaking department would carry her dressmaking chart with her tape and shears attached to ribbons hanging down her skirt, and folds of fancy silk over her arm. The old Gilman building was the last to go down on December 17, 1996, as demolition crews made way for the new Vermont State Office Complex and Waterfront Development.

James R. Hall was born March 22, 1845, to the Reverend Robert V. Hall and Laura Newton. Hall's Drug Store was founded by James Hall in 1869 in the Colburn Block on Main Street, and was the leading drug store when personal attention was given to the prescription trade.

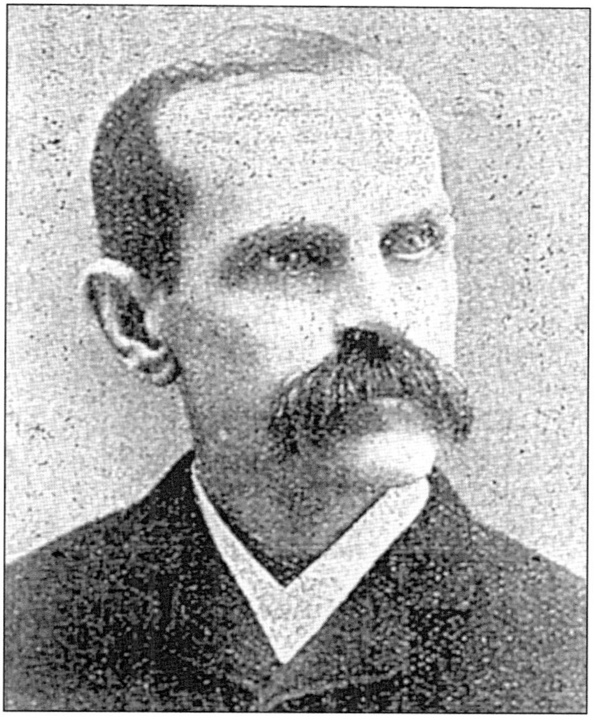

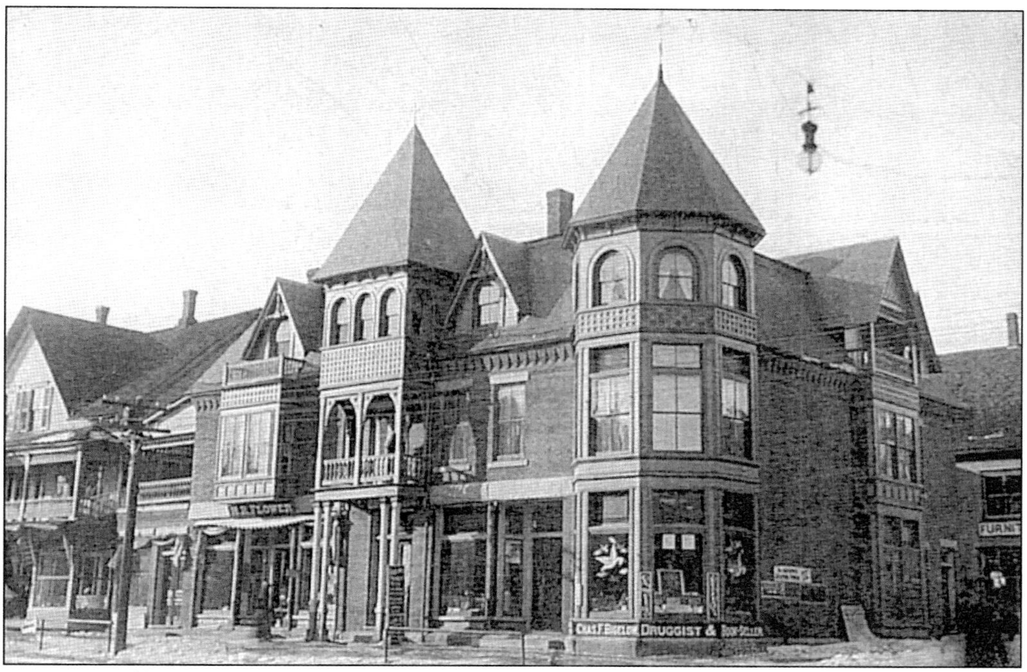

In 1886, Hall erected on the corner of Main and North Avenue a three-story brick- and slate-roof building at a cost of $15,000, with Hall's Drug Store and two other businesses on the first floor. On the second and third floor was the Hall's residence with pleasant views of Main Street and Lake Memphremagog. A suspension bridge ran back to the carriage house and barn.

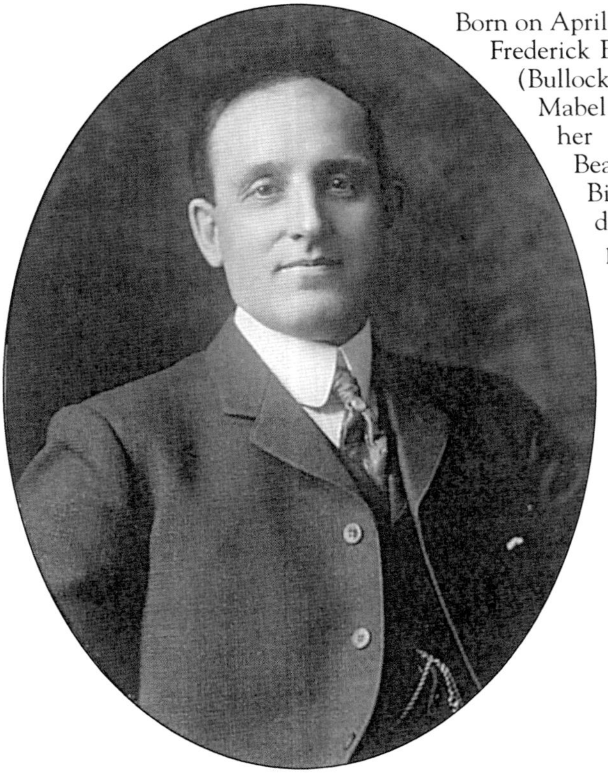

Born on April 26, 1869, in Georgeville, PQ, Charles Frederick Bigelow was the son of Ezra and Mary (Bullock) Bigelow. In 1893, Charles married Mabel Hall and established their home with her mother. They raised two children, Beatrice and Rudolf. By 1910, C.F. Bigelow was a successful business man as director of the National Bank. He was president of the bank at the time of his death on May 6, 1920.

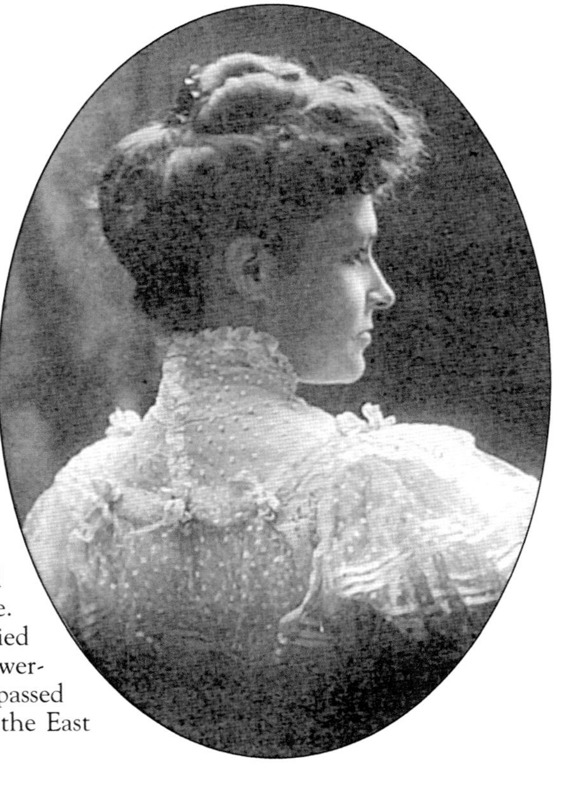

Mabel Harriet Hall, born October 2, 1873, was the daughter of James and Amie Hall. She is shown in this photograph wearing the dress she wore to President William Howard Taft's Inaugural Ball on March 4, 1909, at the White House. On September 13, 1893, Mabel married with 200 guests present in the flower-filled parlor of her family home. Mabel passed away on April 26, 1959, and is buried at the East Main Street cemetery.

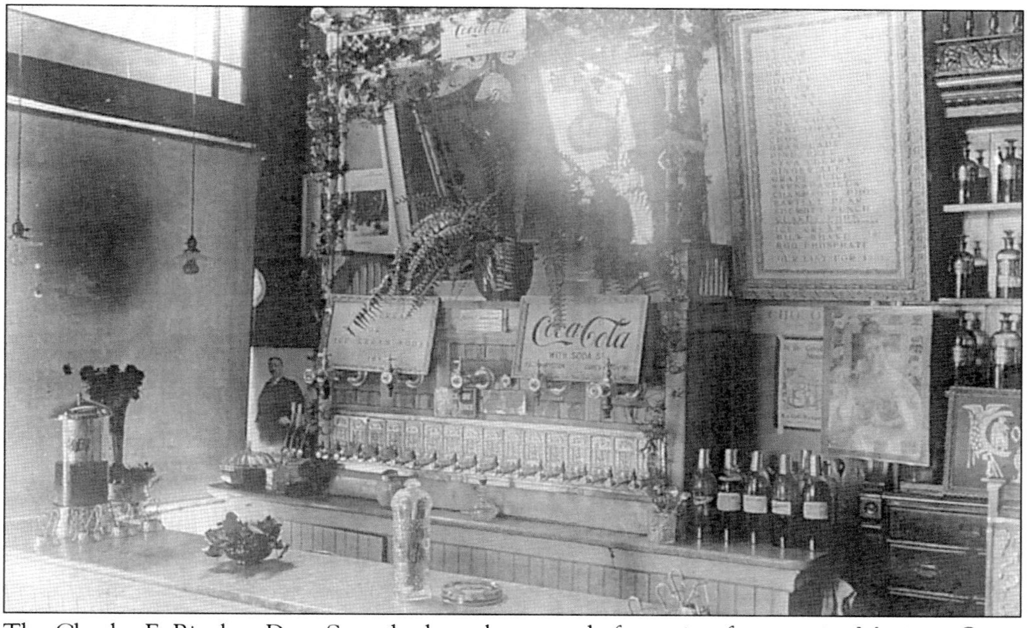

The Charles F. Bigelow Drug Store had an elegant soda fountain of composite Mexican Onyz. When this photograph was taken in 1909, ice cream or an ice cream soda cost a dime, and a Coca-Cola cost just a nickel.

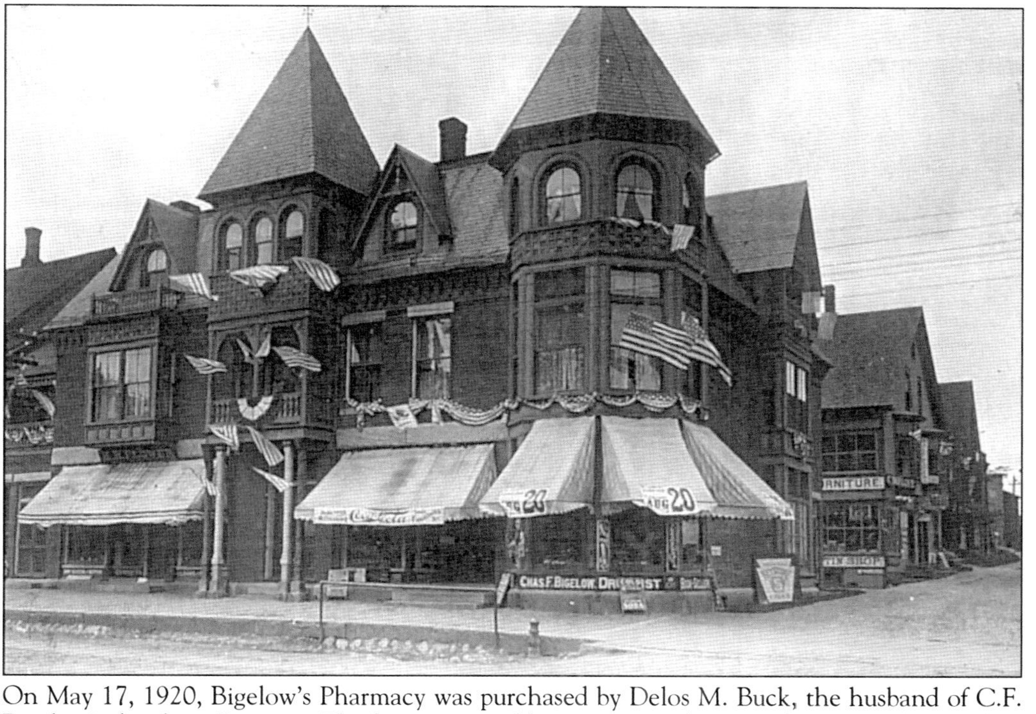

On May 17, 1920, Bigelow's Pharmacy was purchased by Delos M. Buck, the husband of C.F. Bigelow's daughter Beatrice. The business would continue at the same location where it had been for the past 50 years, enjoying the reputation as the leading Rexall Store in Vermont.

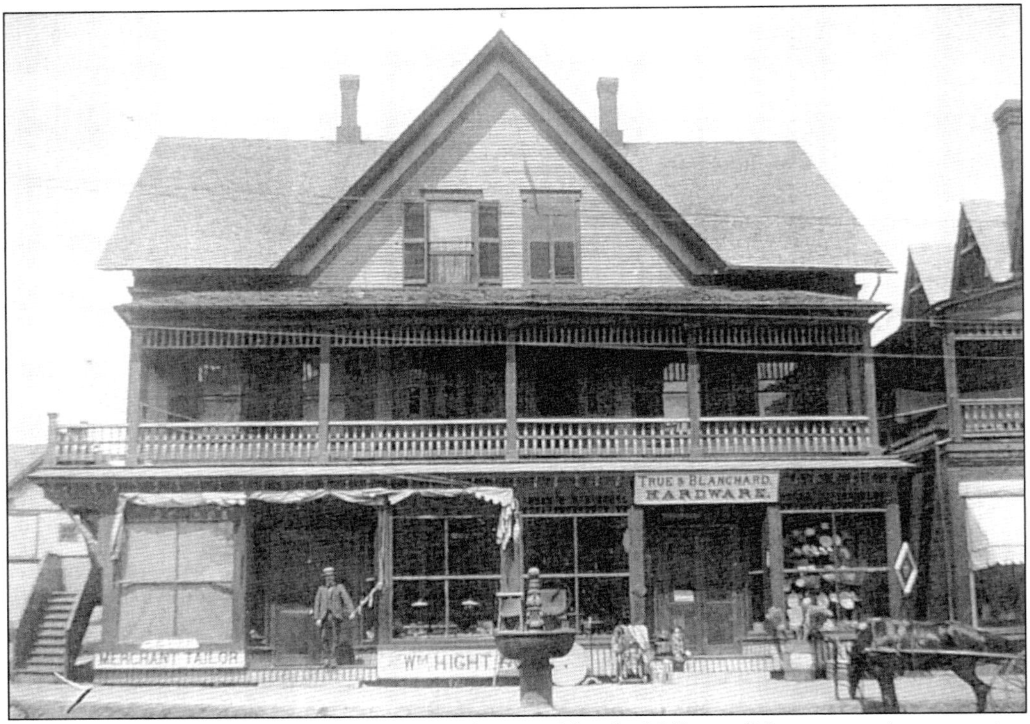

The True & Blanchard Company purchased in 1895 for the Village of Newport an iron watering trough and placed it in front of their store to be both useful and ornamental. A disgruntled businessman suggested the new trough should be on wheels and moved around Main Street to suit the public.

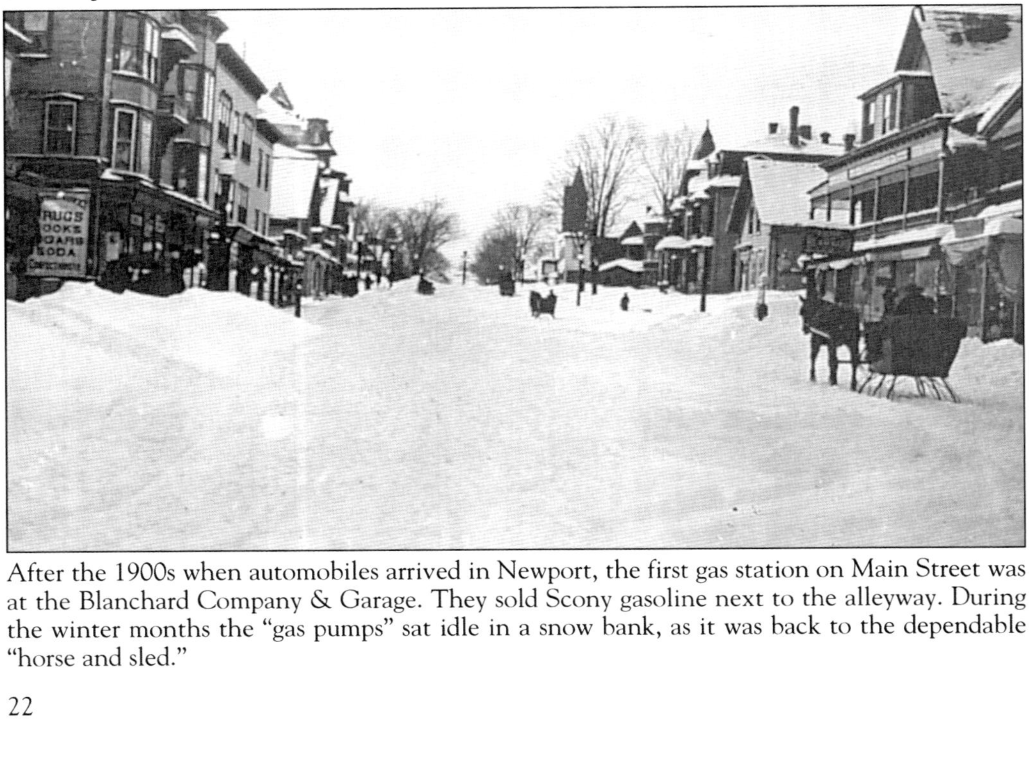

After the 1900s when automobiles arrived in Newport, the first gas station on Main Street was at the Blanchard Company & Garage. They sold Scony gasoline next to the alleyway. During the winter months the "gas pumps" sat idle in a snow bank, as it was back to the dependable "horse and sled."

Dr. John McNabe Currier was born on August 8, 1832, and received his medical degree in 1858 before settling in the Village of Newport. In 1862, Dr. Currier established the first circulating library in Newport and organized the Orleans County Historical Society in 1888. He was the society's first elected secretary.

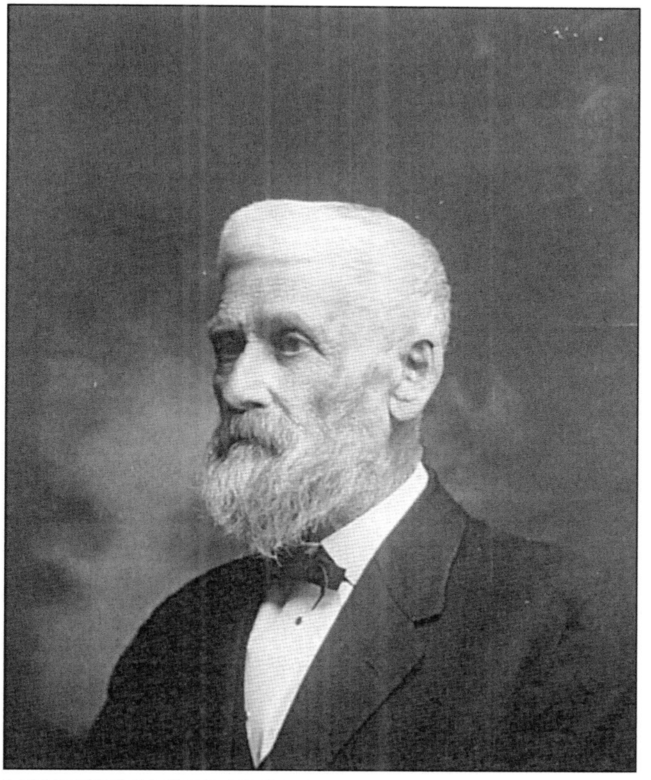

Mr. and Mrs. Converse Goodhue Goodrich, benefactors of the Goodrich Memorial Library, did not live to see the completion of their Queen Anne and Romanesque brick structure. Construction started in 1896, on the corner of Field Avenue, and was completed in 1898. Almira (Howard) died in 1896, and Converse in 1897. They were buried in the Goodrich lot in the East Main Street cemetery.

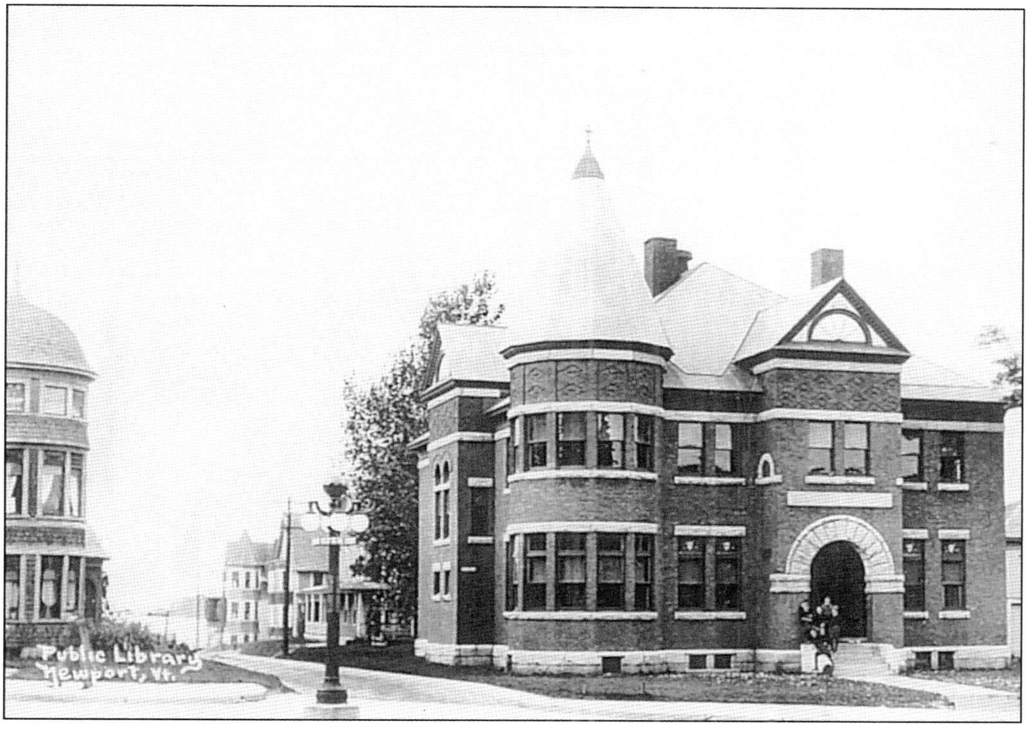

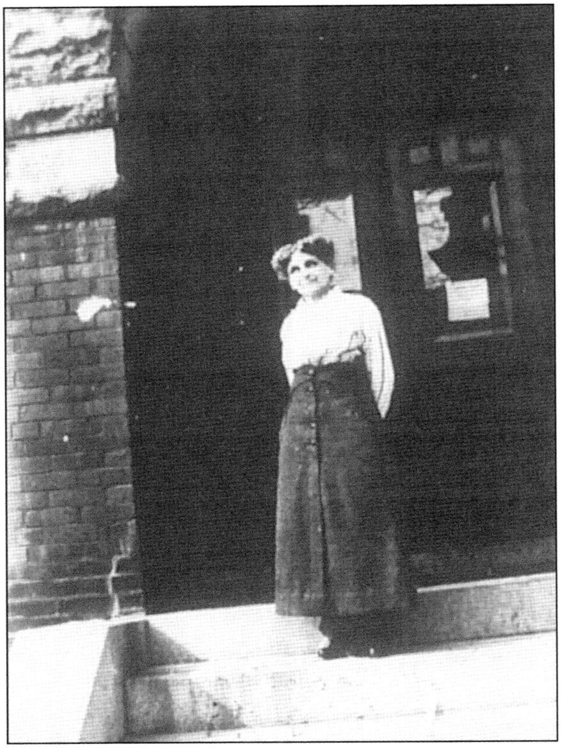

Elizabeth M. Sargent was born in 1856 in Newport, the daughter of Moses G. Sargent and Lucy Gilman Knight Sargent. "Lizzie" was as the first and longest-serving librarian, giving 30 years of her life to the work she loved so well.

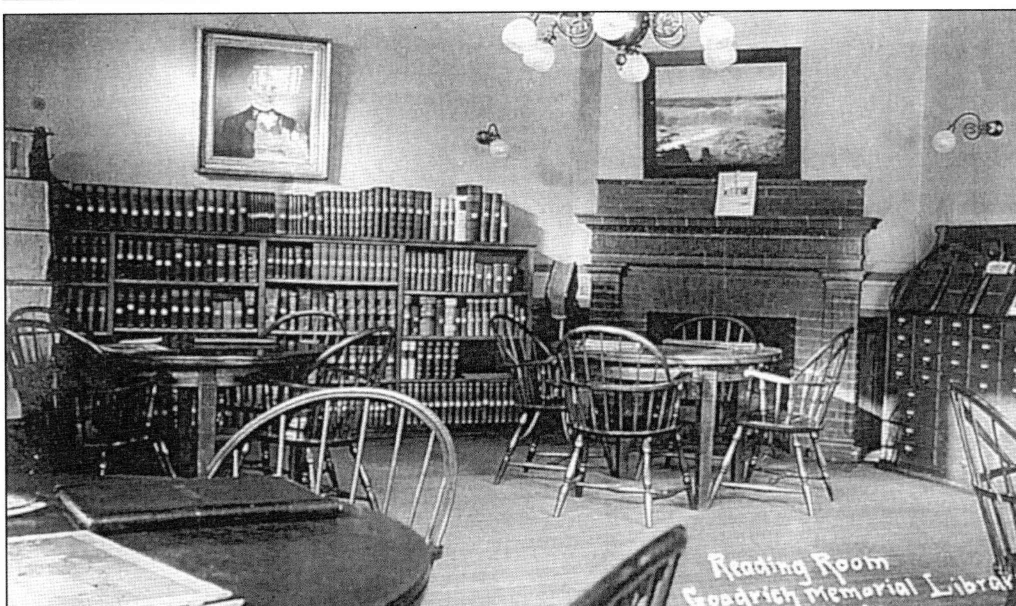

David W. Hildreth, known as an ornithologist and a taxidermist, gave some of his birds, ducks, and owl specimens, including a 10-foot-alligator in the 1920s, to be showcased on the second floor of the library. The reading room to the left of the front door includes a large photograph of Converse G. Goodrich over the bookshelf where it can still be seen today, after 100 years.

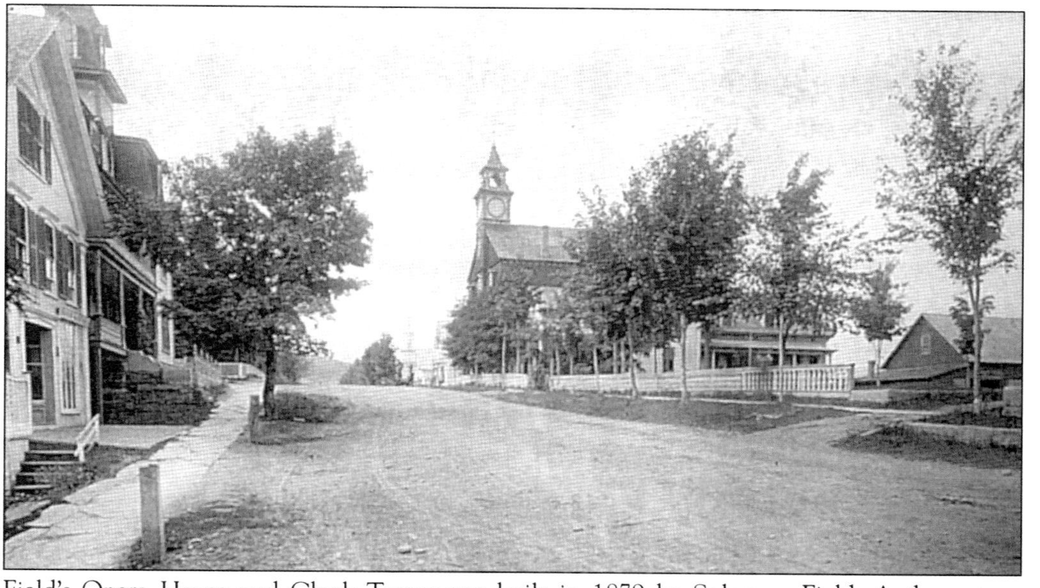

Field's Opera House and Clock Tower was built in 1879 by Solomon Field. A three-story wooden building with a large dance hall on the third floor, it was the site of masquerade parties, concerts, and exhibitions. In 1896, a brisk fire from the building next door consumed the block and the Fields Opera House that once stood across the street from the courthouse.

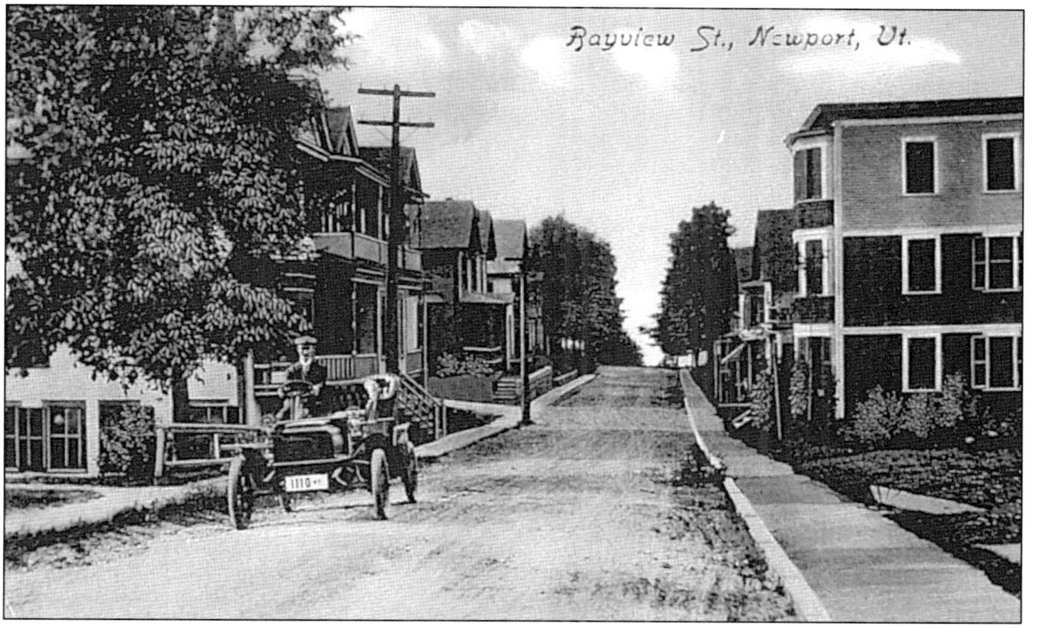

By the early 1900s, "Locomobile Horseless Carriages" attracted attention at the local fairs. One fair-goer said "Before 'it' would be accepted as a household treasure, 'it' will have to despense [*sic*] with that continuous 'buzzying sound' which is worse than a horse with the 'heaves.' "

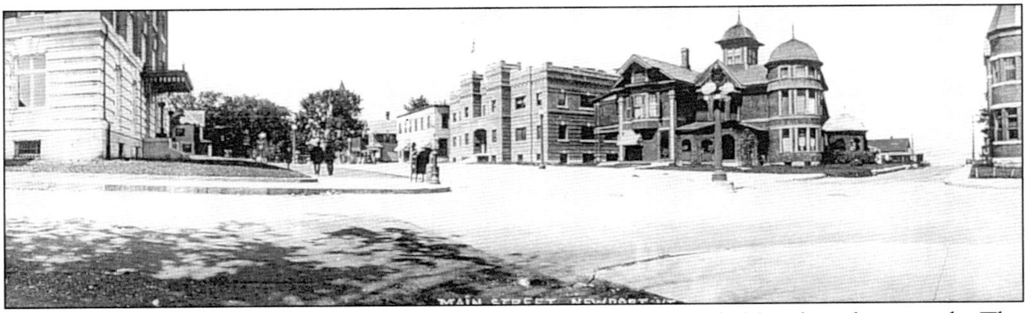

When Newport City was formed, upper Main Street looked much like this photograph. The Charles N. Brady house stood on the corner of Main Street and Fields Avenue. The City of Newport purchased this home for their first offices (1918–1921).

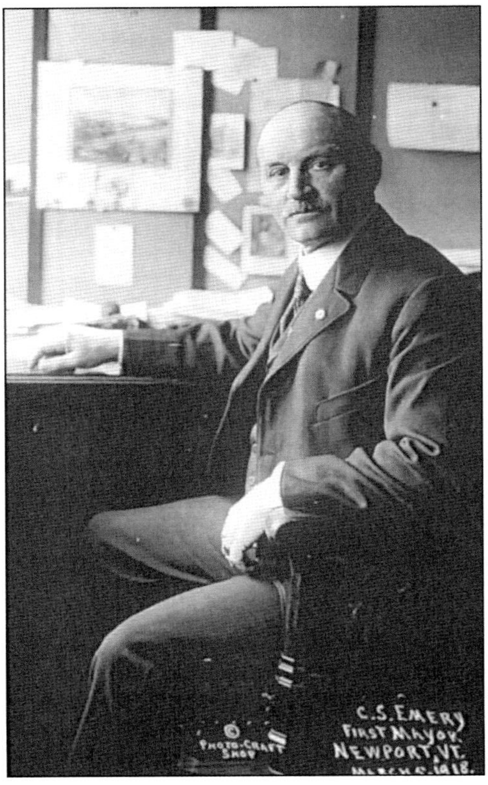

Col. Curtis S. Emery was born in 1861 and admitted to the bar in 1883. In 1906, he came to Newport as Collector of Customs for the Port of Memphremagog. In 1915, he formed C.S. Emery and Company, a Customs Brokers firm, with his son Donald. Colonel Emery had a persuasive manner, and on March 5, 1918, he was elected as the City of Newport's first mayor.

Inez E. Miller was born July 10, 1874, the daughter of Oscar and Alma Miller. She is pictured here with her sister Nellie on the right. With a gracious and friendly manner and a good sense of humor, Ms. Miller made a definite contribution to her home community. On December 3, 1959, she passed away and was laid to rest at the East Main Street cemetery.

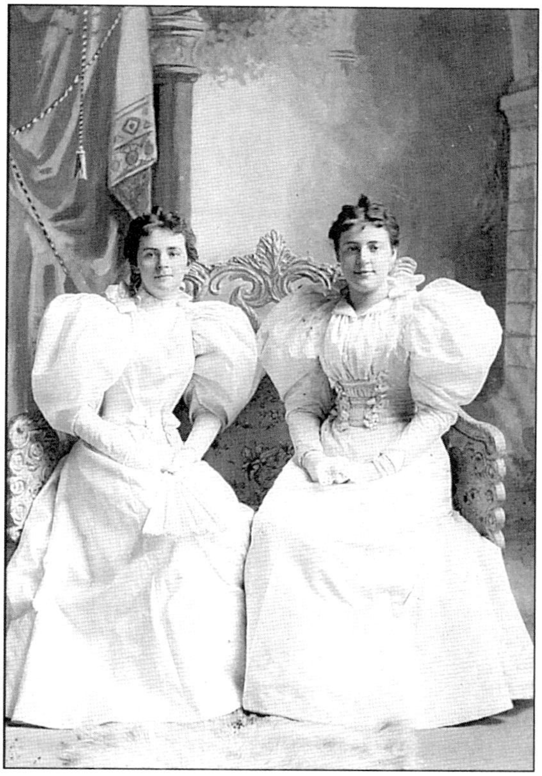

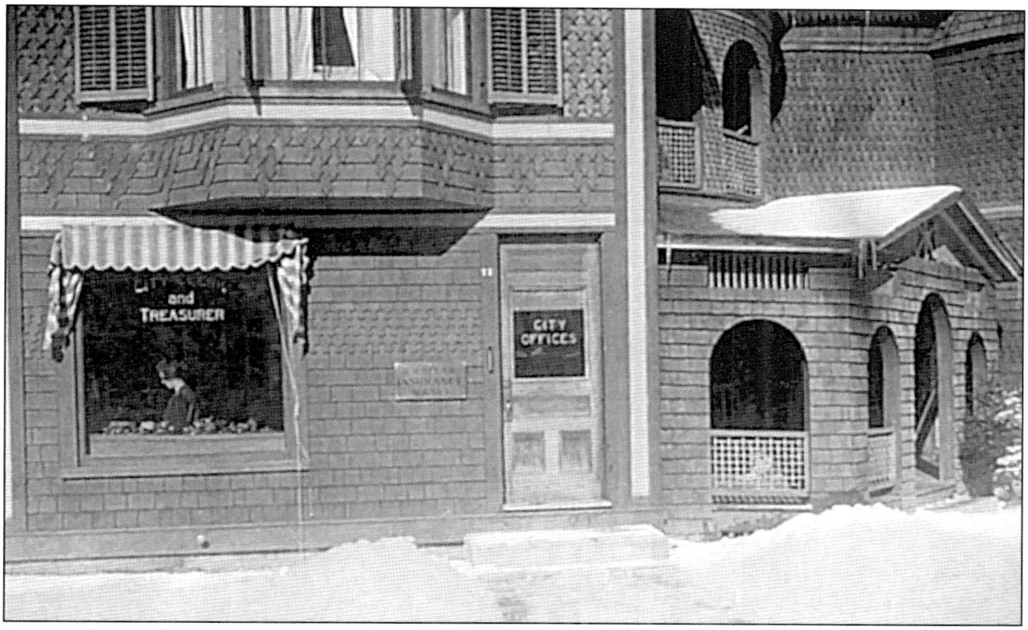

Inez Miller had the distinction of being the first woman to cast a vote in 1918, in the new City of Newport. It was reported that she "roosted" on the steps of the City Hall all night in order to get the lead on the other women.

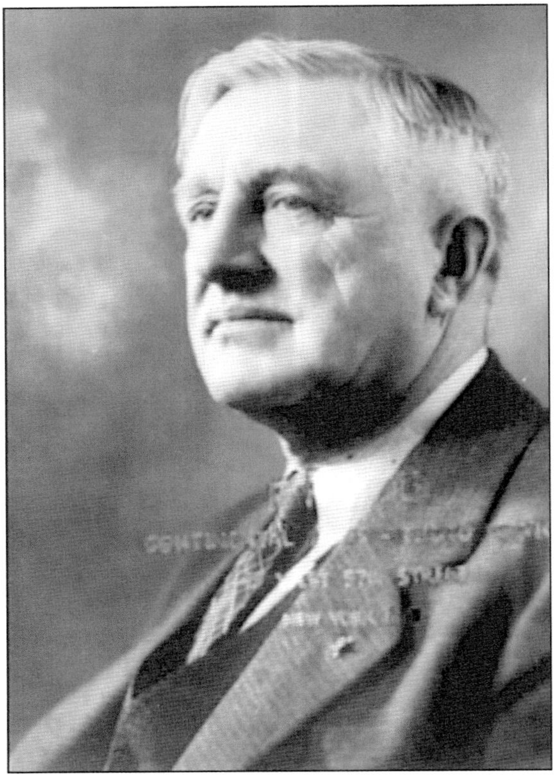

Gardner Park was the brainchild of James T. Gardner, described as a kind man who could inspire others. His greatest ambition, or "Jim's Folly" as the townspeople called it, was to transform the swampy tract of land along the causeway in Newport into a beautiful park.

On the causeway, there was a row of houses built between the Clyde River and the road. Across the river was a big "Muskrat Swamp" which extended straight back to the steep bank just below East Main Street, before Gardner Park was built in the 1920s.

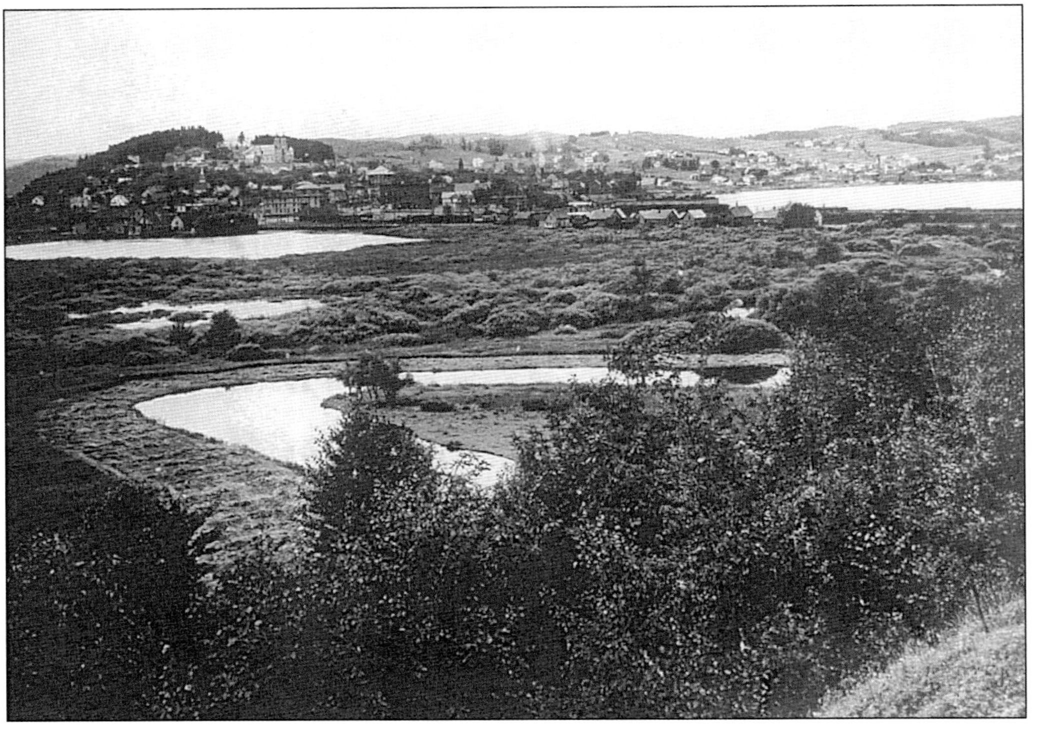

Carolina D. Pratt, the youngest daughter of Deacon Timothy Pratt & Emily Carpenter Pratt, was born on a farm on the Lake Road. In 1874, she married C.F. Ranney, and raised four children. Only one child, William, survived childhood. An old-fashioned woman, Carolina kept a home that was a delight to visit. She joined with the Congregation Church in 1858 and, at the time of her death in 1911, was the oldest member.

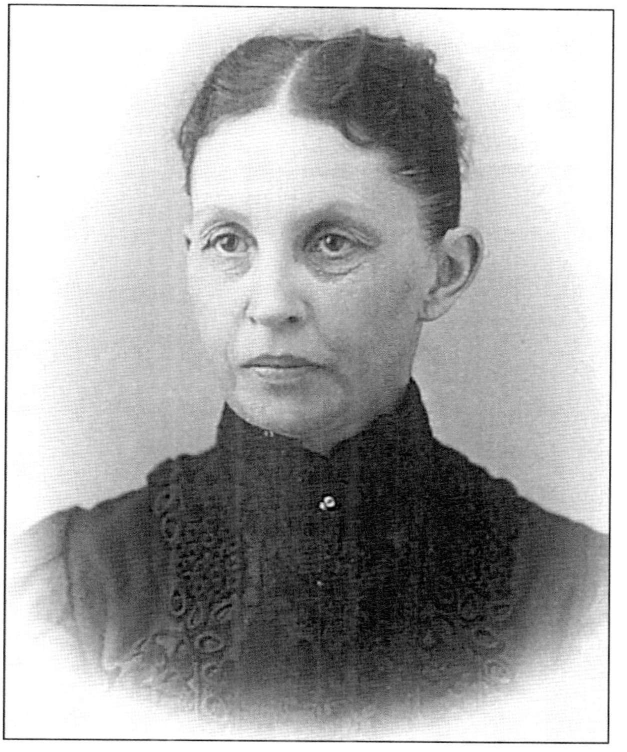

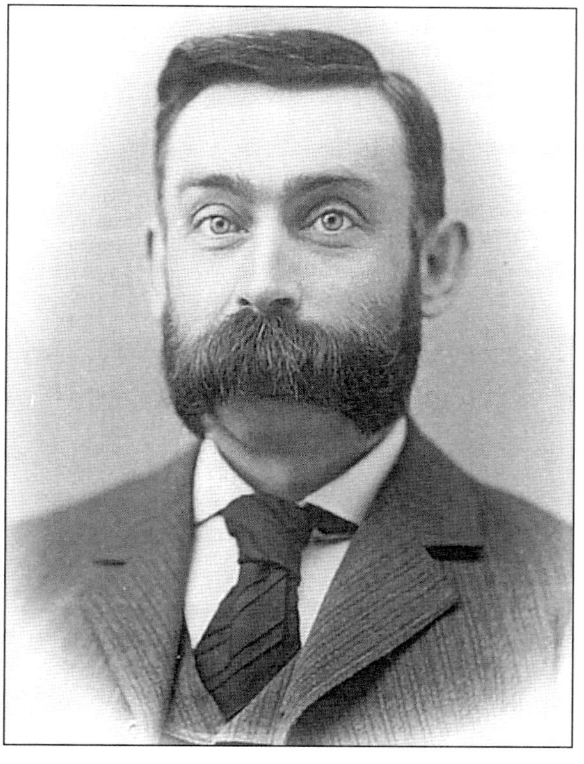

Deacon Charles Freeman Ranney, born in 1851, was connected with the *Express & Standard Newspaper* (1875–1890), and bought the newspaper's job printing and stationery business. Ranney thought that the Village of Newport would be a tourist center, evidenced by his printed brochures. He and his wife, both Congregationalists, built a home on the corner of Main and Bayview Streets. In 1919 the house was remodeled to become the church's parsonage.

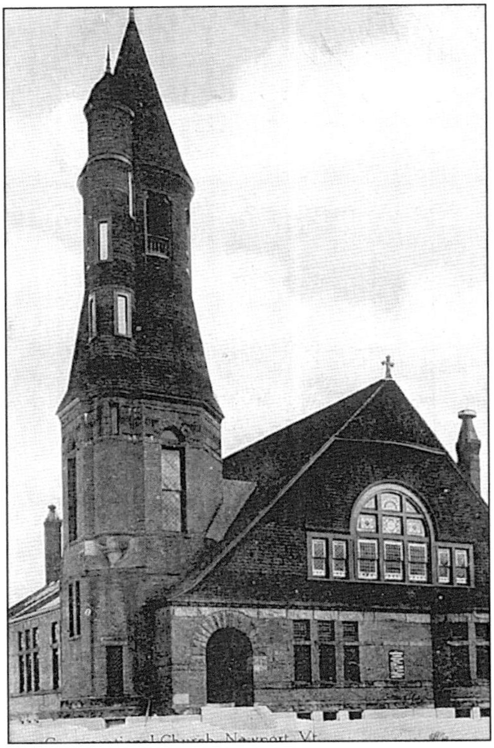

The first Congregation Church in 1861 was a white wooden building located on the corner of Main and School Streets. The last service in this building was held April 14, 1889. On July 27, 1889, the Reverend Robert V. Hall laid the cornerstone for the new brick church building erected on the same site.

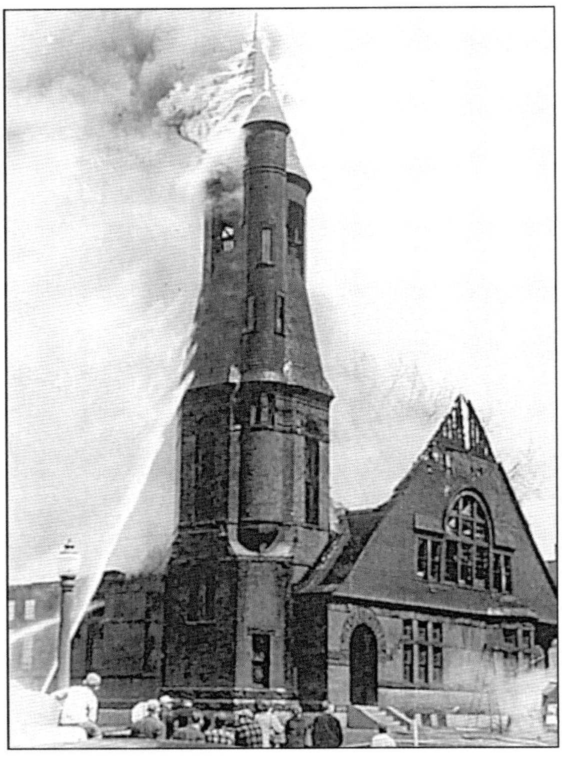

A destructive fire on May 4, 1956, resulted in a tragic loss to hundreds of Newporters. The 80-foot steeple which housed the 3,000-pound bell finally plummeted through the tower and landed with a resounding crash that sent sparks and embers soaring.

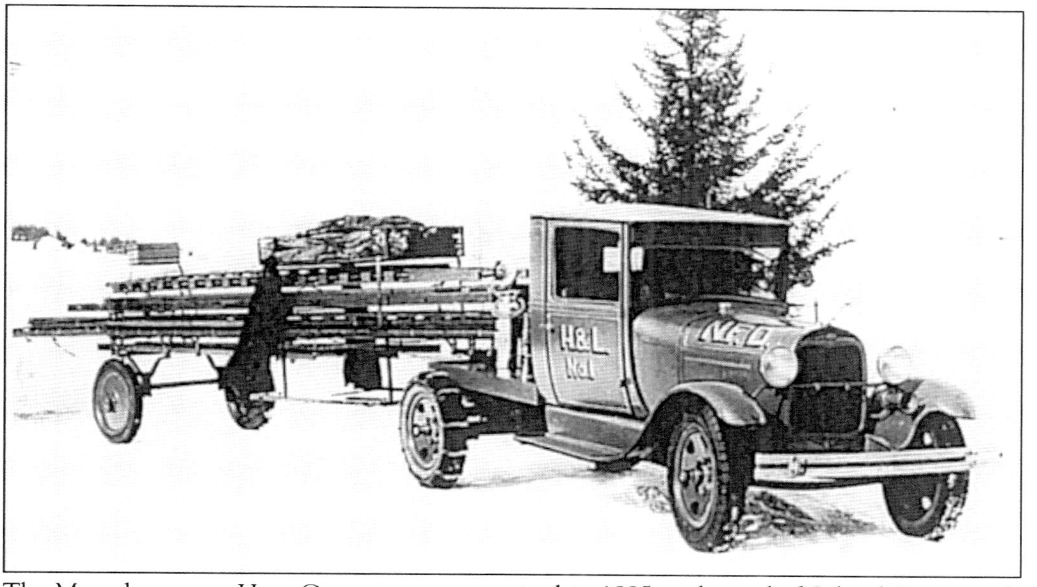

The Memphremagog Hose Company was organized in 1885 at the end of School Street, with Edwin B. True as the first fire chief. Apparatus consisted of one hand tub, one hook and ladder, and three hand-drawn hose carts. A job team trucker contracted with the village of Newport to draw the hose carts for 25¢ per fire.

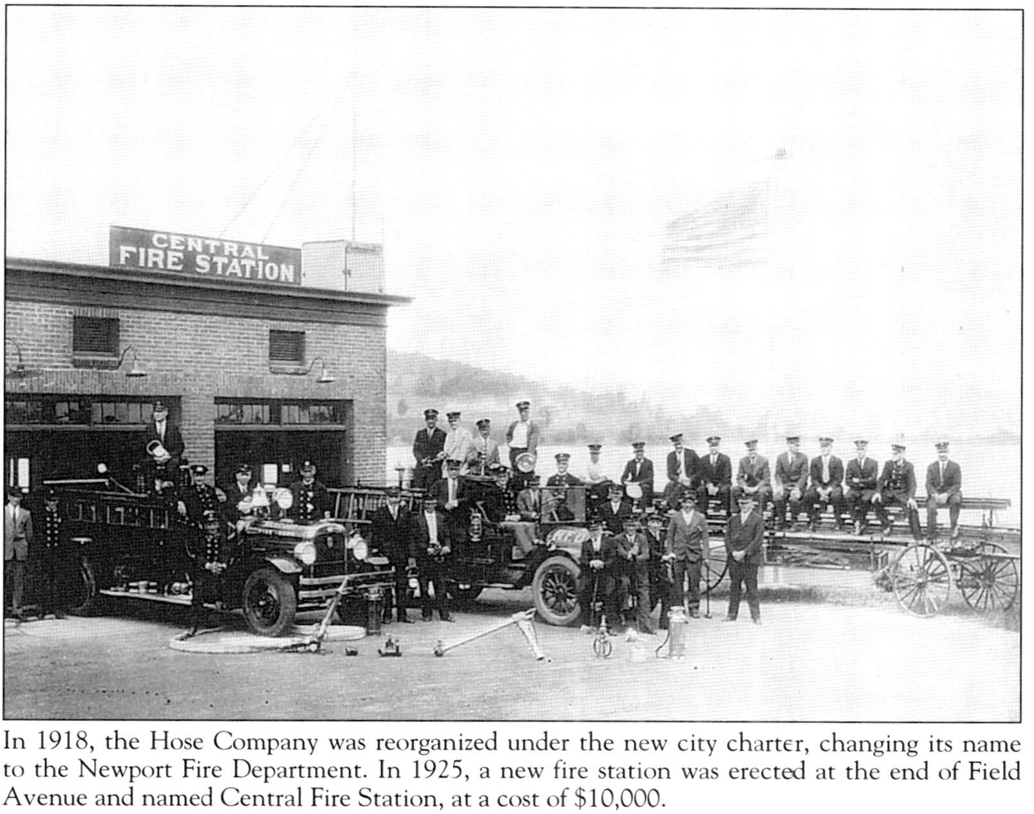

In 1918, the Hose Company was reorganized under the new city charter, changing its name to the Newport Fire Department. In 1925, a new fire station was erected at the end of Field Avenue and named Central Fire Station, at a cost of $10,000.

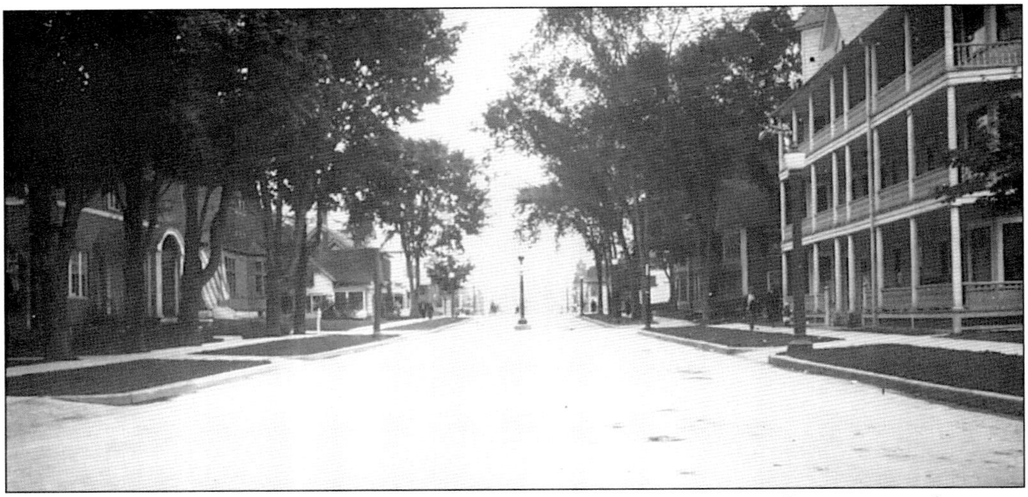

B.F. Moore & Company started in an attic of a general store in Morgan Center, manufacturing "Railroad Overalls" before moving to the Aubin Block in Newport in 1893. In 1896, the company moved to Coventry Street and the block was converted into a YWCA Home in 1916 for teachers and single working girls. In 1935, the Burgess Block, on the corner of Third Street, burned leaving 25 people homeless. (Courtesy of Richardson Cartee Collection.)

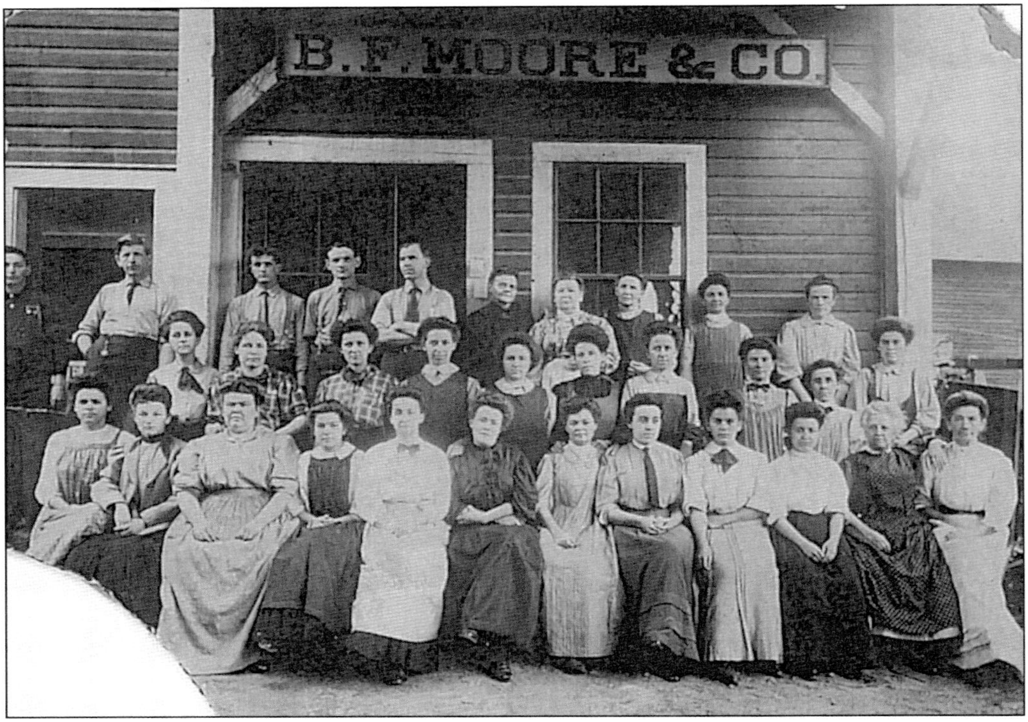

In 1941, B.F. Moore & Company celebrated their 50th year in business. One of the oldest workers was Rodias Lambert, who started working there on September 1, 1894. The others with long years of experiences were: Lucy Tetreault, 1900; Martha Tetreault, 1900; Mrs. Emma Johnson, 1902; Mrs. Sadie Greenwood, 1905; and Miss Emeria Greenwood, 1909. Harold Lewis, factory foreman, celebrated his 25 years of service.

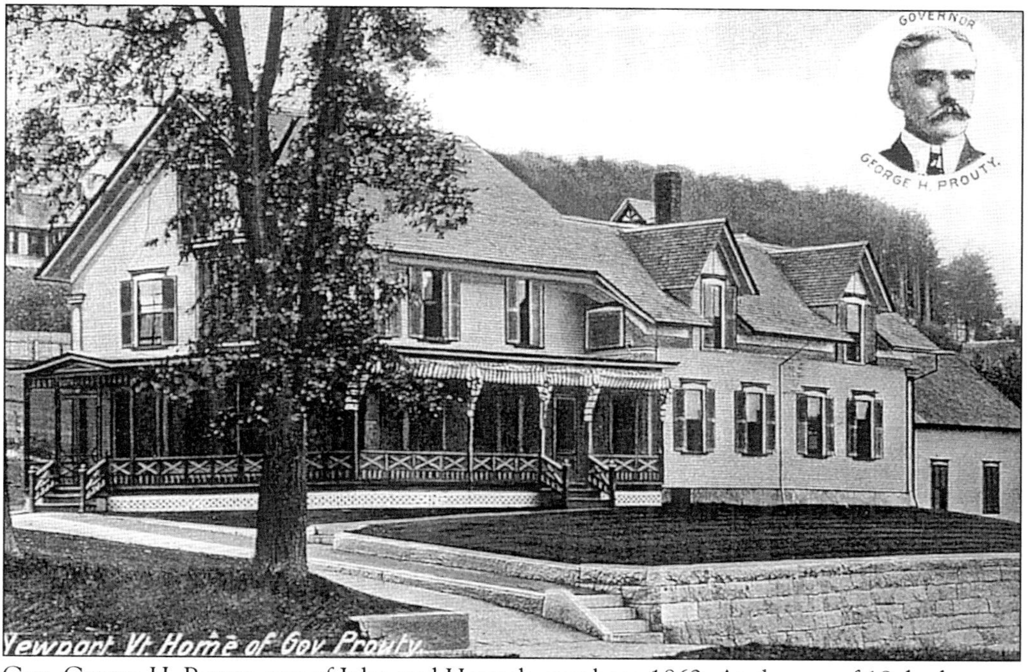

Gov. George H. Prouty, son of John and Hannah, was born 1862. At the age of 18, he became employed by his father's lumber business. In 1890, he married Henrietta Allen. They spent their married life at the Prouty Homestead, a place of gracious hospitality across from Prouty Bay.

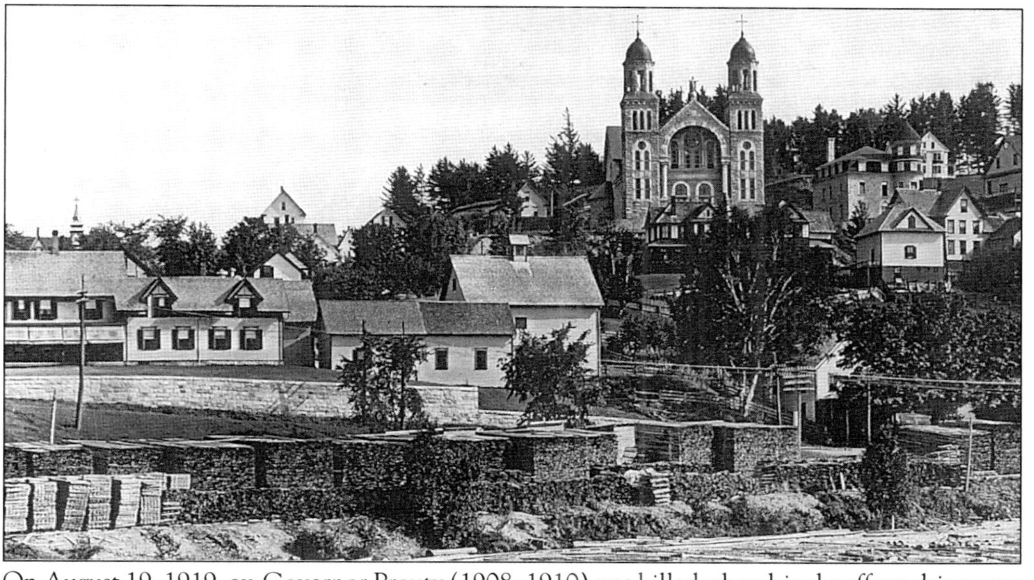

On August 19, 1919, ex-Governor Prouty (1908–1910) was killed when his chauffeur-driven car was hit by a train in Quebec, Canada. Henrietta Prouty passed away on February 18, 1929, on her 64th birthday, and was laid to rest beside her husband at the East Main Street cemetery.

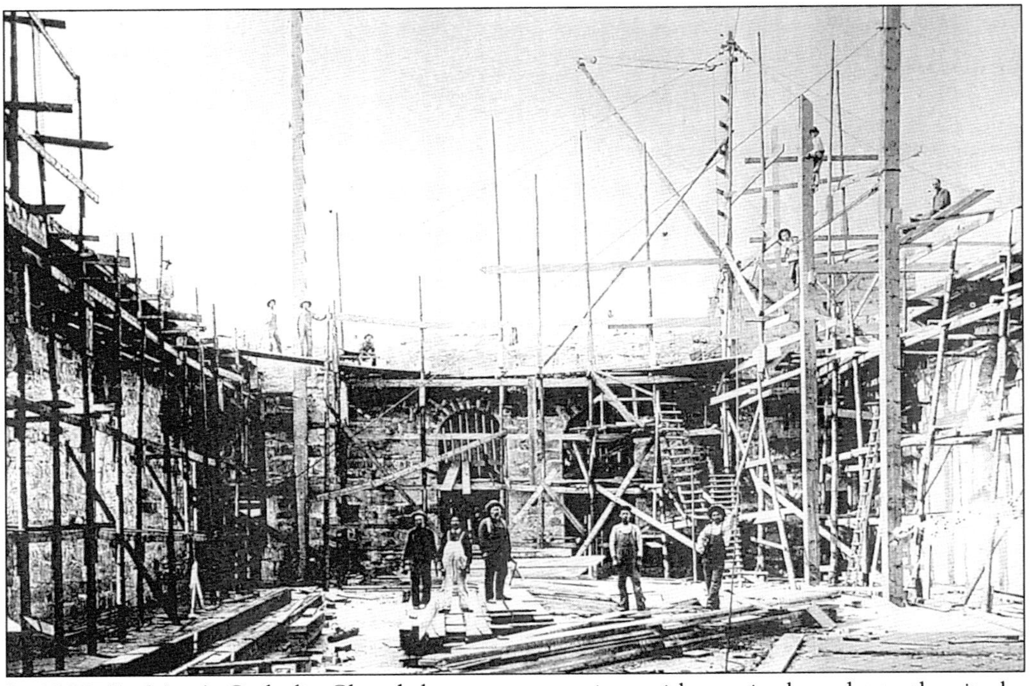

In 1903, St. Mary's Catholic Church began construction, with granite brought to the site by teams of horses pulling wagons with huge iron wheels over dirt roads, then up the narrow dirt road of Prospect Street. The church's Vermont granite, Romanesque in style, was flanked by twin granite towers in which silver bells were hung high above Newport overlooking the beauty of Lake Memphremagog.

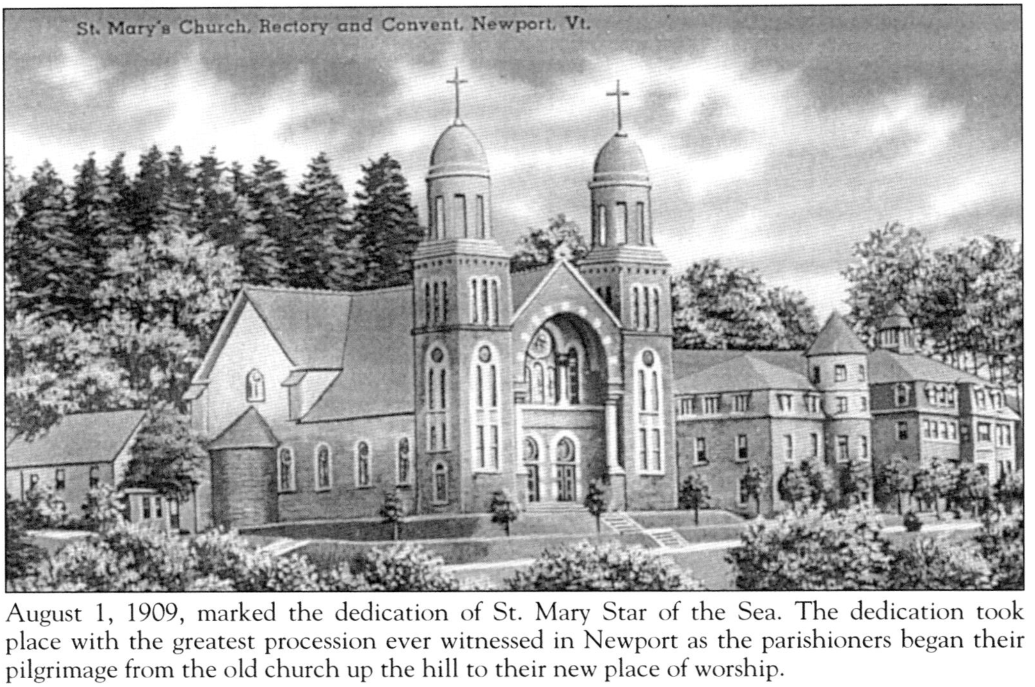

August 1, 1909, marked the dedication of St. Mary Star of the Sea. The dedication took place with the greatest procession ever witnessed in Newport as the parishioners began their pilgrimage from the old church up the hill to their new place of worship.

The Orleans County Courthouse was erected in 1886, commanding a view of the entire Village of Newport and one of the finest scenes of Lake Memphremagog. The courthouse and jail cost $21,000. On the first floor, 12 rooms were rented for law offices at $250 a year each.

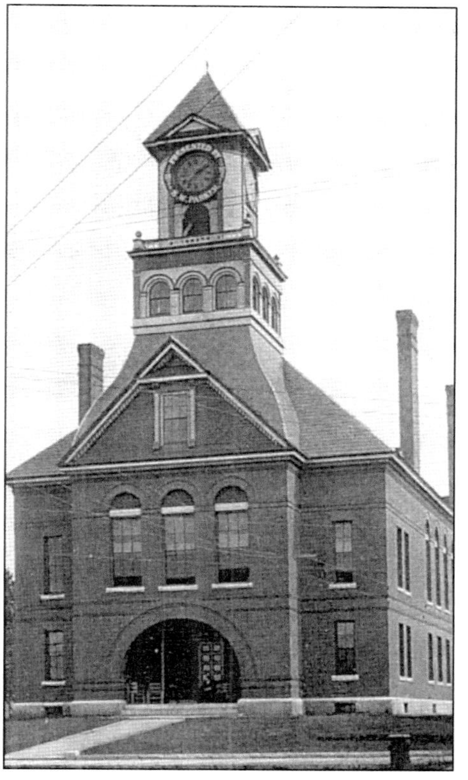

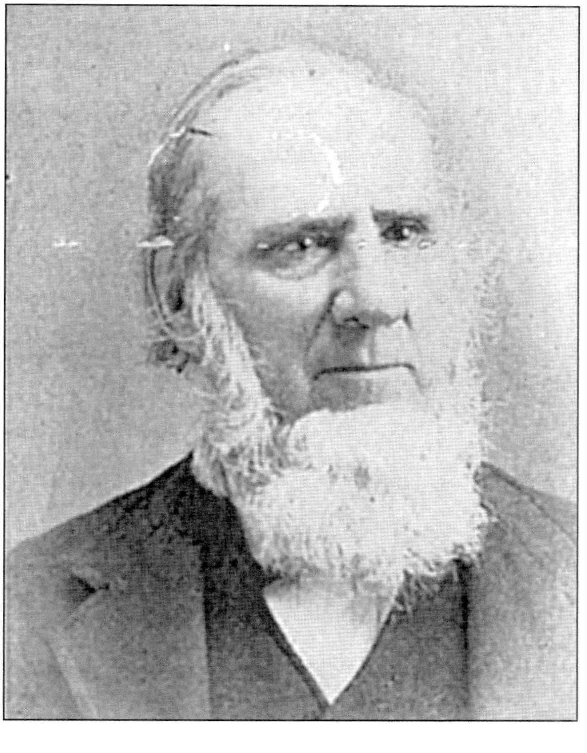

Samuel W. Parker's courthouse clock dials were illuminated for the first time on the night of March 24, 1897, as a gift to the people of Orleans County. This $1,000 Seth Thomas clock weighed 2,214 pounds, had four round glass dials of five feet in diameter, and would run for eight days.

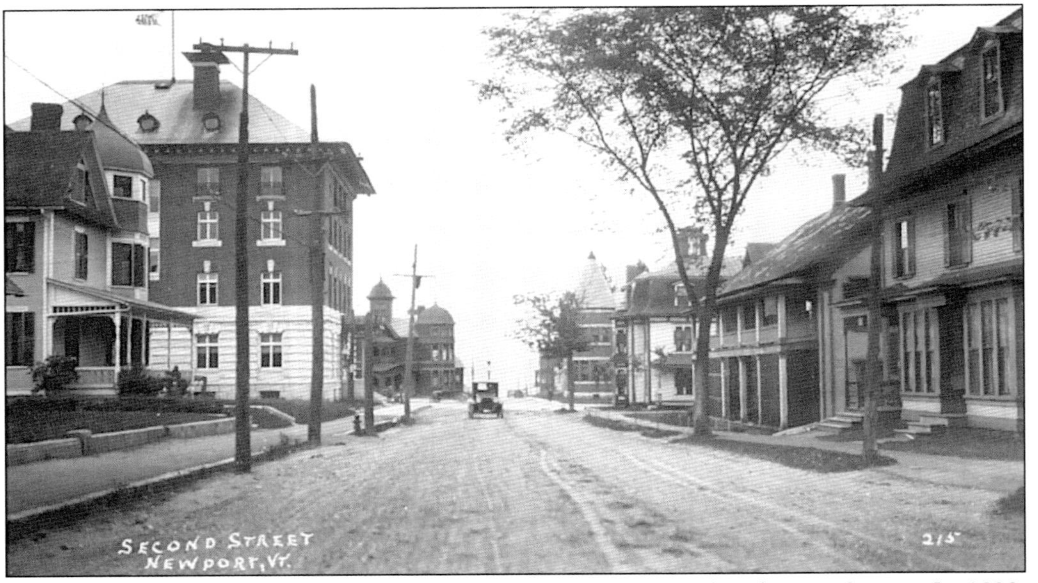

The Avaline Brown House c. 1899 sat on the corner of Second and Main Streets. In 1899, she moved the house and sold the lot for $14,800, for the construction of the new Federal Building, completed in 1903. Colonel Mansur, Hon. Charles Brady, and Congressman W.W. Grout headed the pioneering that saw the United States Post Office, courthouse, and customs house moving into the new building in 1904. (Courtesy of Richardson Cartee Collection.)

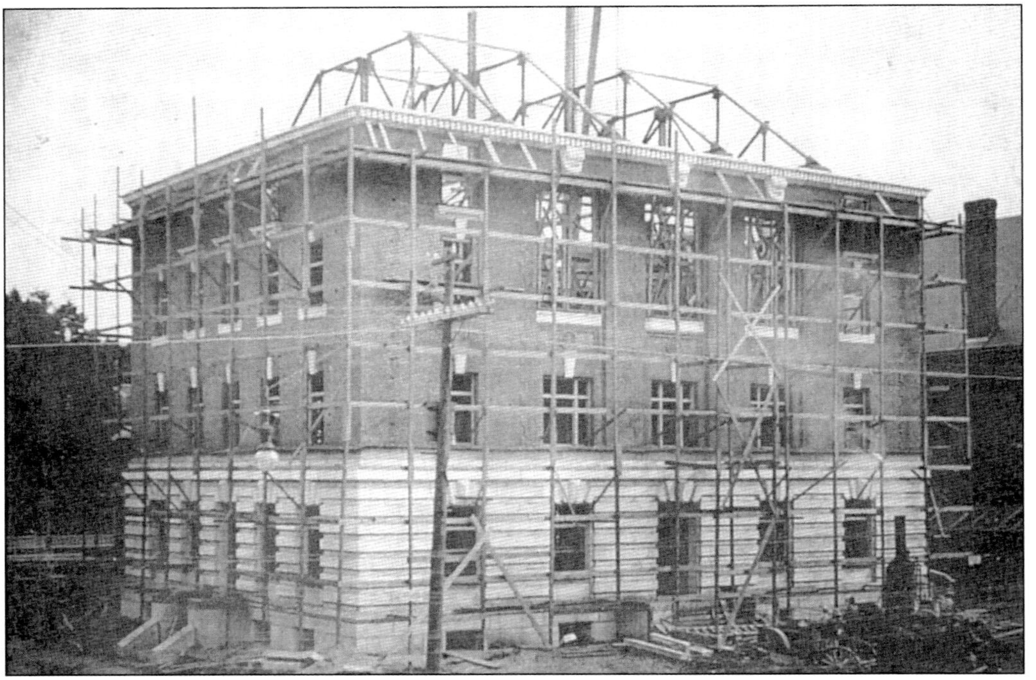

The federal building was later renamed the Lee Emerson State Office Building after the two-term Governor of Vermont (1953–1957).

Gen. Benjamin W. Lee and his wife Sara Jane came to Newport where they ran a boardinghouse in the 1860s, in the old Arlington Block. Gen. B.W. Lee was first master of the Memphremagog Lodge #65 in the Village of Newport (1864–65). The Memphremagog Masonic Lodge #65 charter was granted on January 12, 1865.

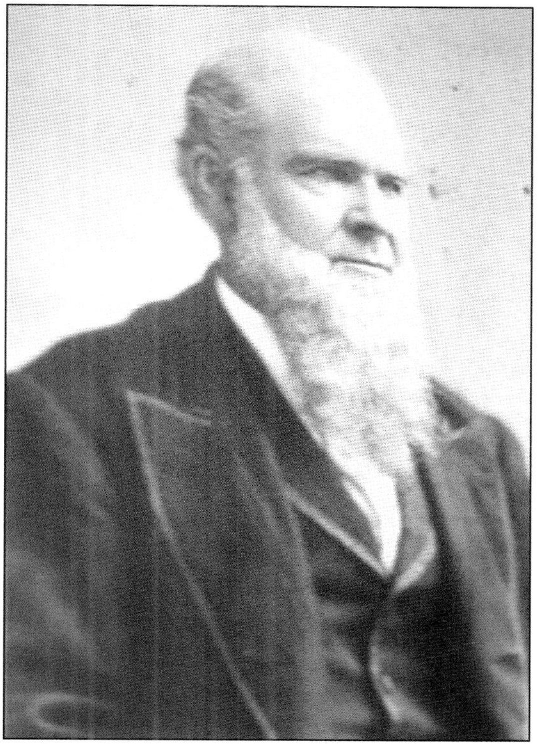

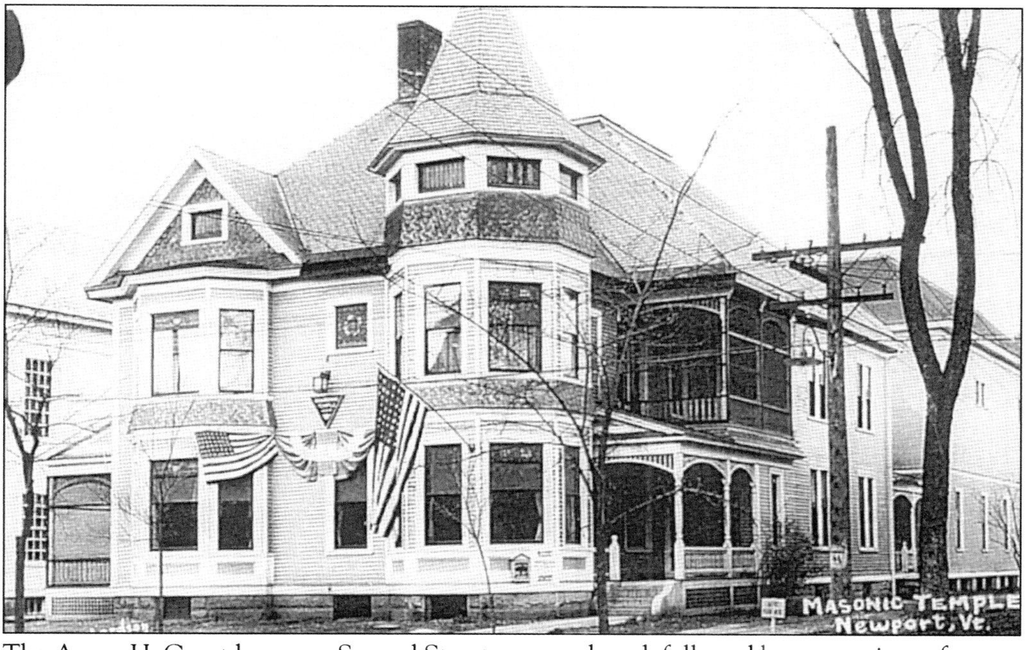

The Aaron H. Grout home on Second Street was purchased, followed by renovations of a two-story addition at the rear. The first floor held the club rooms along with a banquet hall to seat 300 people. On the second floor, the Eastern Star Ladies occupied the front rooms with the Lodge Room in the rear. Dedication ceremonies were held in May of 1926.

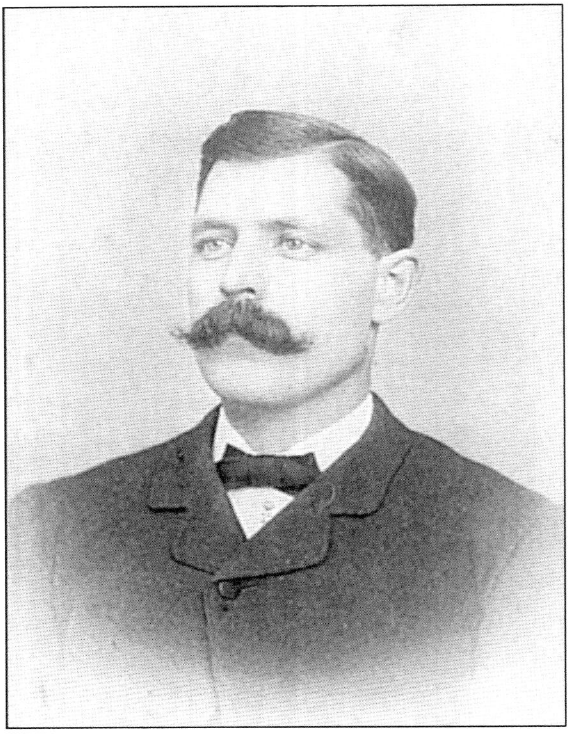

Charles C. Davis was born in 1854, the son of Nelson and Sarah (Colburn) Davis. His father settled on the Clyde River, West Derby, in 1840 and worked at his mills and farmed. Three children were born to Nelson and Sarah: Ellen, who married Seymour Lane; Eva, born in1852, who married John W. Redmond; and Charles, who married Nettie Bradley in 1892, and had two sons, Bradley and Donald.

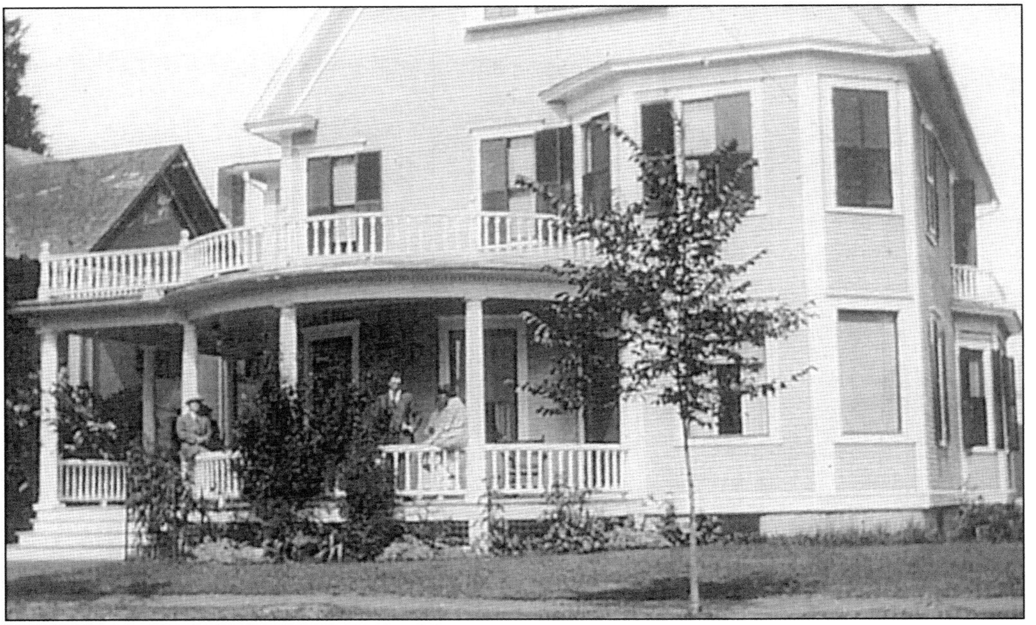

C.C. Davis formed a partnership in the mercantile business with Seymour Lane, his brother-in-law. It was known as Lane & Davis in 1881, occupying a store in the Field Opera House Block. In 1887, they purchased a lot on the corner of Main Street and Lane Avenue. C.C. Davis is pictured here standing on his porch along with his son Bradley and his daughter-in-law Gladys.

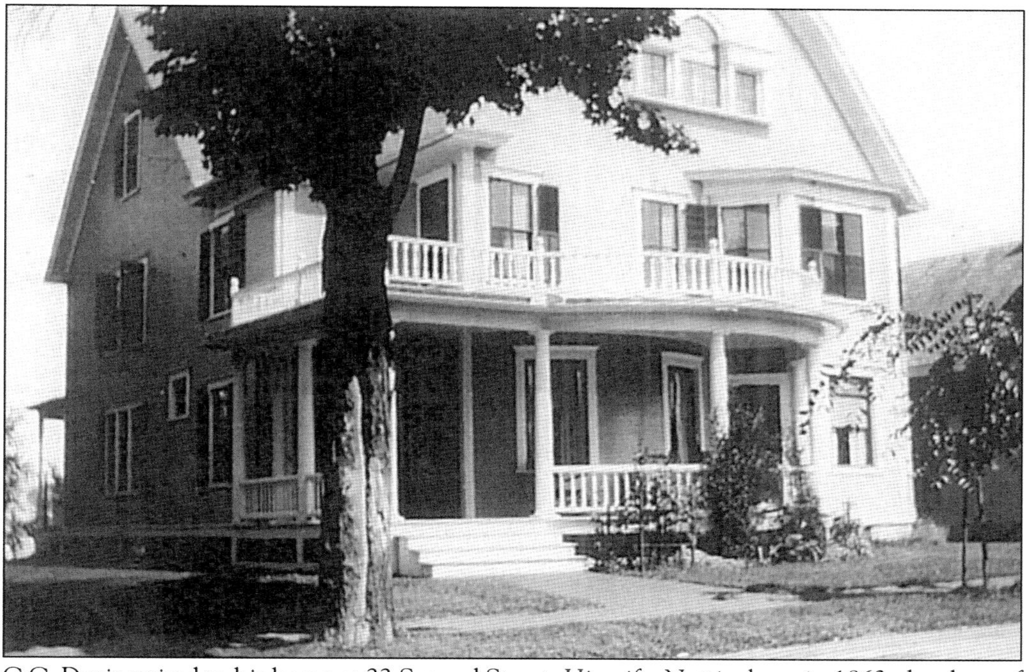

C.C. Davis retired to his home at 22 Second Street. His wife, Nettie, born in 1863, daughter of Addison and Sara (Rood) Bradley, passed away on May 29, 1926. Charles C. Davis, a resident of Newport for 60 years, passed away on January 28, 1942. Funeral services were held at his late home with burial at the Davis family plot at the East Main Street cemetery.

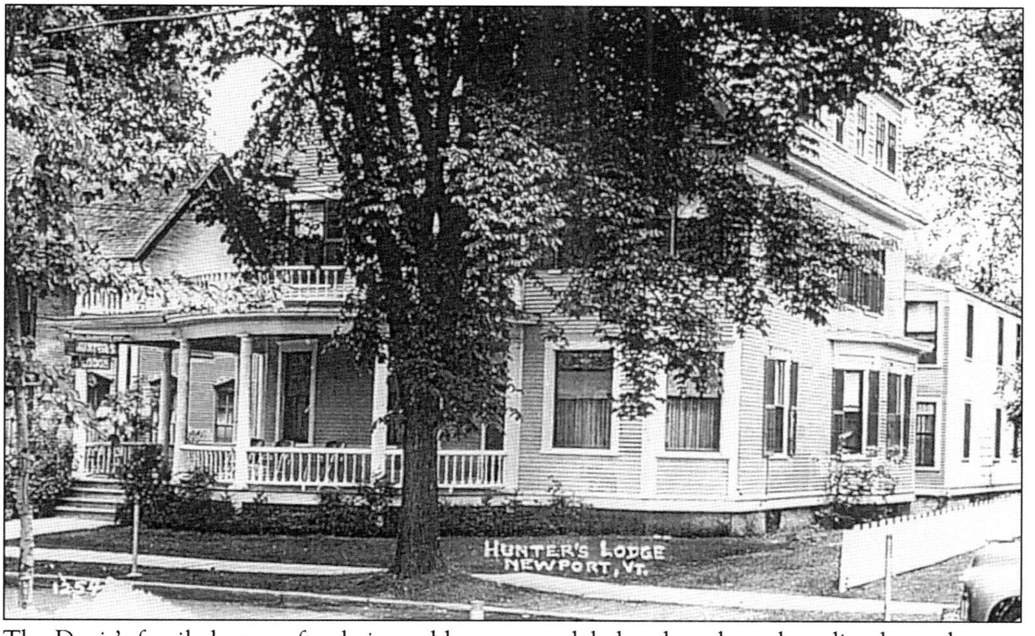

The Davis's family home, after being sold, was remodeled and used as a boarding home known as Hunter's Lodge. A fire destroyed this landmark of Newport on December 2, 1989.

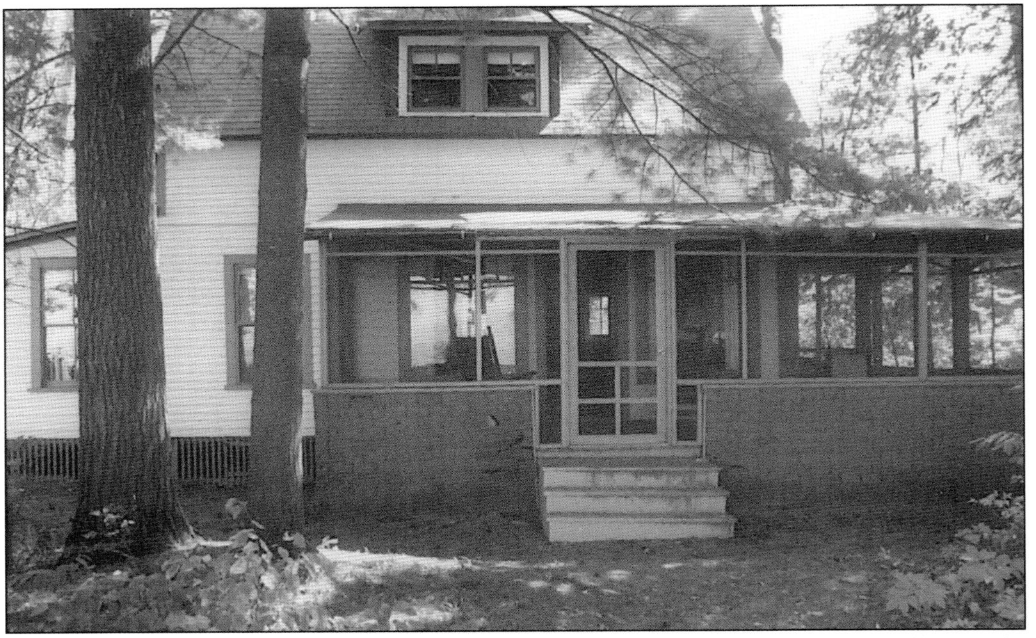

Manila Cassa was built in 1901 on The Bluff's by Sophia Merrill, her daughter Nellie Smith, and Lieutenant Carlos Pierce. Sophia was the wife of the late George C. Merrill, once a purser on the first steamboat the *Mountain Maid* in 1850. This cottage, now owned by the Davis family, was once furnished with rustic furniture and articles the soldier brought back after the Spanish-American War.

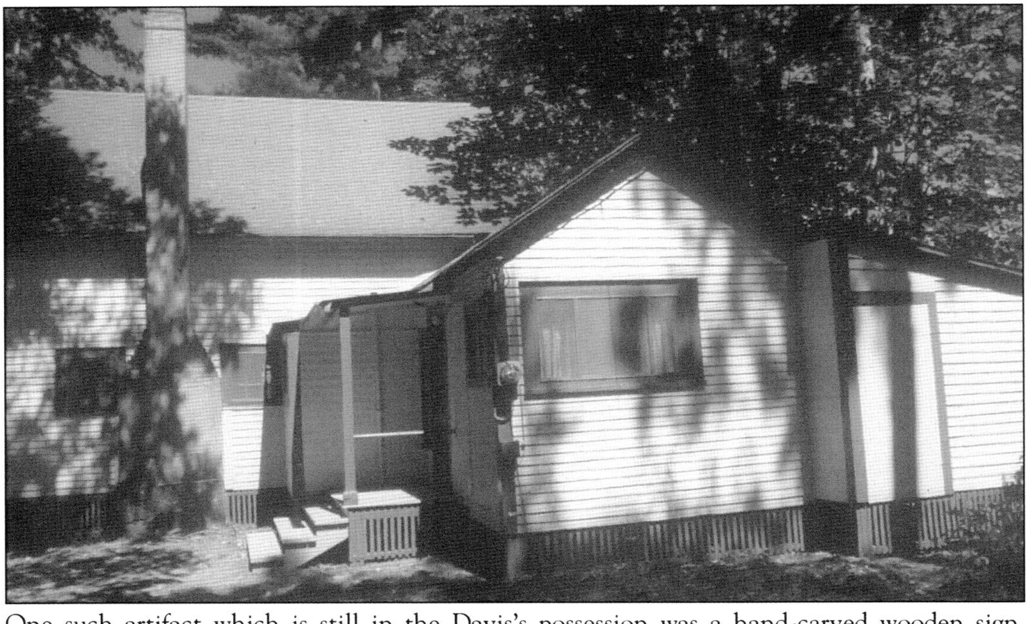

One such artifact which is still in the Davis's possession was a hand-carved wooden sign, originally placed over the fireplace with the words "We Keep Guard." Lieutenant Carlos Pierce was born in 1853 and passed away in 1905. He is buried in the Pierce family plot in the Browington cemetery.

Samuel B. Horton was born in 1827, the son of Abraham and Sarah (Bingham) Horton. By the age of 24, he possessed skills in sketching and was a lover of nature and landscapes. In the1880s, he was foreman of the paint shops for the Railroad Company in Quebec. Horton was full of humor and kindness, and always in demand for stump speeches, especially on the Fourth of July. He died on January 4, 1904.

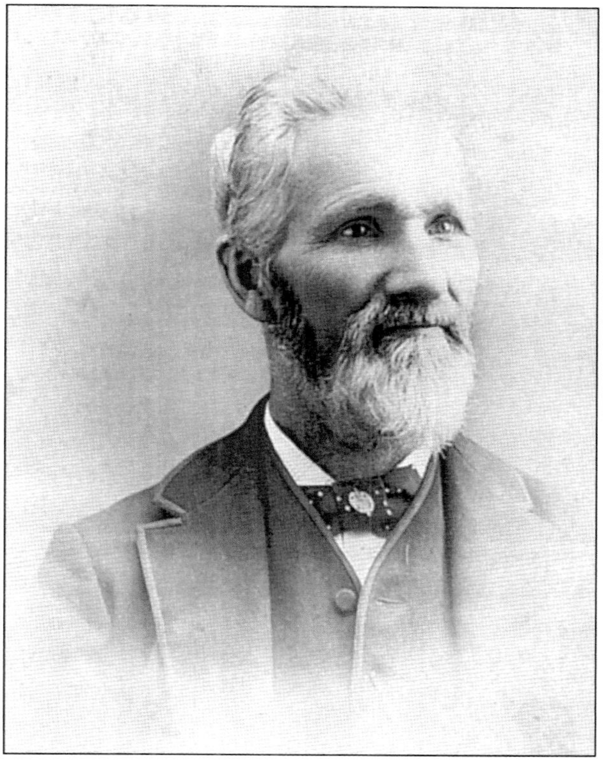

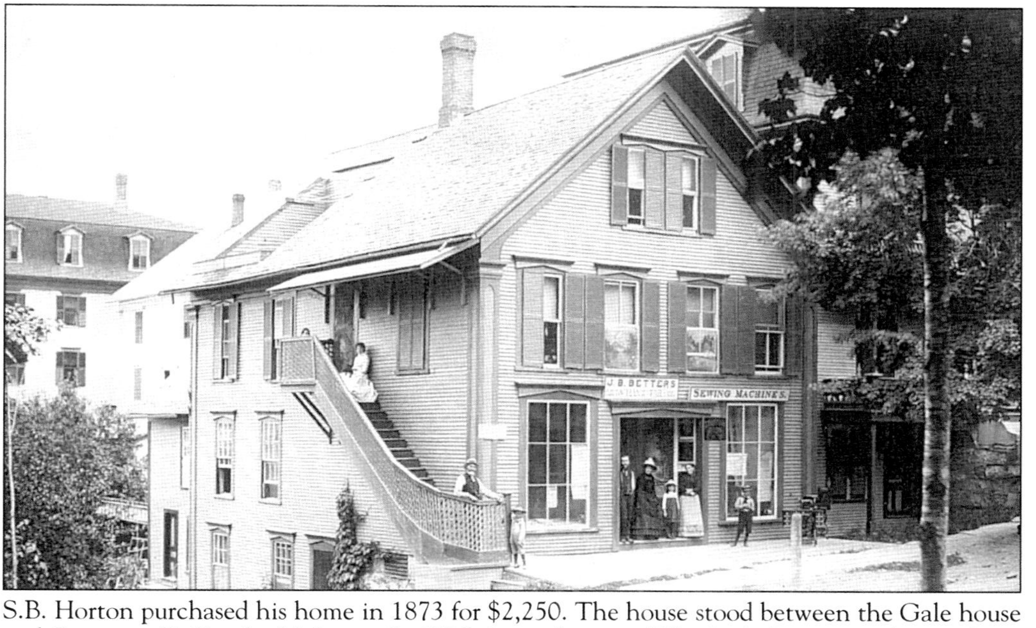

S.B. Horton purchased his home in 1873 for $2,250. The house stood between the Gale house and Converse G. Goodrich's home. In 1856, Samuel married Elizabeth Severans, who was born in 1832. A woman of rare quality, she was lovingly called "Gram Horton" by the younger ones. She died in 1913 at her Main Street home, which she shared with her daughter Jennie and husband Charles Tarton.

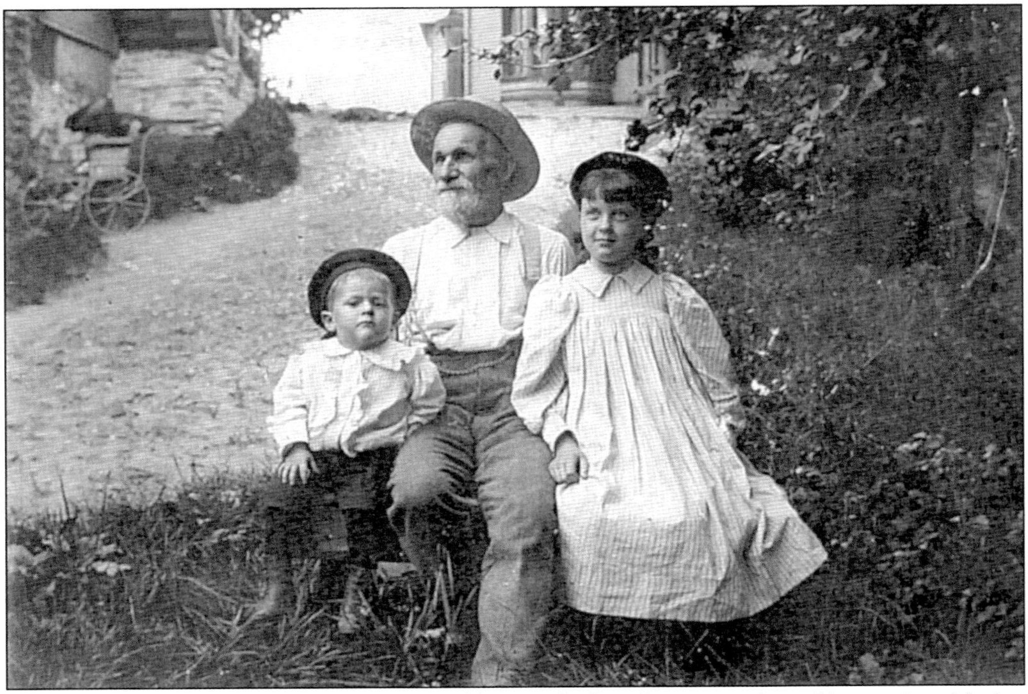

Samuel B. Horton was fond of children and known for his pleasant smile and hearty handshake. He is pictured with his two grandchildren in this photograph, Arthur Horton, son of William, and Natalie, daughter of Jennie and Charles. To Samuel, home was the dearest spot on earth.

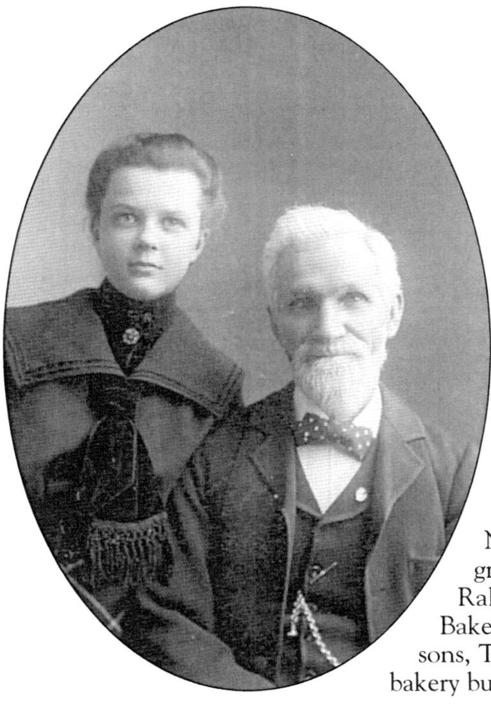

On November 15, 1912, guests assembled at the home of the bride's parents for the marriage of Natalie and Ralph Hamblett. She was the only granddaughter of the late Samuel Horton. In 1916, Ralph Hamblett opened his first store, the Newport Bakery, home of "Lucky Bread." By the 1930s, his two sons, Tarlton and Robert, joined the family grocery and bakery business.

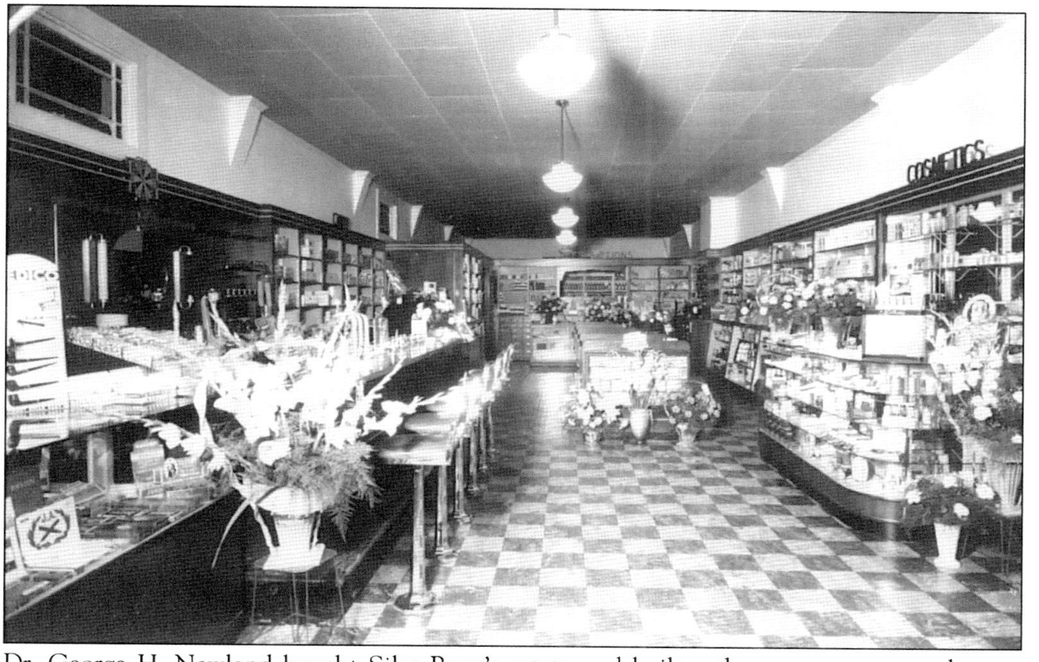

Dr. George H. Newland bought Silas Bean's estate and built a three-story structure known as the Newland/Central Block in 1892 on the corner of Main and Central Streets. In 1902, Ara W. Livingston was proprietor of the pharmacy. He had a shipment of 150 pounds of pure spruce gum, right from the tree, and sold it in small amounts for $1.60 per pound. (Courtesy of Richardson Cartee Collection.)

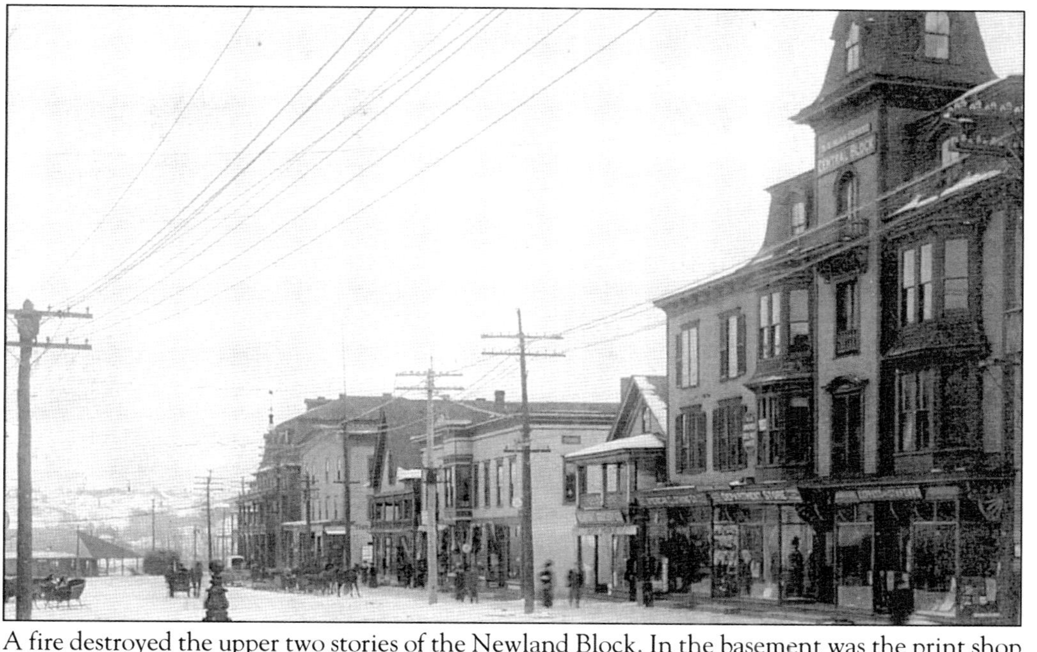

A fire destroyed the upper two stories of the Newland Block. In the basement was the print shop of C.F. Ranney in the 1890s. It is from Ranney's shop that the last circulating public library in Newport existed before the Goodrich Memorial Library was built in 1898.

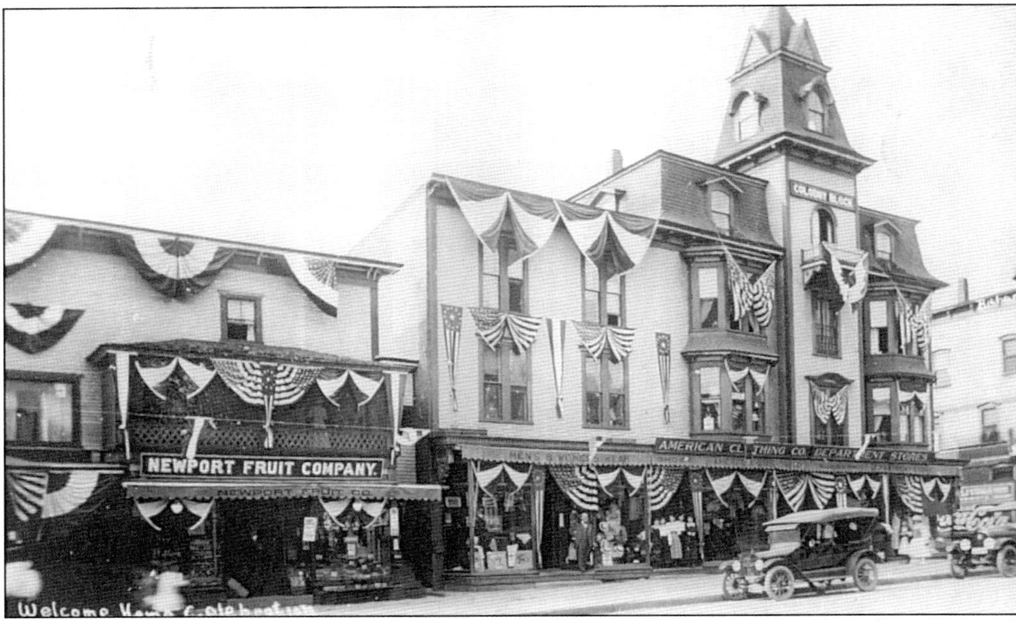

The American Clothing Company in the Colodny Block celebrated 25 years in business, with Leon Colodny as proprietor in 1923. The company was sold in 1925 to two brothers from New York City, Louis and Nathan (Ed) Needleman, with Colodny retaining the block.

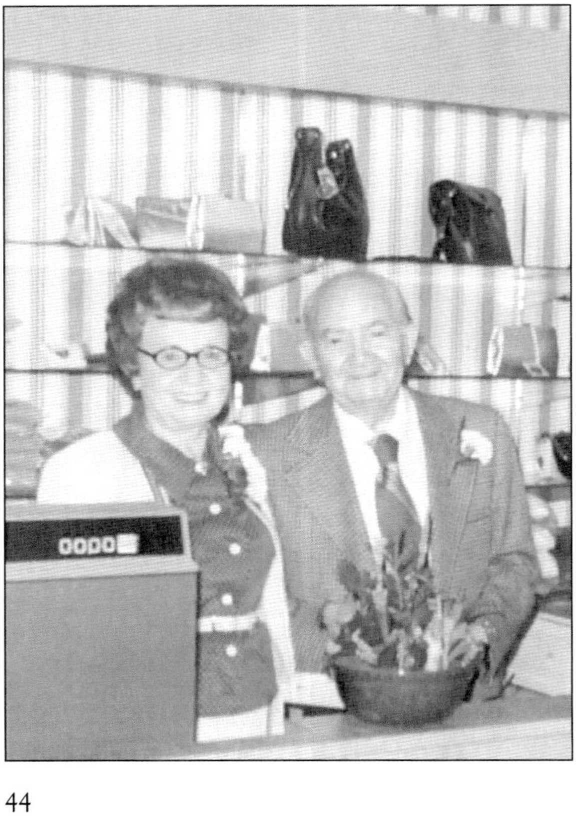

In 1936, Ed and Martha Needleman opened their own clothing store on the corner of Lane and Main Streets, running a successful business at this location for 36 years. In 1964, the family business included bridal and formal wear, and by 1995, Needleman's was assisting a fifth generation of brides. Ed Needleman passed away in 1974 and Martha died in 1985, with the Needleman family continuing on Main Street after 74 years in business.

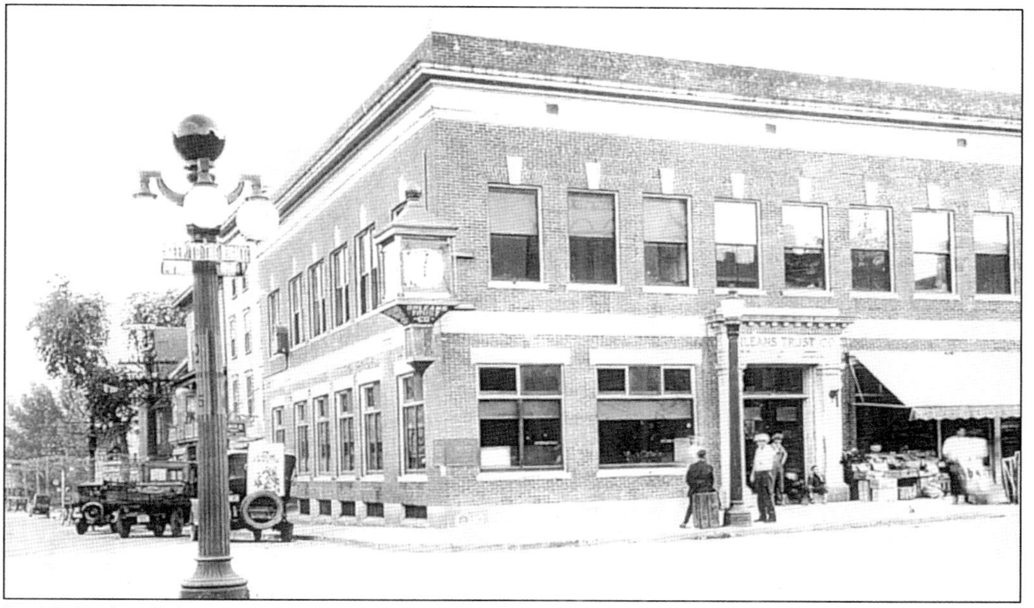

In 1915, the Orleans County Trust Company was interested in rebuilding on this site a brick structure and removing the last "hitching postrails" on Main Street. The bank took heed to good customers' word and left their hitching posts, until construction of their new building on the corner of Main and Coventry Streets in 1918.

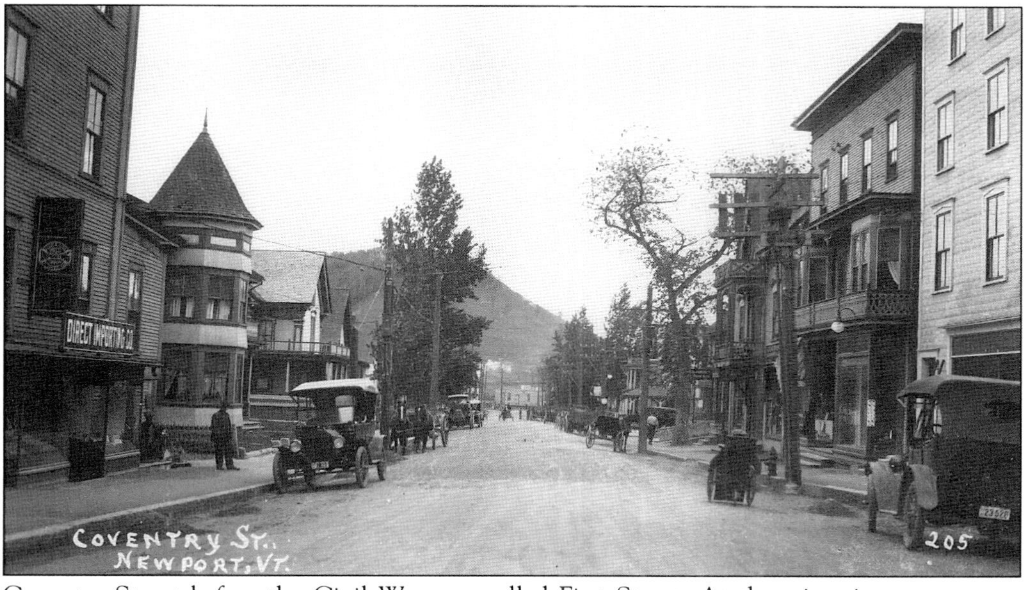

Coventry Street before the Civil War was called First Street. At that time it was no more than a cow pasture roadway leading to the Village of Coventry. (Courtesy of Richardson Cartee Collection.)

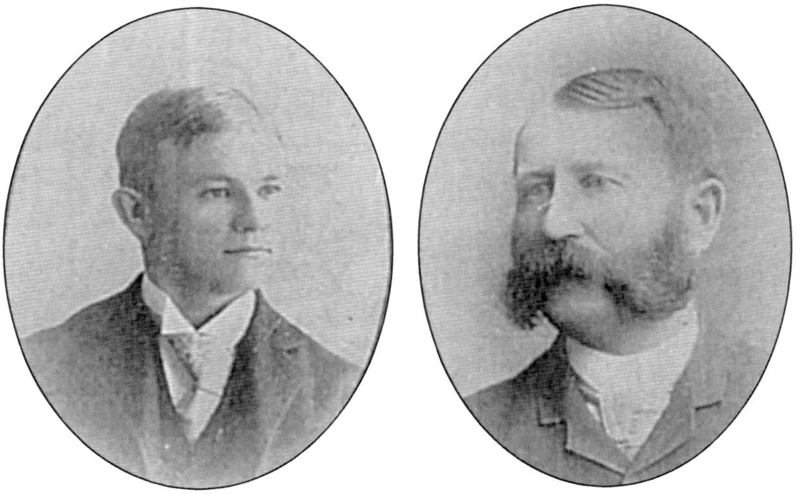

Henry S. Root, born in 1839, entered into the hardware, crockery, and furniture business in 1865 on the corner of Main and Coventry Streets, with his son George entering the firm in 1870. H.S. Root and Son's in 1898 had a Christmas sale logo, "We have the goods you need, you have the money we want, come in and exchange."

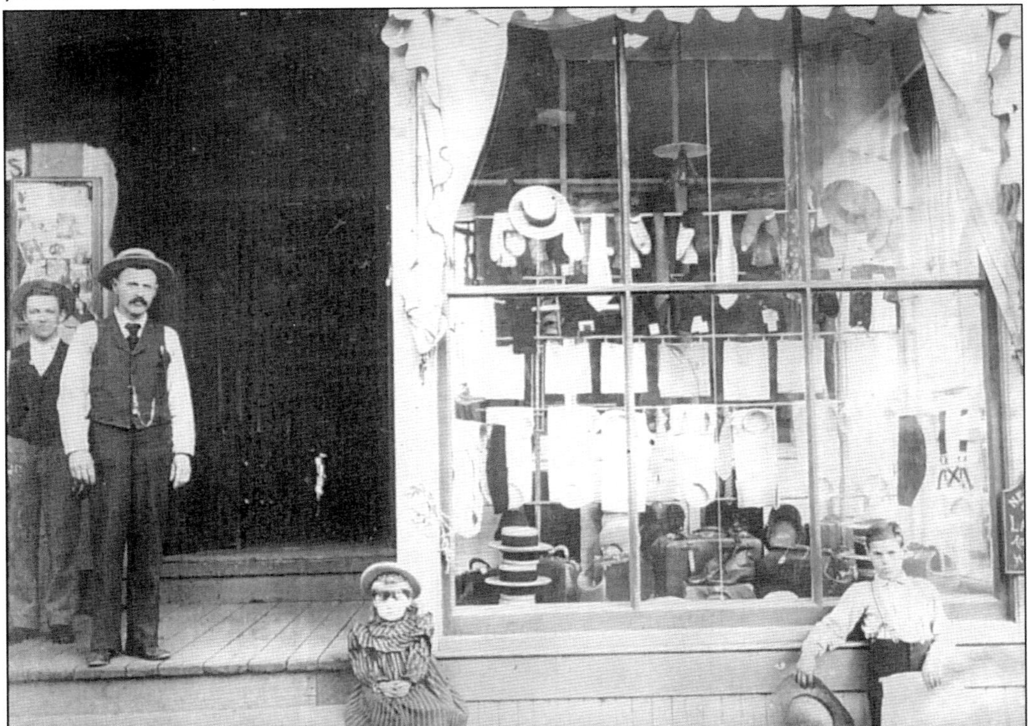

Homer Thrasher in 1883, shown here second from the left, launched into the Gent's Clothing Business, located in the Root Block. He was also a dealer in footwear, mackintoshes, trunks, and traveling bags for 36 years. Thrasher was born in 1841 in Vermont, married Josephine Bowles in 1868, and lived at 14 Second Street. He died in 1922.

H.S. Root, a Mason for 65 years, was Newport City Clerk and Treasurer for 46 years (1872–1918). He is shown here on his 90th birthday in front of his home on Main Street. H.S. Root & Son closed on May 1, 1929, with Henry S. Root passing away in 1930.

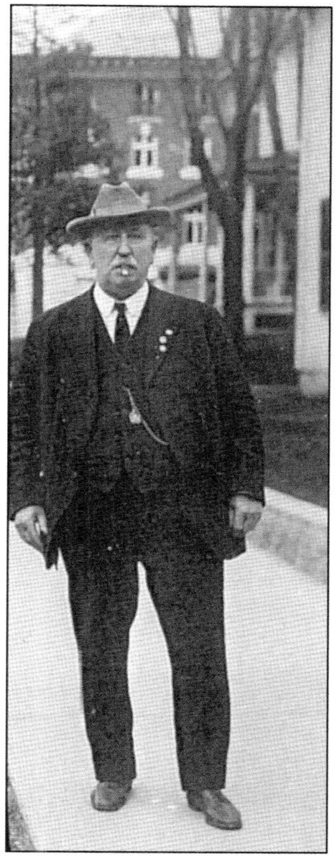

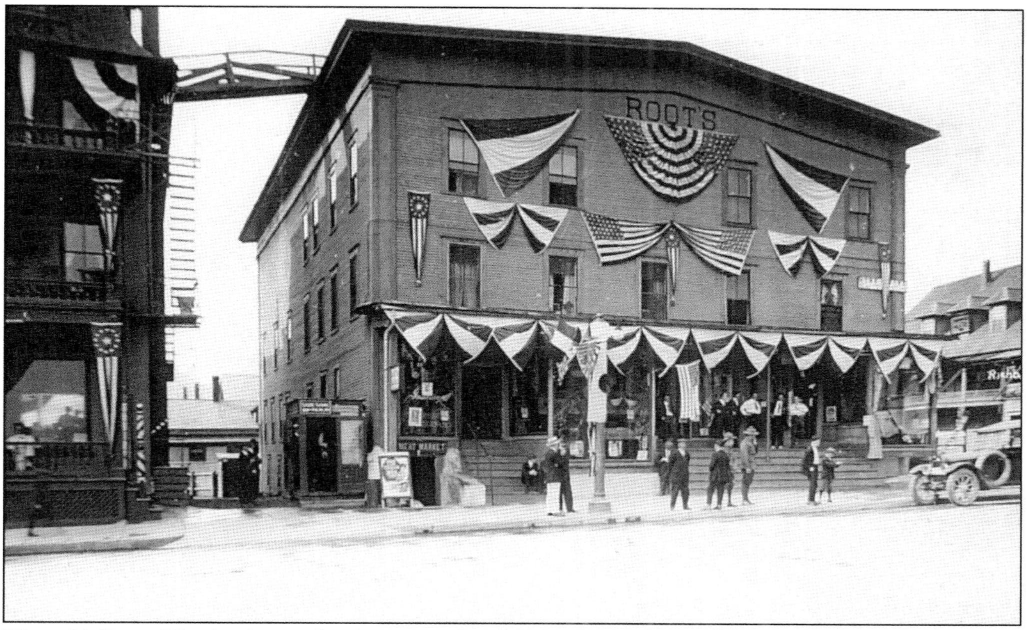

The old Root Block, dating back to pre-Civil War days when all living necessities could be obtained under its roof, was destroyed by a fire on May 20, 1968, that started in the building known then as the Branon block, that left only a shell of the over 100-year-old building.

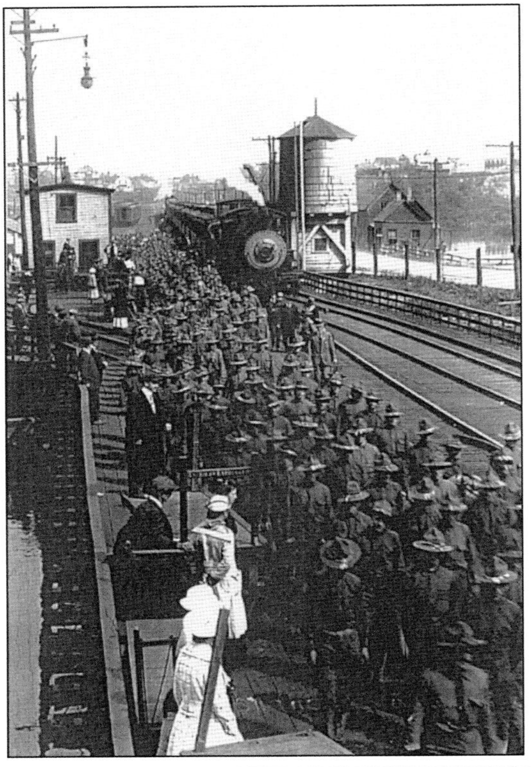

The German ultimatum to Russia on August 1, 1914, caused a war that broke out into a world-wide conflict. The United States sent 1,284,000 men to aid in this conflict. "Local Boys" boarded trains in Newport, to join the war efforts in Europe.

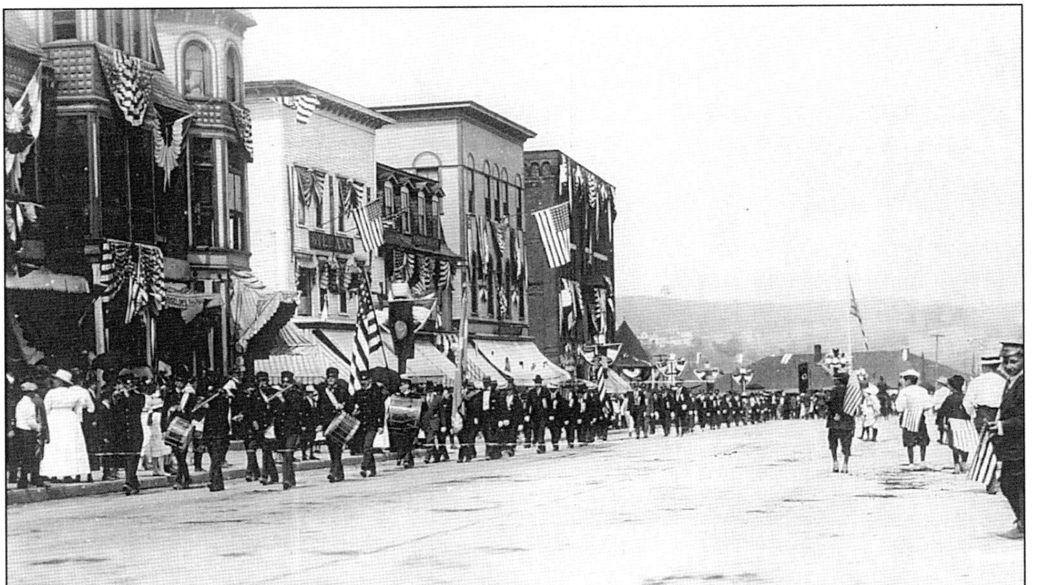

On June 3, 1919, a homecoming celebration took place on Main Street with crowds estimated at 10,000 for the return of 250 U.S. Soldiers and Sailors and 50 Canadians. All the buildings on Main Street were decorated by experts from New Hampshire, resulting in the best piece of work ever seen in the country in tribute to the soldiers returning.

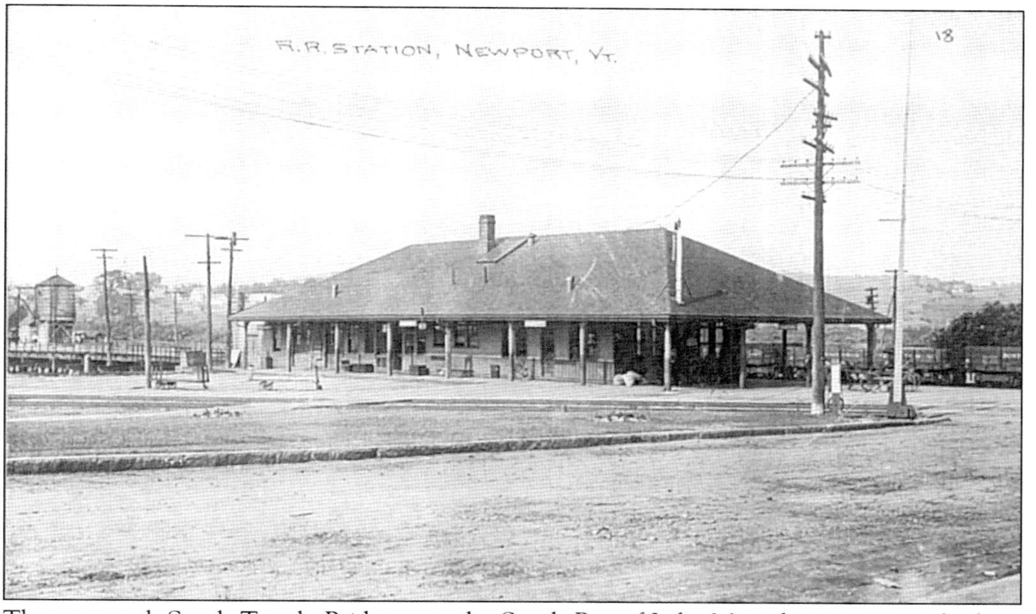

The one-track South Trestle Bridge over the South Bay of Lake Memphremagog was built in 1863 when the first passenger train entered the Village of Newport. By 1869, the Passumpsic River Railroad Company built the first passenger depot at Railroad Square, during the era of wood-burning engines. After the first railroad depot burned in 1902, a new depot would be placed in front of the Memphremagog Boat Wharf, in the open space between the Canadian Pacific Railroad tracks and the Boston & Maine tracks at a cost of $10,000. (Bottom Image Courtesy of Richardson Cartee Collection.)

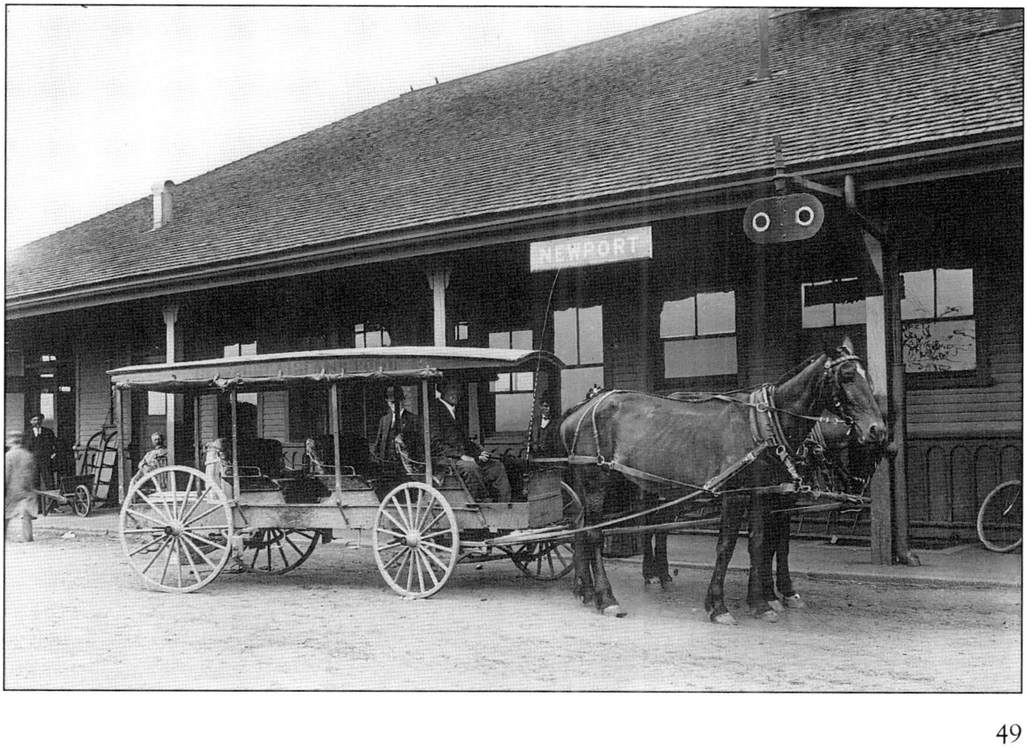

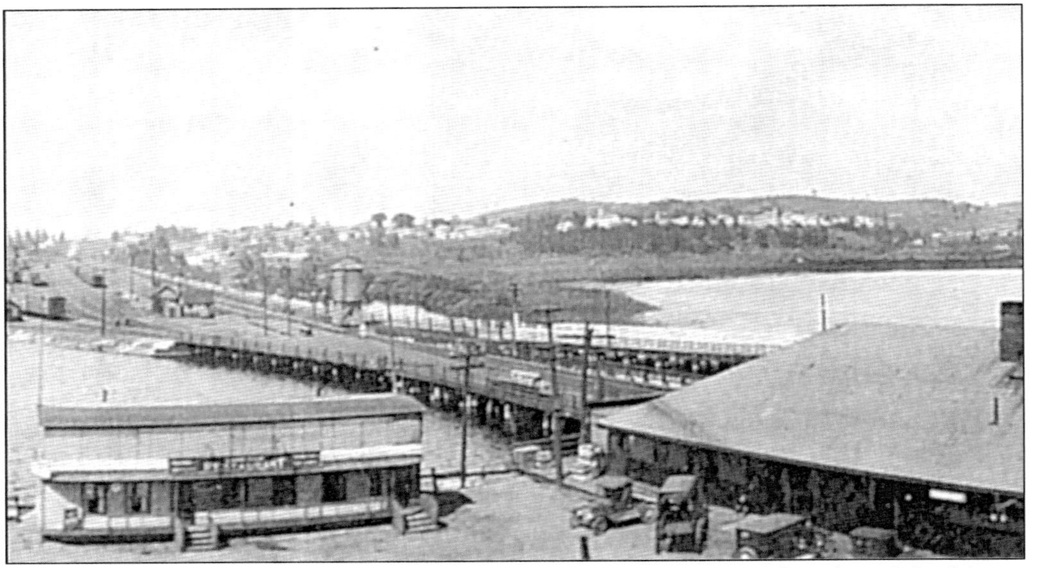

Spauldings Floating House Boat was placed on a solid foundation at the edge of the lake in 1921, near the Railroad Station, and opened as the Lakeside Restaurant. The lower floor had seating for 60 people in the dining room, and the upper deck had a polished dance floor.

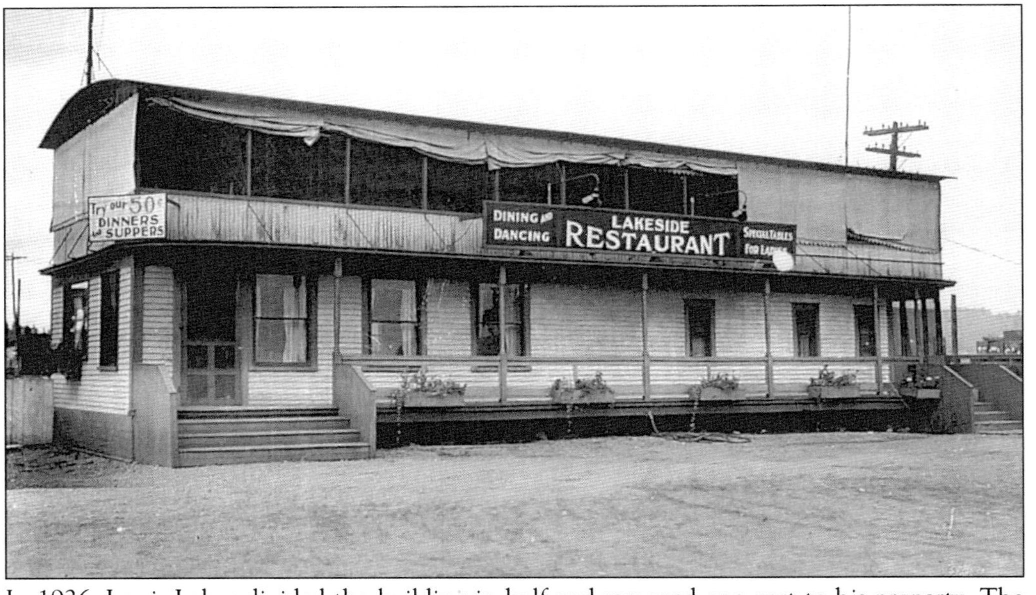

In 1926, Lewis Lahar divided the building in half and removed one part to his property. The other half he moved next to the Long Bridge. Lahar continued the Lakeside Restaurant, known for home cooking and quick service, along with boats and canoes for rent. (Courtesy of Richardson Cartee Collection.)

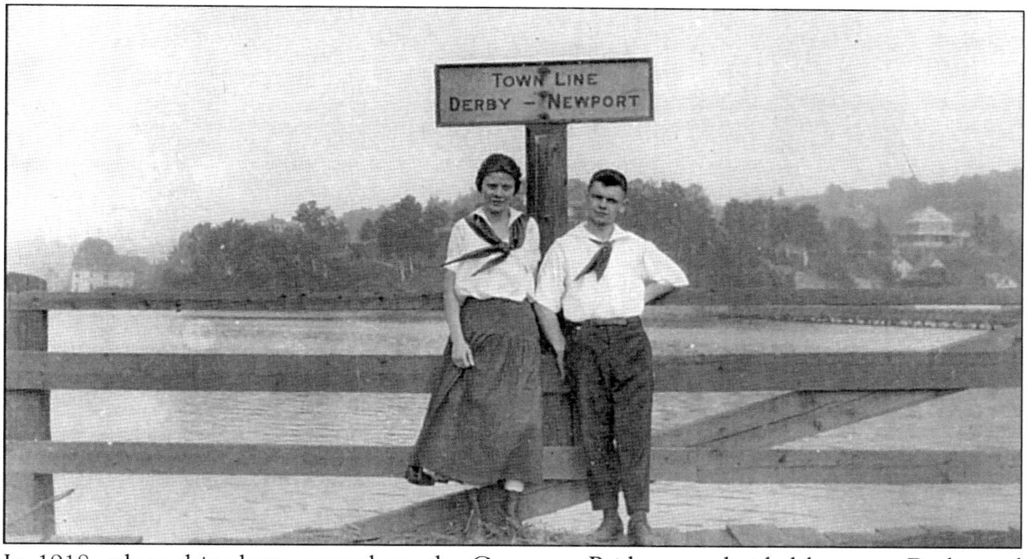

In 1918, when this photo was taken, the Causeway Bridge was divided between Derby and Newport with Mt. Vernon Street and the Long Bridge in the background.

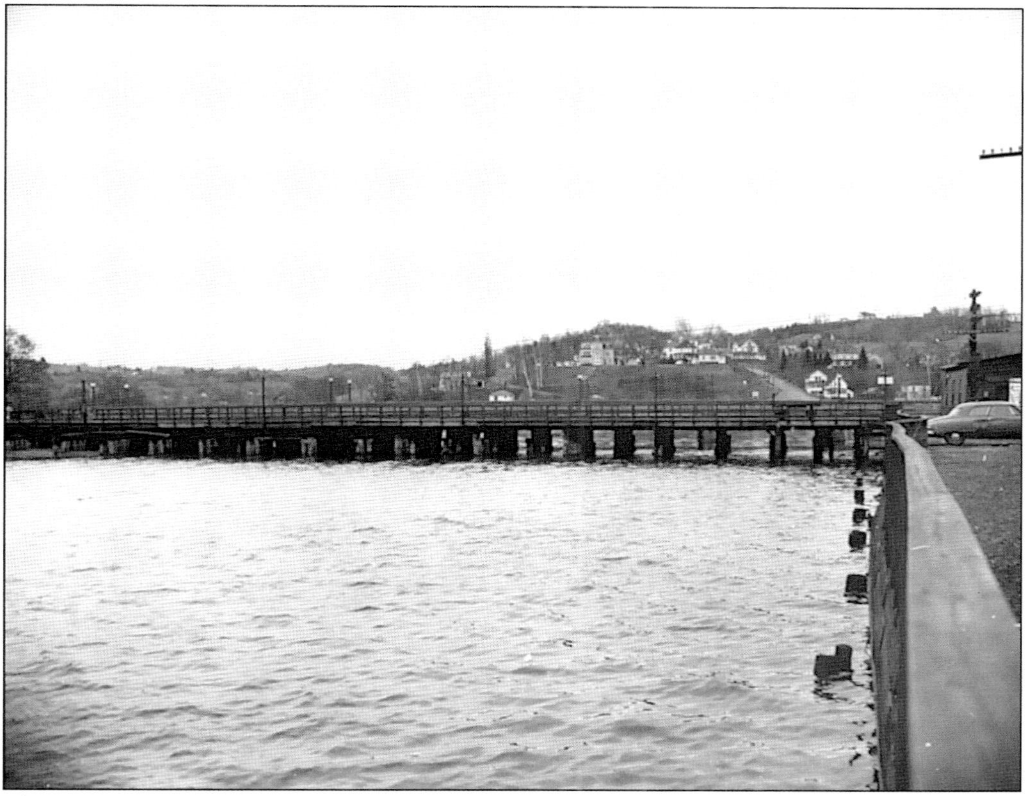

The Connecticut & Passumpsic Railroad rebuilt the old log bridge with a wooden road bridge for teams and people. This bridge washed out in the 1927 flood and was replaced by the present concrete Causeway Bridge in 1932. (Courtesy of Richardson Cartee Collection.)

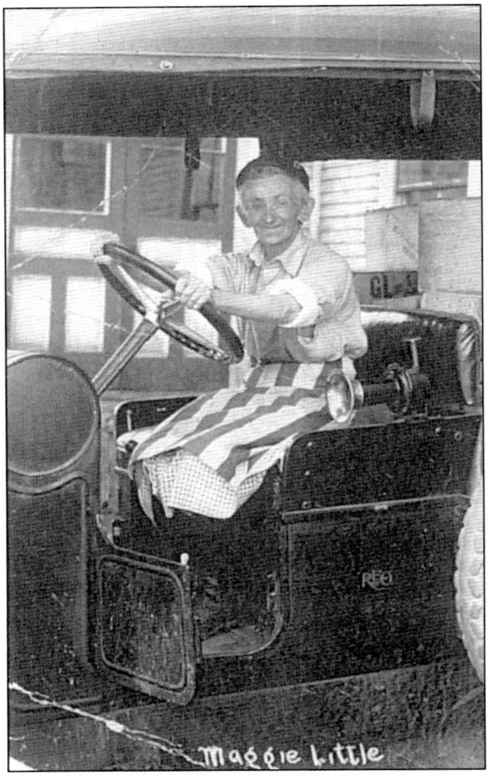

Maggie Little, Newport's fisherwoman of Lake Memphremagog, was born in 1842 and began to "wander" from the age of 12. Maggie dressed at times in long shirts or a man's coat with a cap. She would work up a woodpile or split a cord of wood with a little money the "wanderlust" would come upon her.

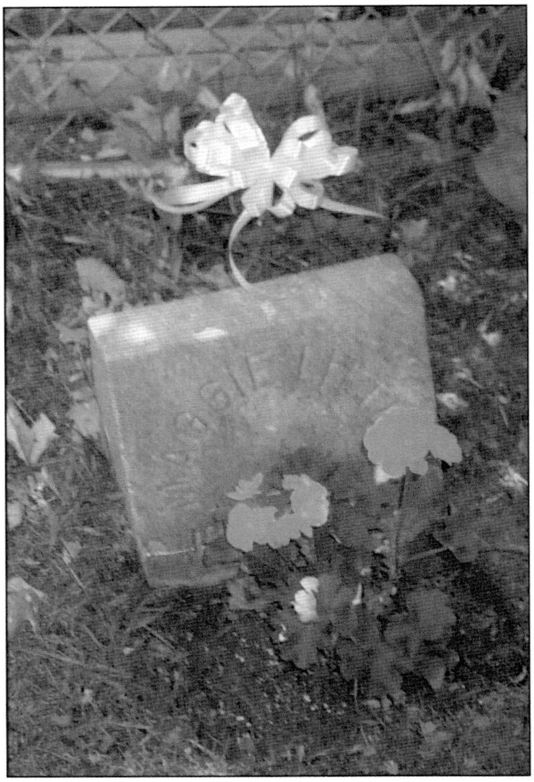

Fishing was both a means of livelihood and a pastime. With her fishing pole and pipe, she chose her place near Newport's railroad bridge. Maggie died in 1934 and went on one more adventure—her last one. She was buried in pauper's row, laid to rest in a pretty blue dress at the East Main Street cemetery.

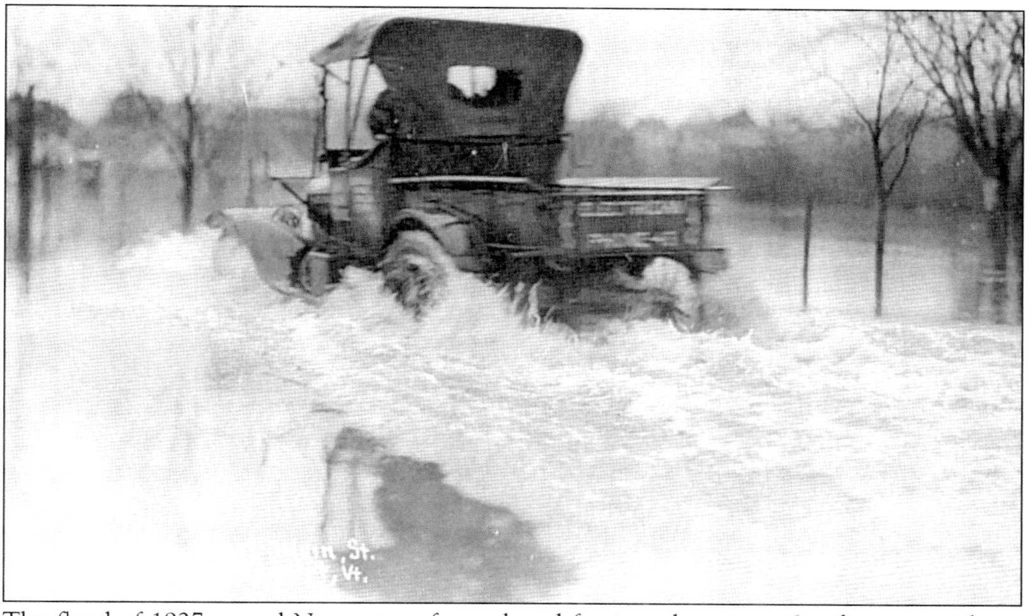

The flood of 1927 caused Newport to face a bread famine when a supply of yeast ran short. Ralph Hamblett's Bakery was short on yeast, and some was being sent by airplane to Newport. Lieutenant Walter Cleveland from Coventry arranged to land on the Roeder Farm in West Derby but the plane failed to arrive. The flood saw a foot of water fall in 40 hours, transforming streams into mad torrents. Old-timers recalled the Flood of 1869 when a severe "freshet" visited Vermont, on Sunday October 3, and continued until Monday night of October 4.

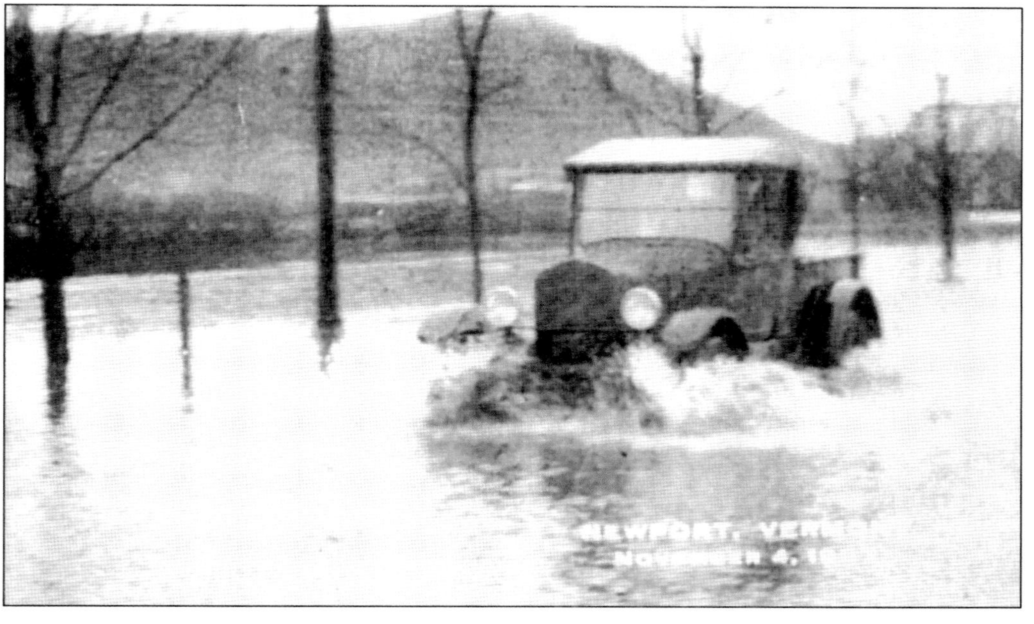

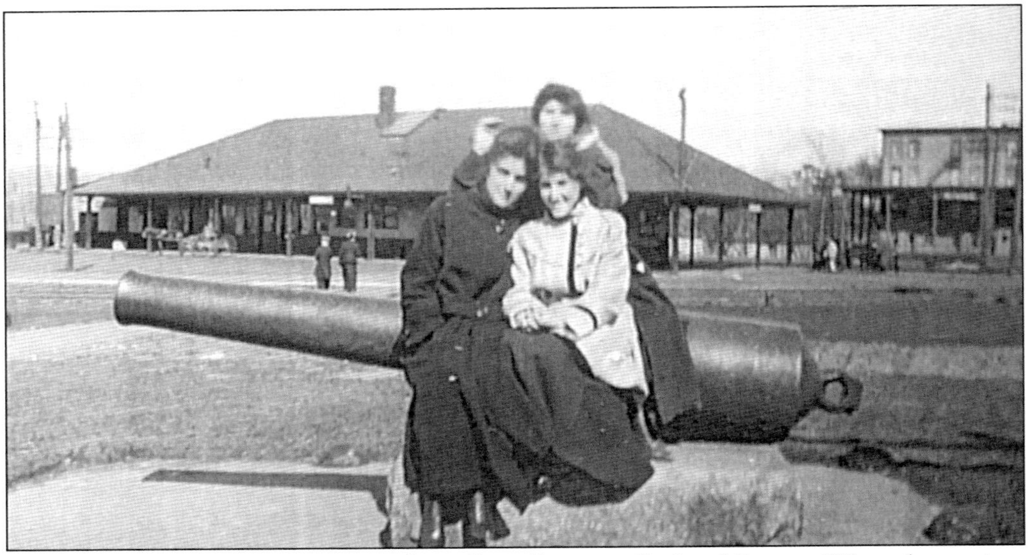

Newport had a cast iron cannon on the Village Green, at Railroad Square. When the carriage rotted away, it was mounted on granite blocks. The city fathers sold the cannon to the Japanese for scrap iron about two years before Pearl Harbor.

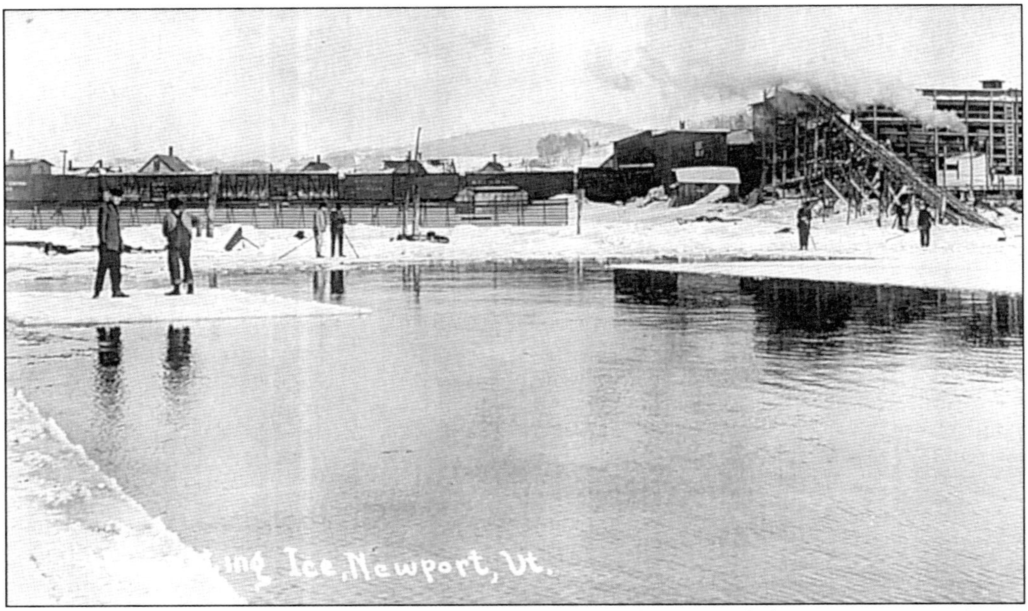

Ice harvesting is pictured on Lake Memphremagog near the turn of the century as workmen engage in the task of filling the Railroad's Ice House, located in the area of the present Waterfront Plaza on the Causeway. Instead of using horses to pull the ice up the slip, they used a small steam engine called a "donkey" and a wrench that wound up the rope, as in this 1910 photograph.

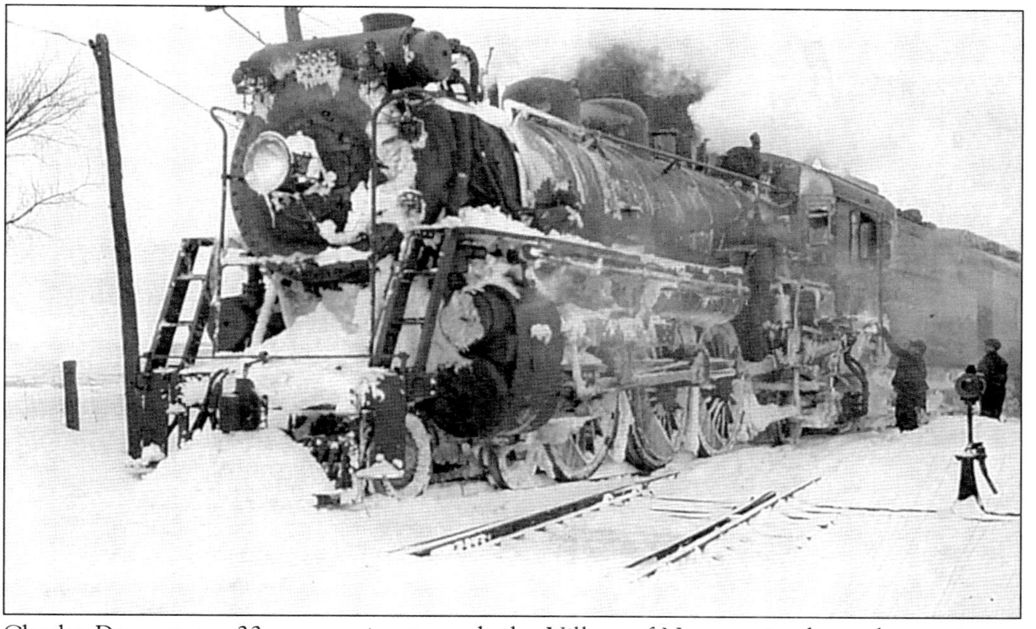

Charles Drew at age 33 was coming towards the Village of Newport in the early evening in January of 1888, when he discovered a heavy timber sticking out of a culvert. It was too heavy to remove as he heard the express train that whistled at the crossing below. With no lantern to attract attention he took off his coat, twisted it around a stick, and set it on fire as he ran down the tracks. The engineer saw something was wrong and slowed the train down. Drew was presented with a new suit of clothes and many thanks for his heroic act.

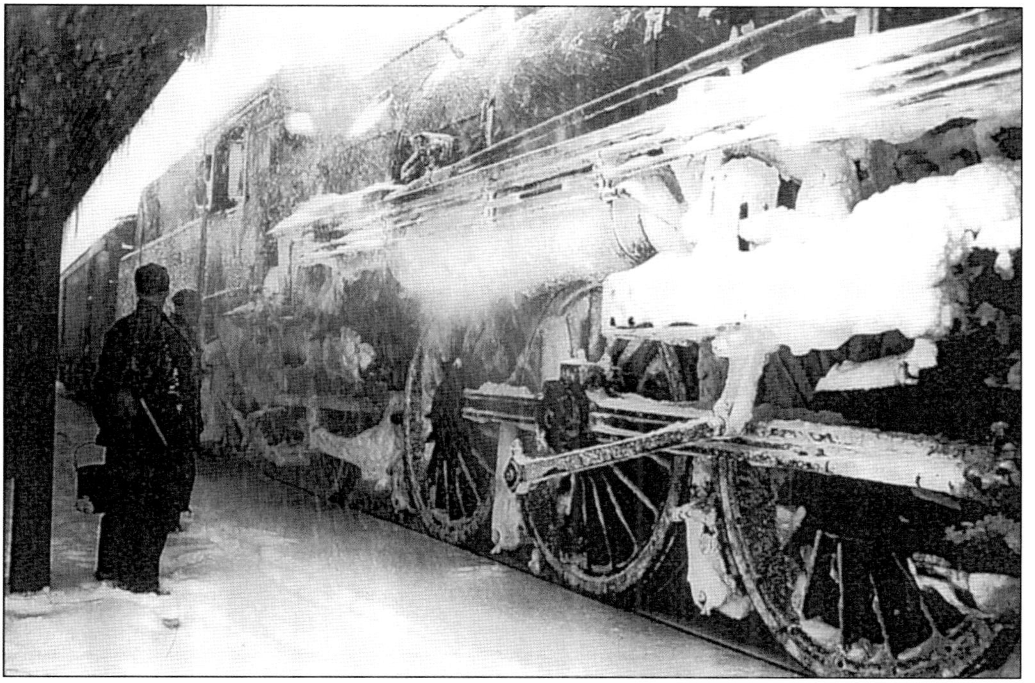

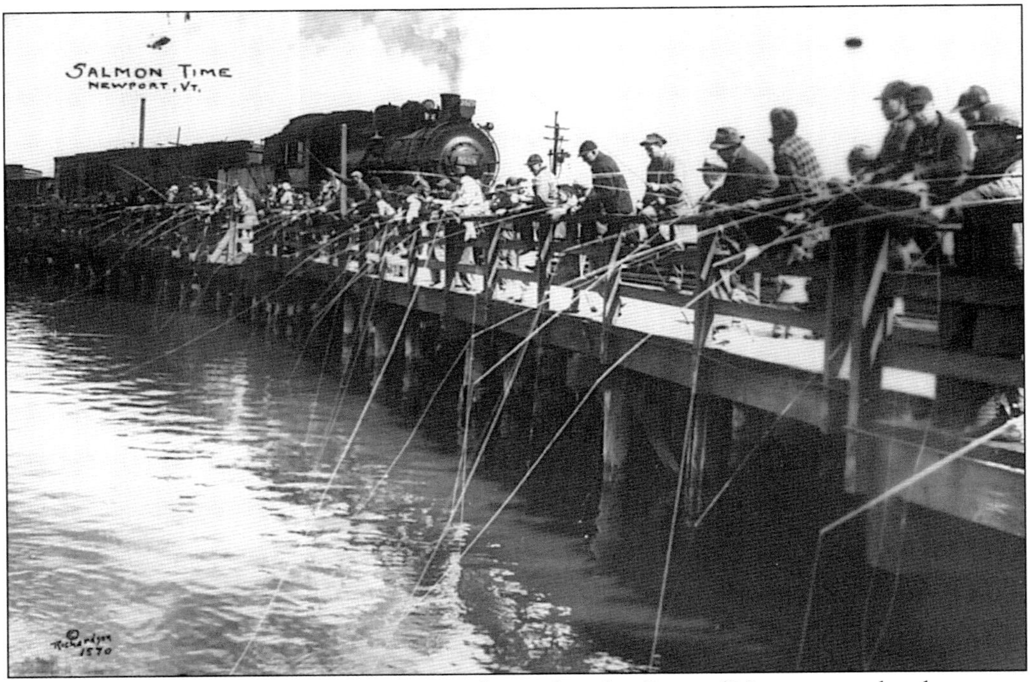

The "Land of the Sky Blue Waters" was a phrase that the State of Vermont used to lure game fisherman to the abundant fishing in the Northeast Kingdom from the early 1900s until the mid-1950s. It truly was a fisherman's paradise when "Salmon was King." Sportsmen registered at the local hotels and stood shoulder to shoulder with their fishing rods on the Canadian Pacific Railroad Bridge, over Lake Memphremagog. In 1935, 279 pounds of fish were caught from the railroad bridge in the first three hours of fishing on opening day. (Courtesy of Richardson Cartee Collection.)

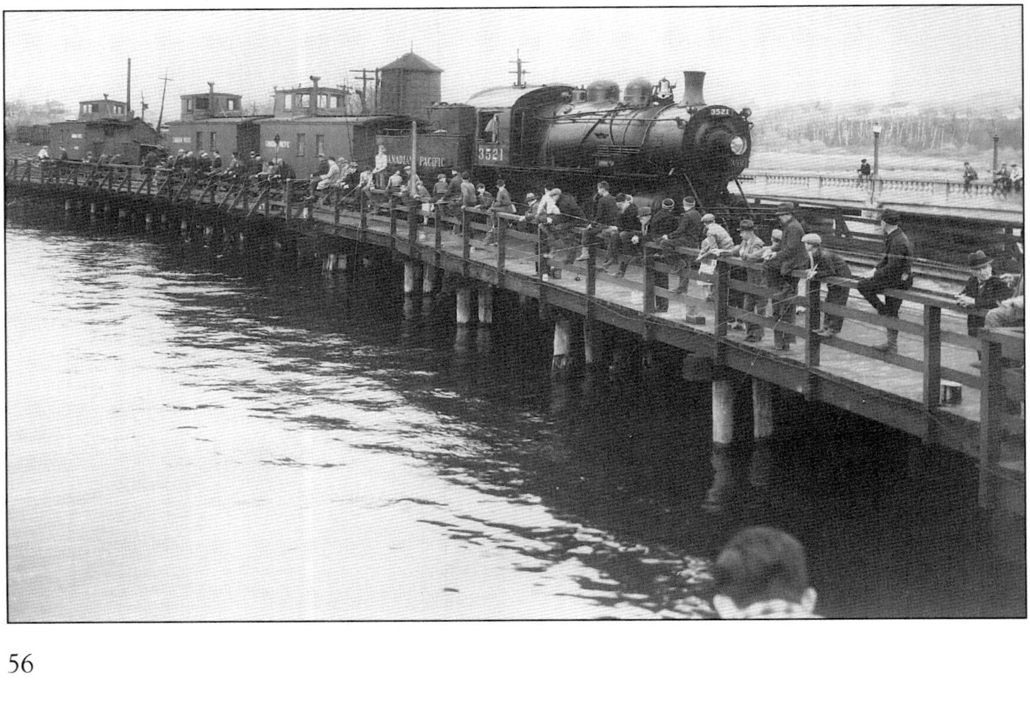

Fred Fauch, who ran the Amaco Gas Station on Main Street, shows off his trophy of a fish. Another fish story goes: when a train pulled into the station a passenger gave a kid a dollar to let him try his fishing rod. With his first cast he got a strike and landed his fish. He returned the rod hauling his prize fish aboard just as the train pulled out. He then sent it to the diner to be prepared for his dinner.

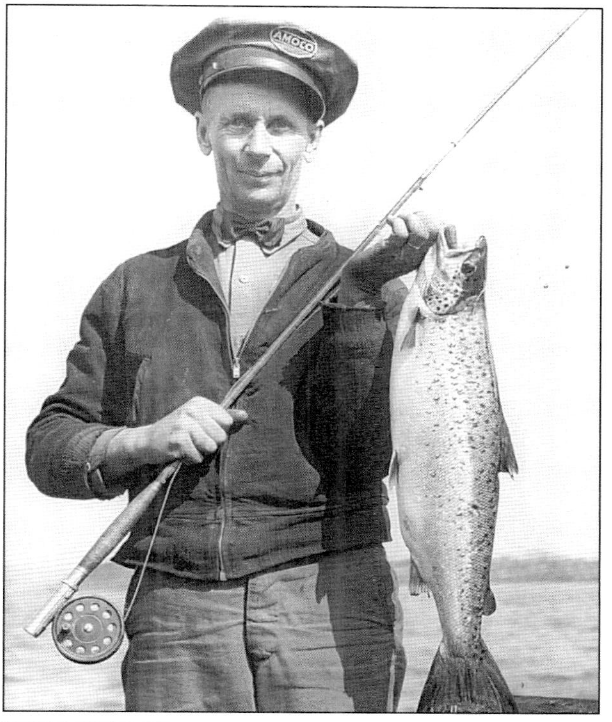

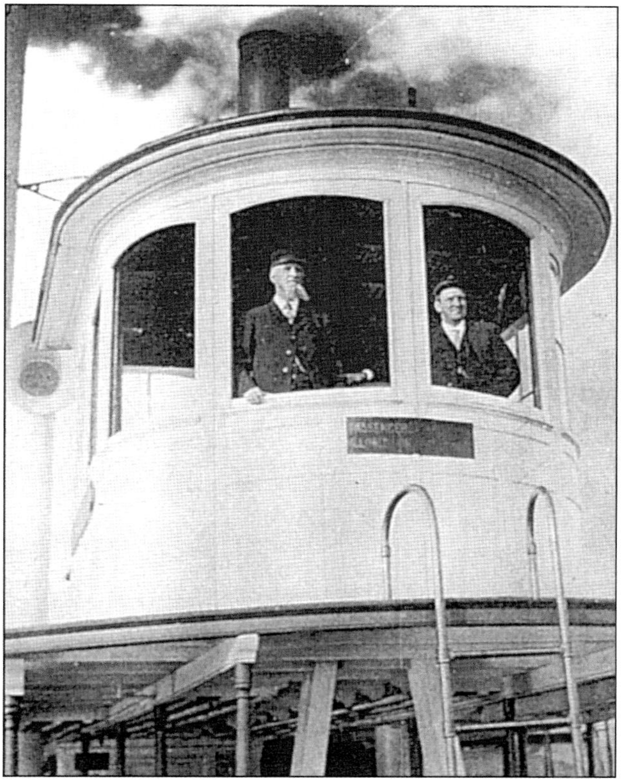

Pictured here is the *Lady of the Lake* with Captain C.C. Bullock and Pilot John McEwan. After the death of Captain Fogg in 1885, Captain Bullock was in charge until his death in 1916, when the famous steamer laid idle. Bullock was a good navigator and in his fog-horn voice he would yell out to his passengers, "Get back on the other side or you'll dump us all in the lake."

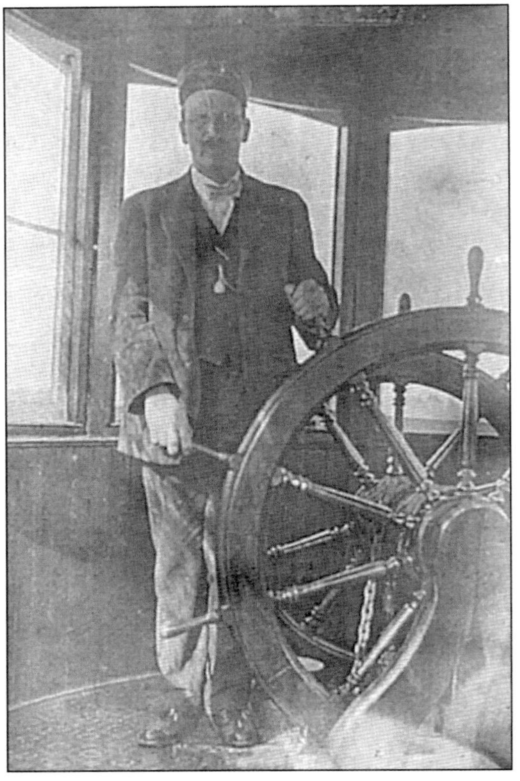

Pilot John (Jack) McEwan in 1935 retired as a railroad conductor after 48 years of service. He passed away in 1951. Born in 1871, he was the son of Scottish parents. He married Laura McShane and had one child, Mary. Jack was not a tall man but was sturdy and much liked for his work and service on the famous *Lady of the Lake*.

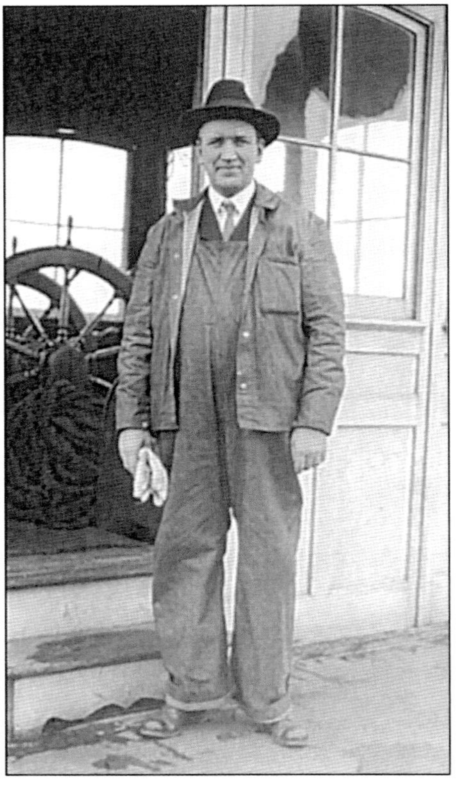

Jack McEwan of Newport was one of the last pilots of the *Lady of the Lake*, about the time when old-timers were recalling the last years of the famous steamer.

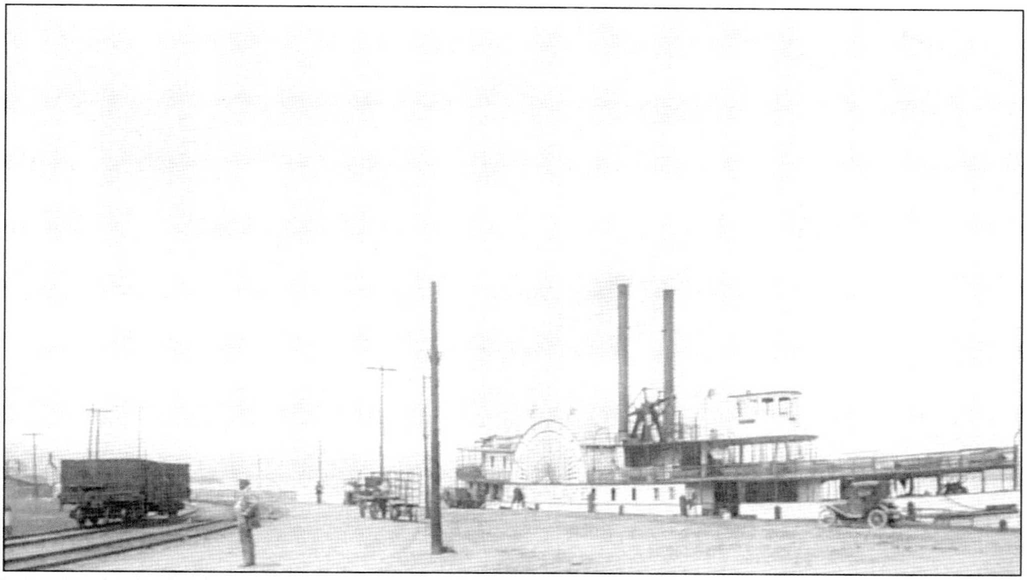

John Beebe had a booth on the historic old boat and sold tobacco, refreshments, and peanuts during the last excursion days.

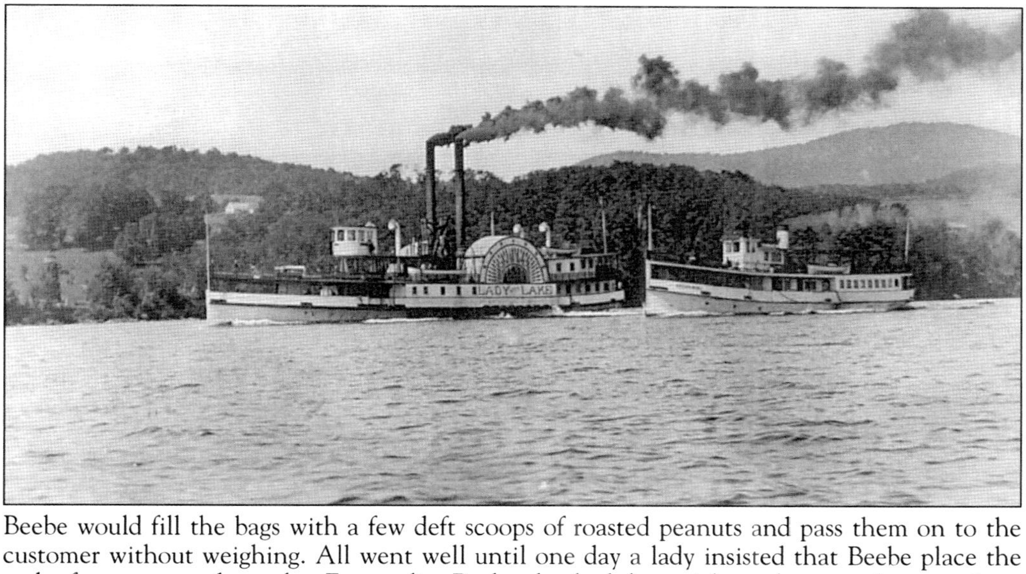

Beebe would fill the bags with a few deft scoops of roasted peanuts and pass them on to the customer without weighing. All went well until one day a lady insisted that Beebe place the sack of peanuts on the scales. Ever-polite Beebe checked the weight and removed two or three peanuts from the bag as the purchaser viewed the proceedings with a bit of chagrin.

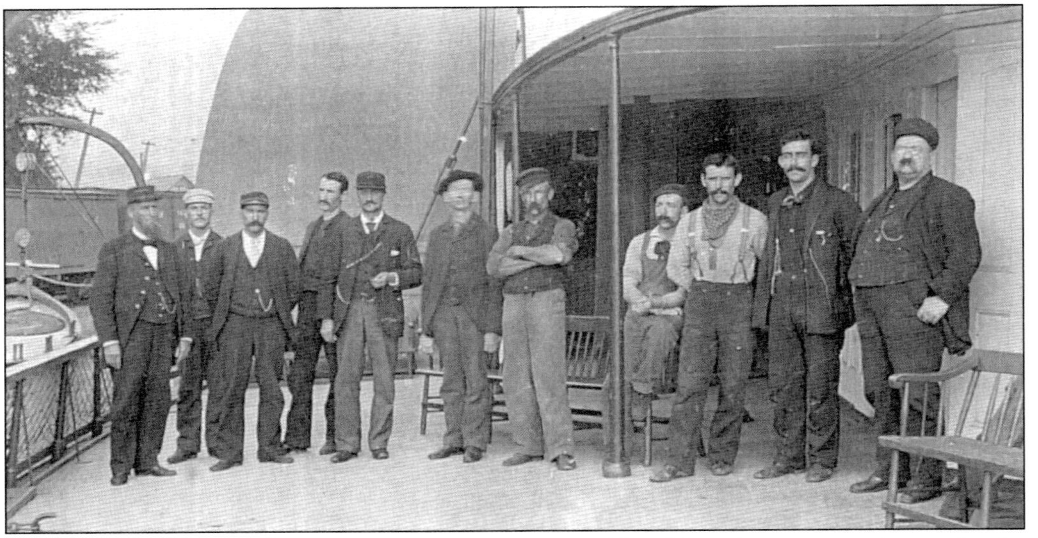

The old steamboats had a crew to assist its captains, like this unknown captain on the far left. It could be one of several men, including Capt. George W. Fogg (1819–1885), who in 1868 was appointed and many considered him "Father of Commercial Navigation." He resided in Newport at his Lake View Farm overlooking Lake Memphremagog. It could also be Capt. George C. Merrill (1836–1900) or Capt. Charles C. Bullock (1837–1916).

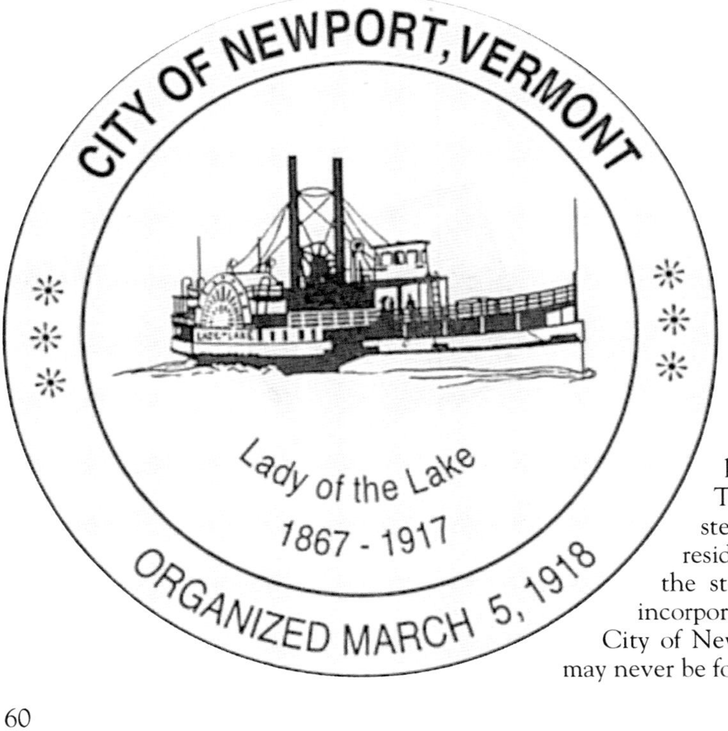

The *Lady of the Lake* was the largest paddlewheel steamer on Lake Memphremagog, carrying 500 passengers. She made her maiden voyage in 1867. The handsomely appointed steamer was so loved by the residents of Newport that the steamer's likeness had been incorporated into the seal of the City of Newport in 1918, so that she may never be forgotten.

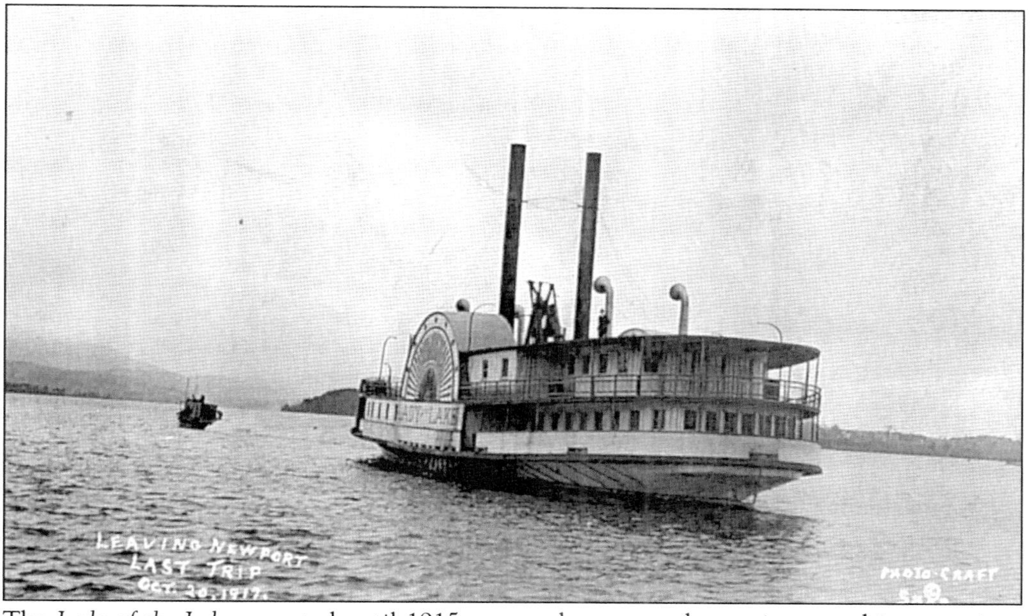

The *Lady of the Lake* operated until 1915, as people were no longer interested in excursions when the automobile was introduced. On October 20, 1917, the steamer who endeared itself to the hearts of thousands of people was towed from the Newport Wharf, and passed out of sight as it bade Newport a last farewell.

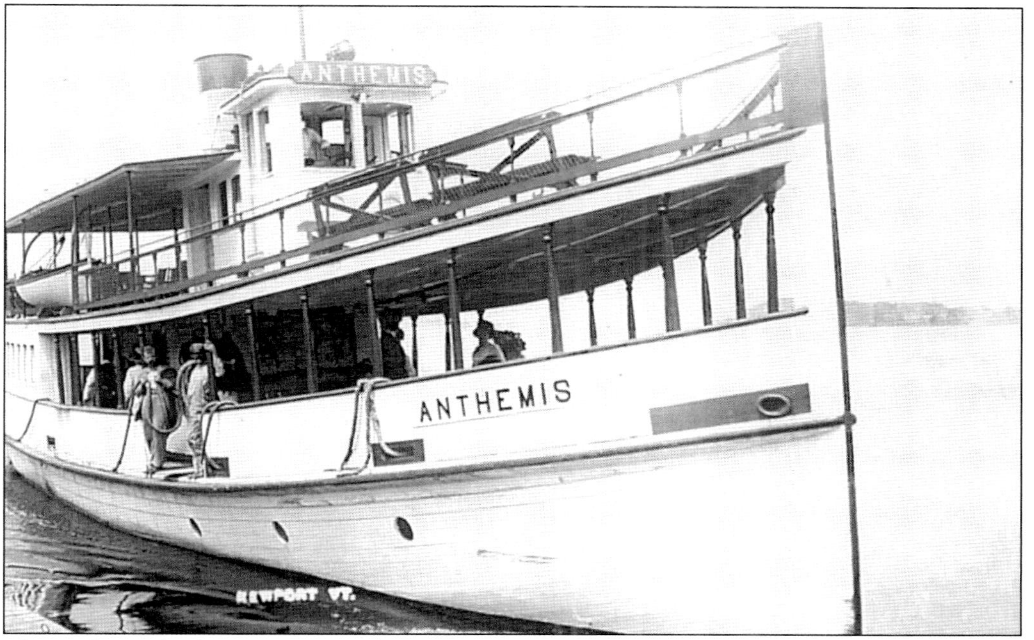

The *Anthemis*, built in 1909, named after a greek word meaning "The Goddess of Steam," was the last wood-burning steamer on Lake Memphremagog. The *Anthemis* berthed at Railroad Square, and on July 24, 1931, no less than 16 nationalities were represented among the passengers when it departed from the wharf.

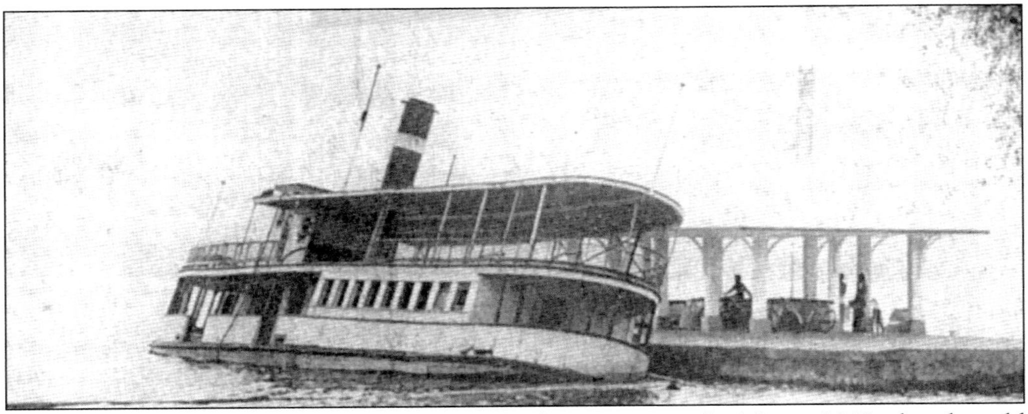

Capt. Alexander Clarke, born in 1877, spent his last season on the lake in 1947 when he sold the *Anthemis* to Canadians. In 1954, the *Anthemis* was scrapped and stripped by vandals where she rested on her side at the Magog Wharf, Quebec, Canada, before sinking in eight feet of water to the bottom of her beloved Lake Memphremagog.

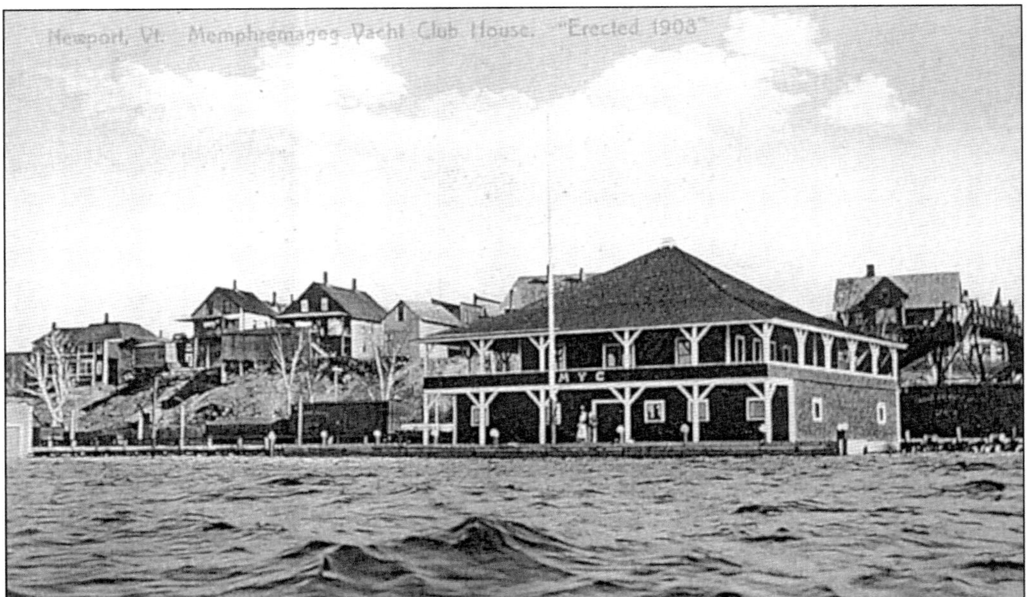

The Memphremagog Yacht Club was constructed in May of 1908 on piles at the water's edge, and was reached by a steel bridge at the end of Field Avenue, extending over the railroad tracks.

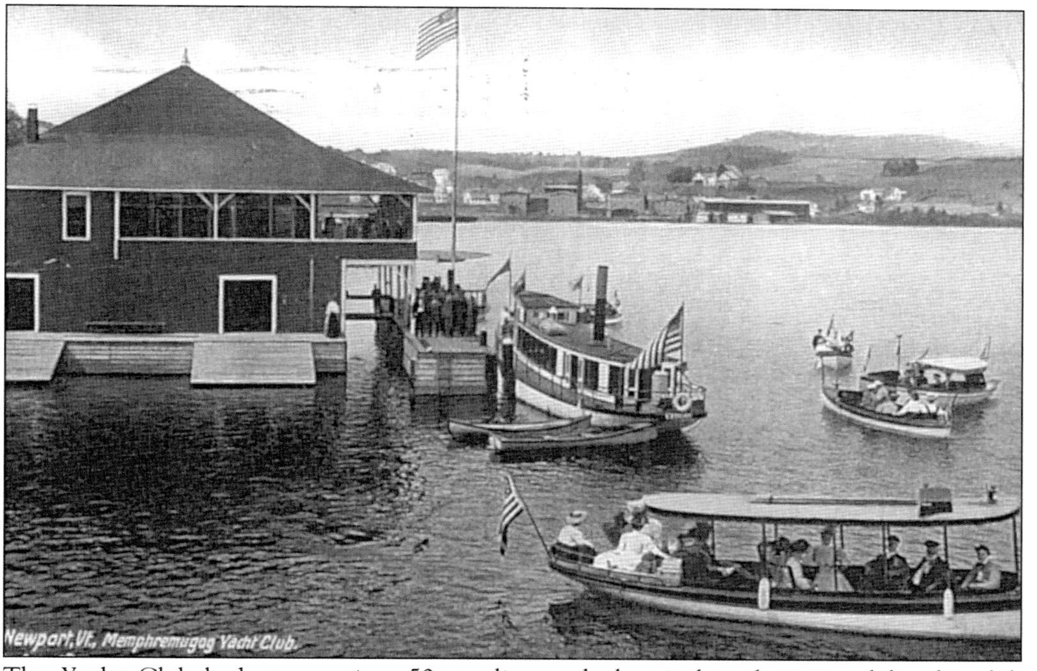

The Yacht Club had at one time 50 gasoline and electric launches owned by the club members, and the club was the home to the Black Arrow Canoe Club. In 1921, Charles Garrett purchased the building from the last MYC Directors and Commodore Carroll A. Davis for $1,000.

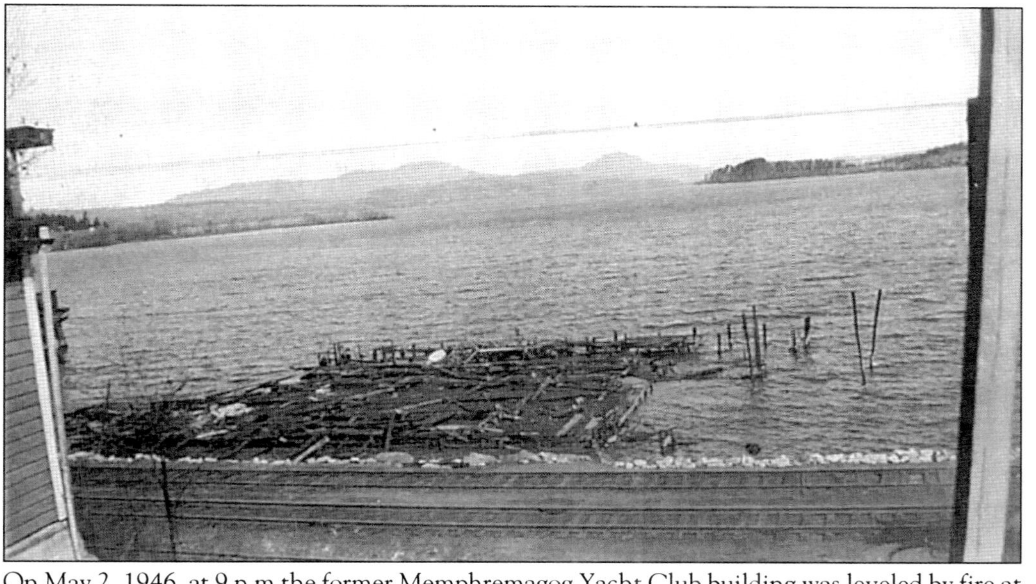

On May 2, 1946, at 9 p.m the former Memphremagog Yacht Club building was leveled by fire at a loss of $3,000. Courageous members of the fire department who sought to carry hose line over the steel overpass bridge to the doomed building were driven back by the flames and smoke. The timber-dry building burned for an hour before the walls caved in, and by 10:45 p.m. the building was gone.

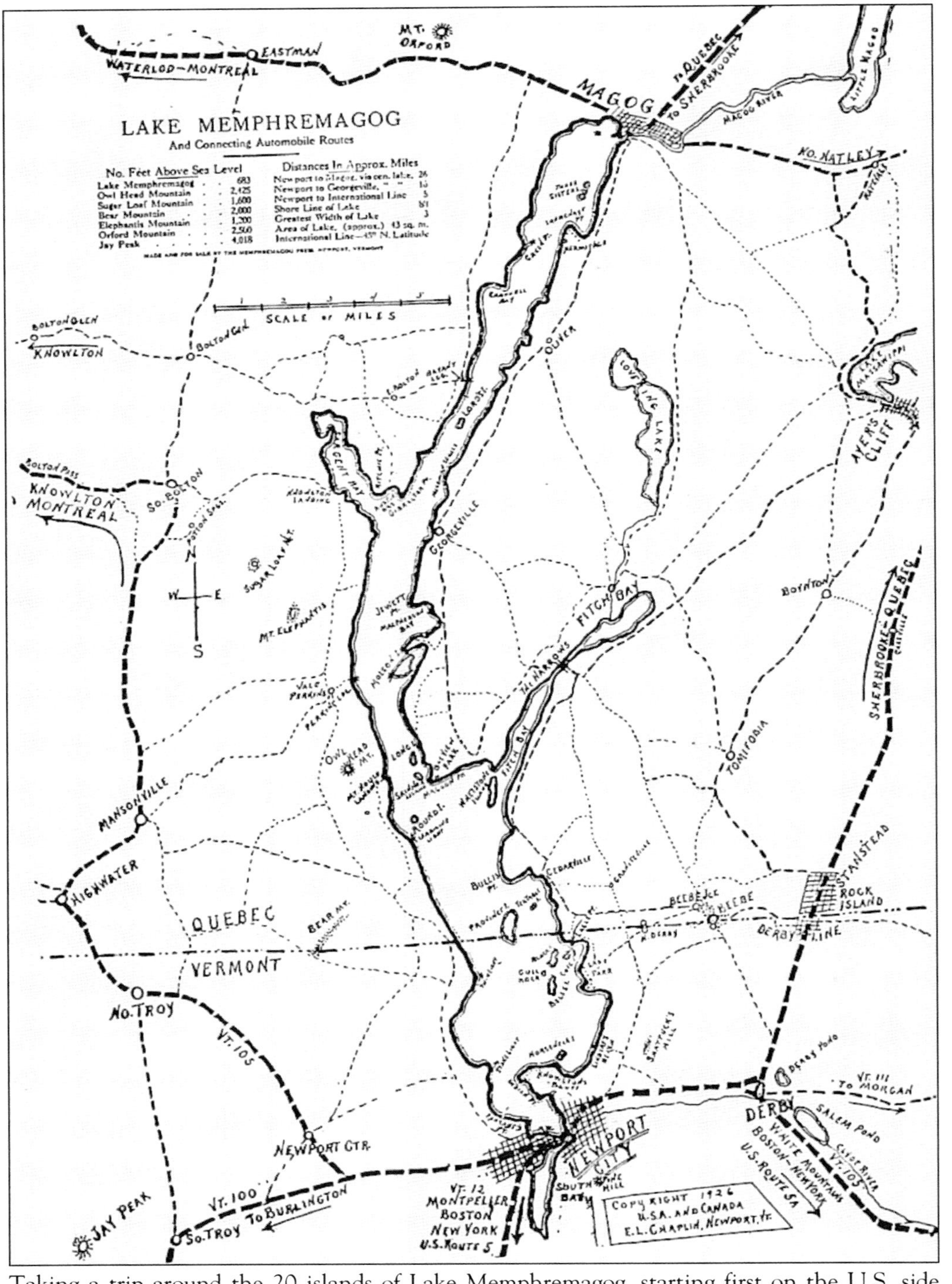

Taking a trip around the 20 islands of Lake Memphremagog, starting first on the U.S. side of the border, there is Horseneck Island. Here the author and her two daughters, Kelly and Heather, had a sighting in 1983 of the now famous Memphre, the friendly lake creature seen by many eyewitnesses since 1816 on both sides of the border.

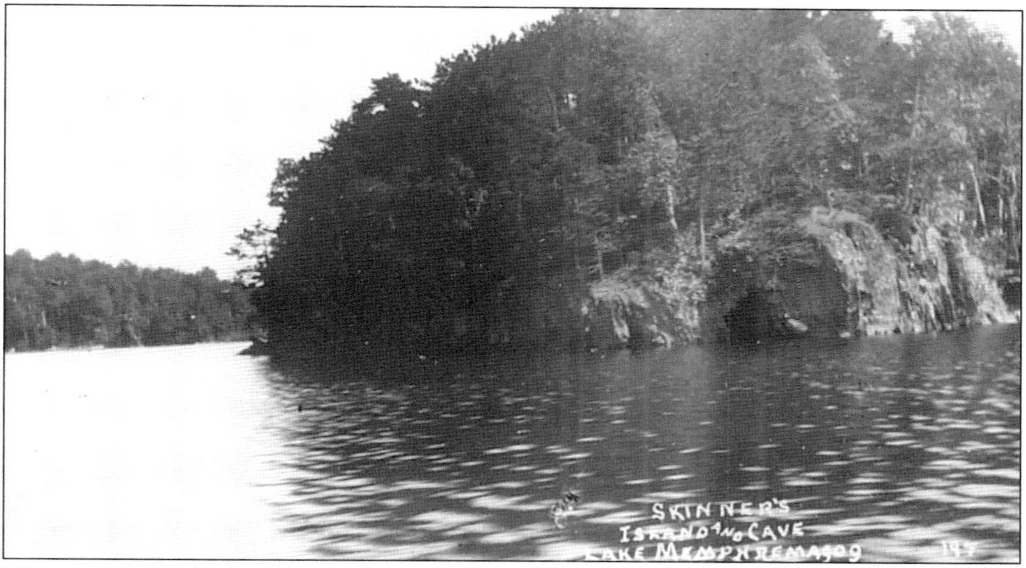

The rest of the islands going north are Belle and Black; Cove Island; Province Island, where the southern tip is in the U.S. and the rest in Canada; Tea Table, Loon, and Gull Islands; Whetstone, Round, and Minnow Islands; Skinner's Island, where Skinner's cave is located, 60 feet long and 8 feet wide, used by smugglers; Long, Molsons, Lords, and Eagle Islands; the Three Sisters and the last Charest Island in Magog, Quebec, Canada. (Courtesy of Richardson Cartee Collection.)

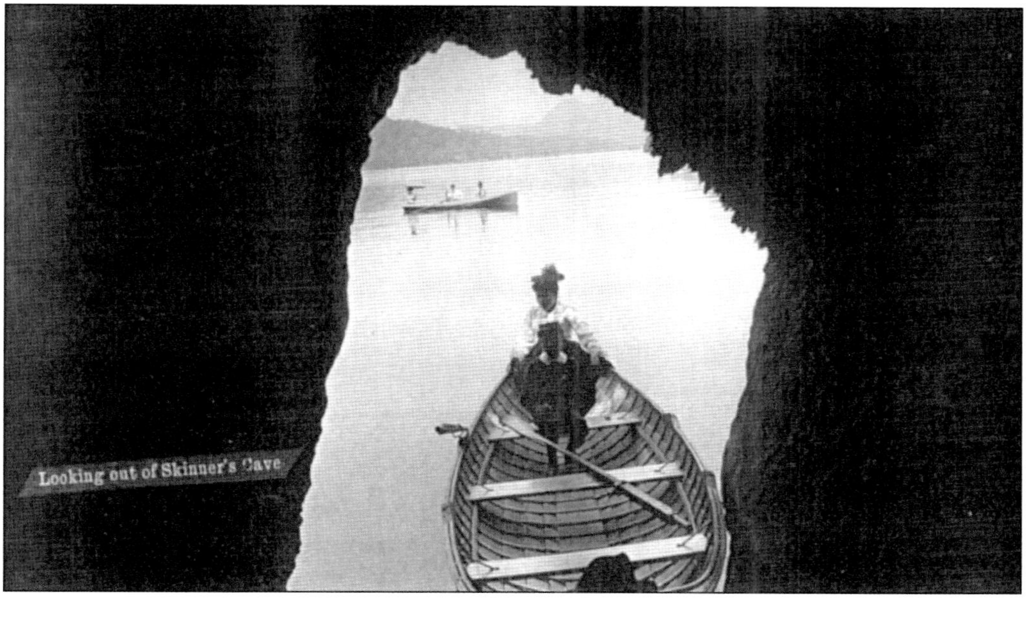

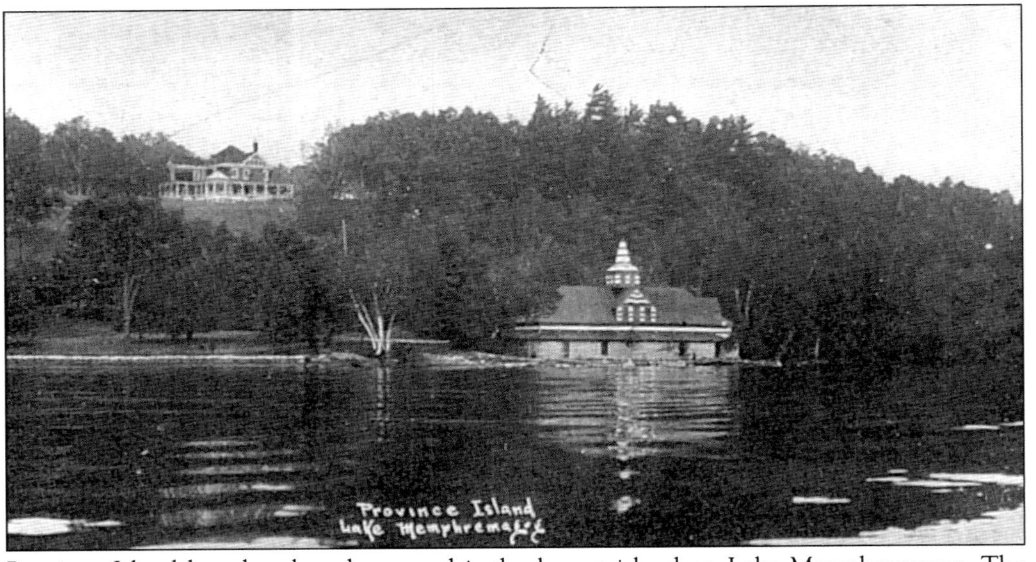

Province Island has shoreless shores and is the largest island on Lake Memphremagog. The International Boundary between the U.S. and Canada cuts through the island with the largest portion being in Canada. Andrew C. Zabriskie of New York City purchased the island and built a summer residence on the summit in 1886. He also erected a boathouse and wharf where he kept his steam yacht named "Dodo."

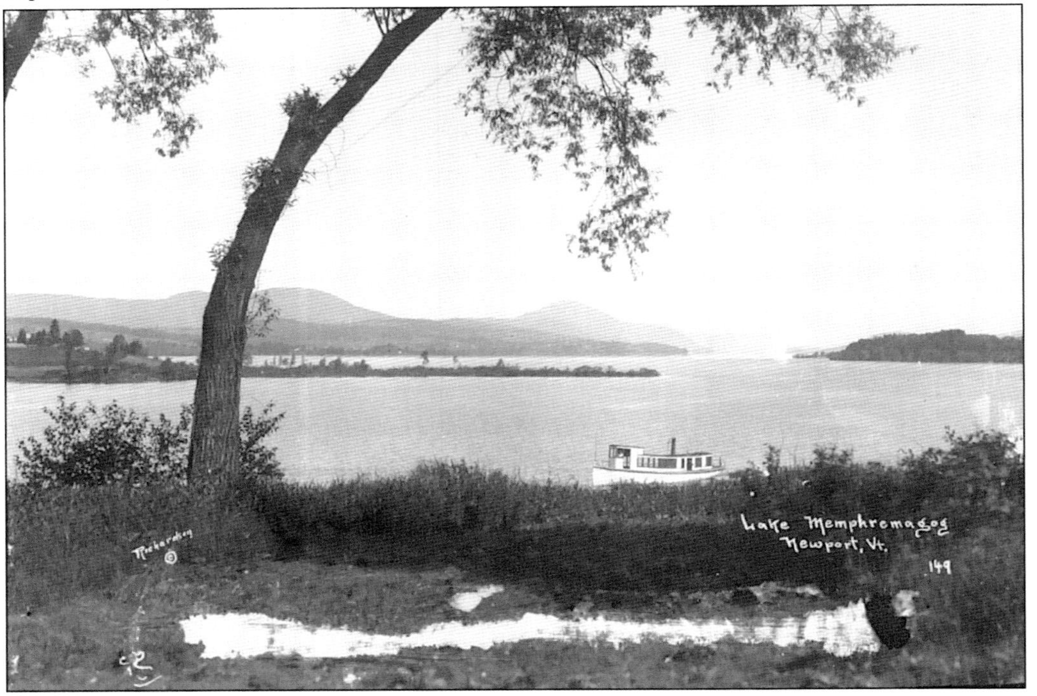

Zabriskie's cottage on Province Island, the noblest of the island kingdoms, sits on the 45th parallel, with 100 acres. The southern end of the islands, facing Newport, is in the domain of Uncle Sam, USA, and the remainder is that of her Majesty's, Canada, on the Vermont/Canadian border. (Courtesy of Richardson Cartee Collection.)

Charles Robert Moore, engineer and Newport inventor, was born in 1863, in Barnston, Province of Quebec, the son of George & Clara (Peck) Moore. He came to Newport at the age of 23 to work in the lumber mills and married Tattie Rocque. They raised four sons and lived on Summer Street. Moore died in 1933 and his wife died in 1940. Both are buried at the Pine Grove cemetery.

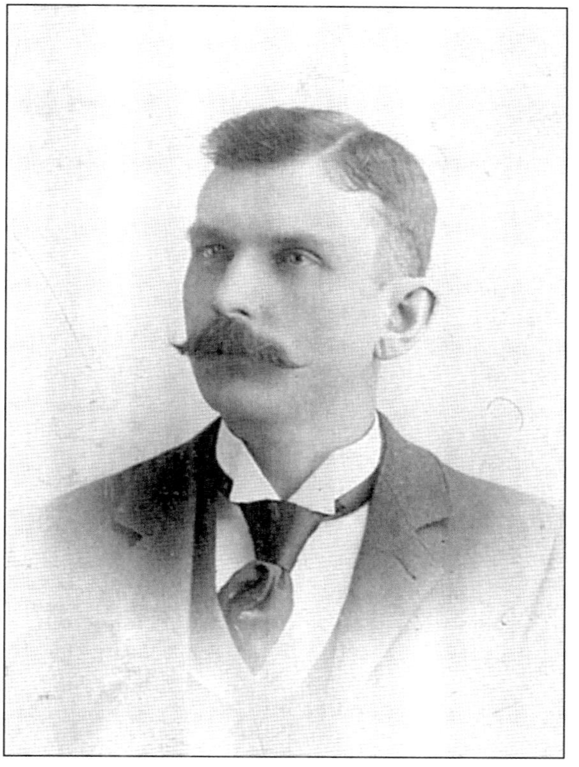

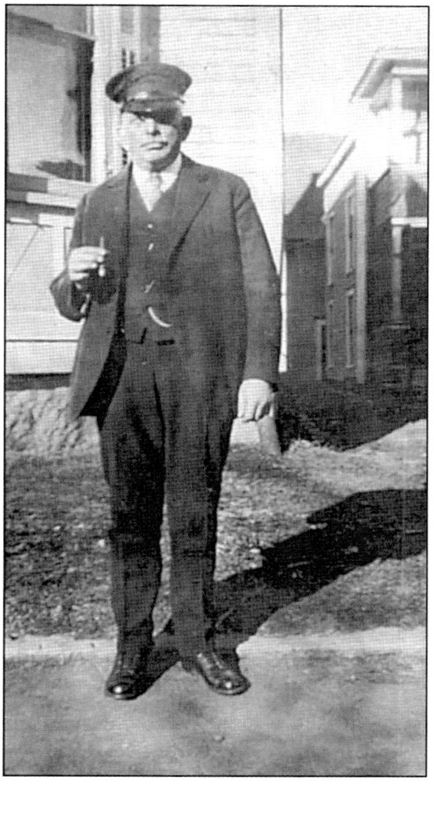

C.R. Moore invented and patented in 1883 the combination storm and screen door that remains permanently attached to the house, and is used worldwide. From a woodworking shop on Lane Avenue in 1898, these doors were manufactured. Once again, Moore's invention did not make him rich or famous.

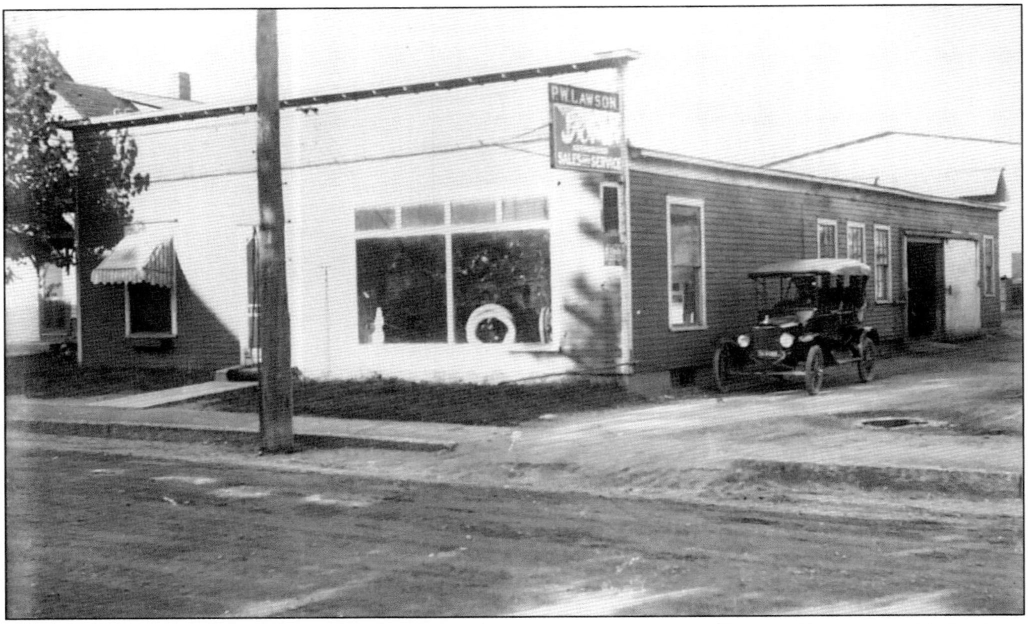

In 1916, Percy W. Lawson was an auto salesman on Coventry Street. Some recalled when Henry Ford in 1924 stopped by P.W. Lawson's Ford dealership. Ford admired a set of stained-glass windows and asked if he could take them back to his museum in Dearborn. Today, the Henry Ford Musem's records have a set of windows in their collection that remains unidentified as to provenance. (Courtesy of Richardson Cartee Collection.)

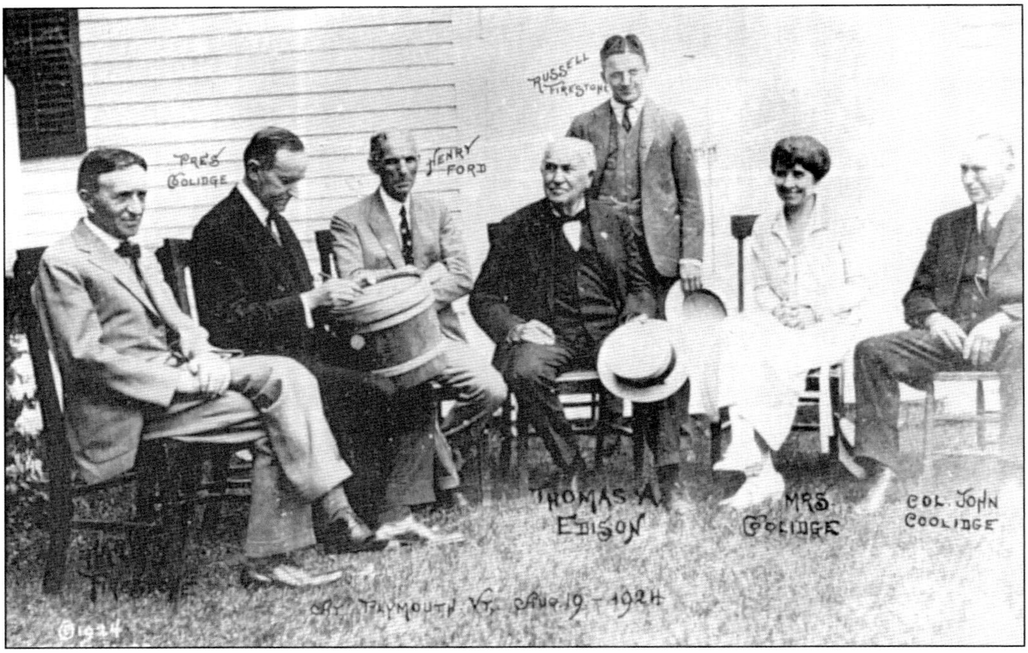

Henry Ford, along with Henry Firestone, President Coolidge, Thomas Edison, Russell Firestone, Mrs. Coolidge, and son Col. John Coolidge were presented with a sugar sap bucket in a signing ceremony for the President at Plymouth, Vermont, in 1924.

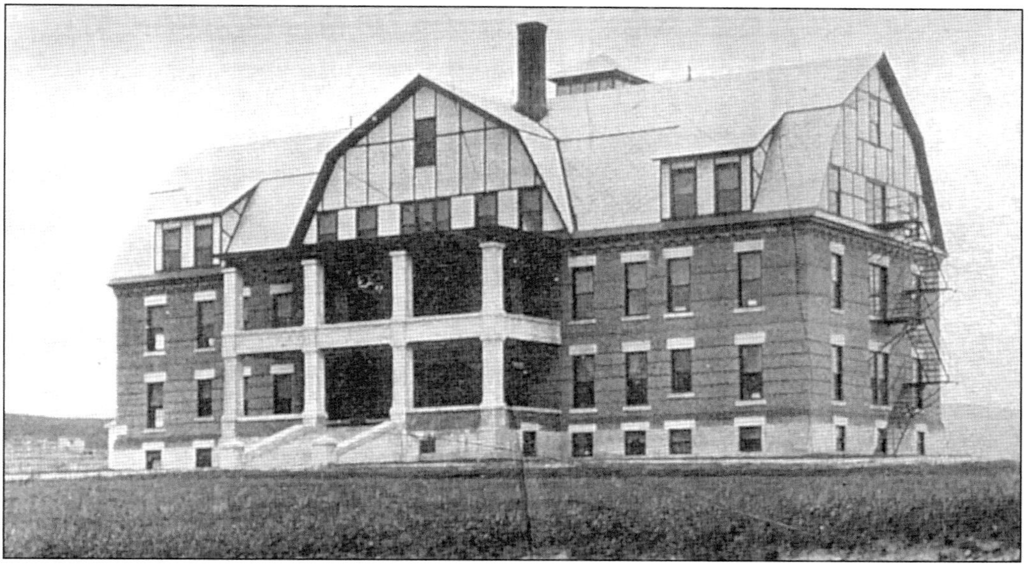

Dr. Joseph C. Rutherford, born in 1818 in New York, was commissioned a surgeon during the Civil War. In 1892, he opened the Memphremagog Clinic in Newport. Until a hospital could be built, the idea for such a hospital was born in the Newport Woman's Club in 1917. The Orleans County Memorial Hospital opened in 1924 with 24 beds.

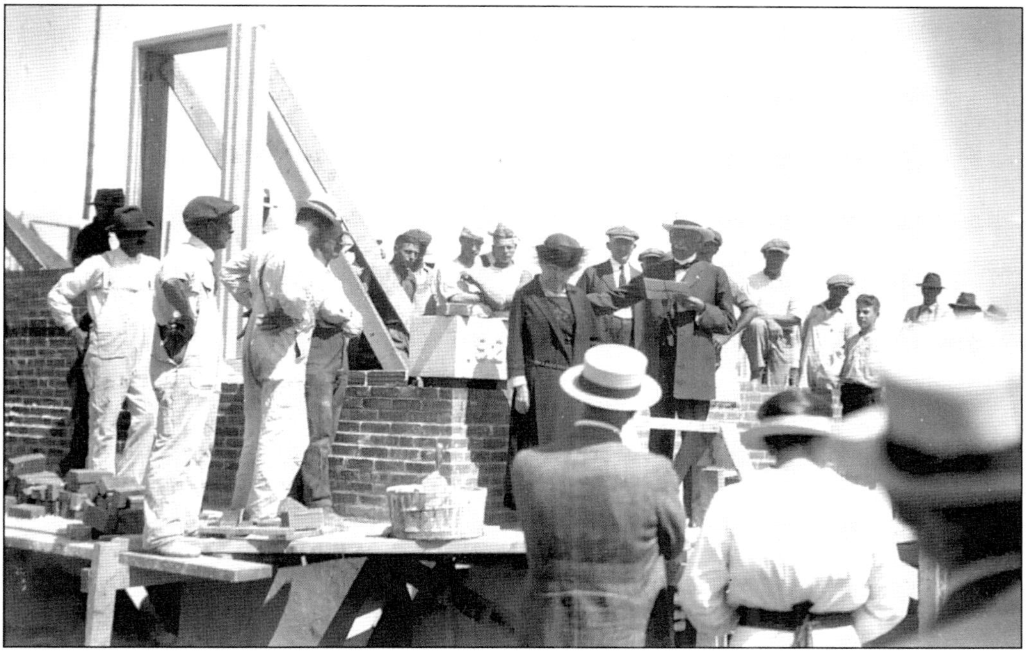

On July 30, 1922, the cornerstone of the hospital was laid by Mrs. John (Augusta) Young, seen standing in the center of the photograph on the property she donated on Longview Street for the first hospital. In 1972, dedication ceremonies were held for a new North Country Hospital and Health Care Center on land purchased from the old Coffin Farm estate, located on Prouty Drive, where the hospital just celebrated its 75th anniversary in 1999. (Courtesy of Richardson Cartee Collection.)

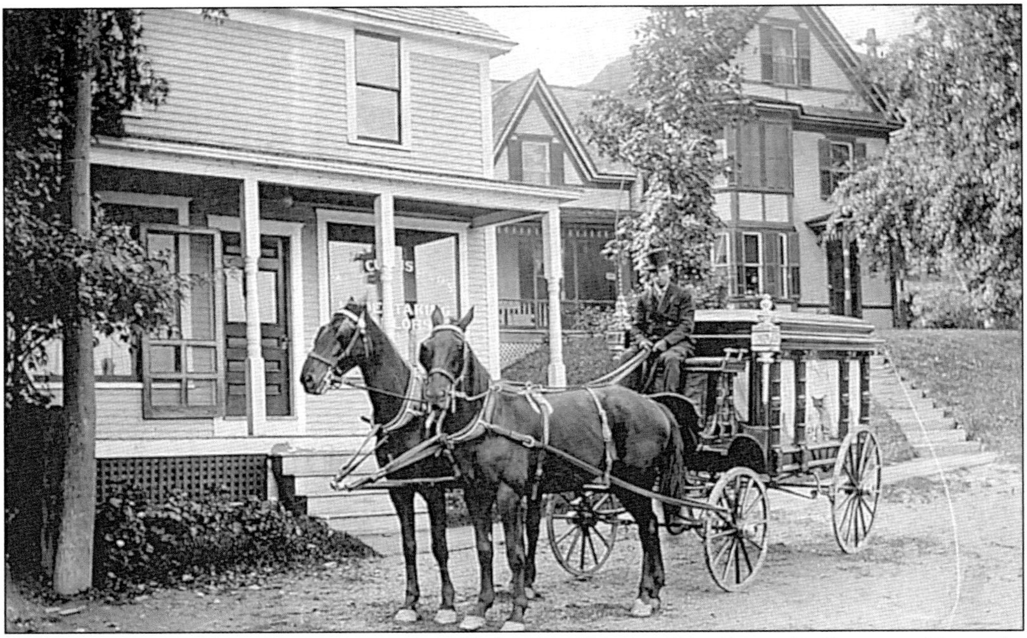

The Curtis Funeral Home in 1894 was established and operated by Bryon S. Curtis and his wife, Augusta. The home continued to serve Orleans County for over 100 years. In 1904, the James Haslet home and property at 5 Bay Street was purchased, and the Curtis Funeral Home became the first fully equipped funeral parlor in Northern Vermont.

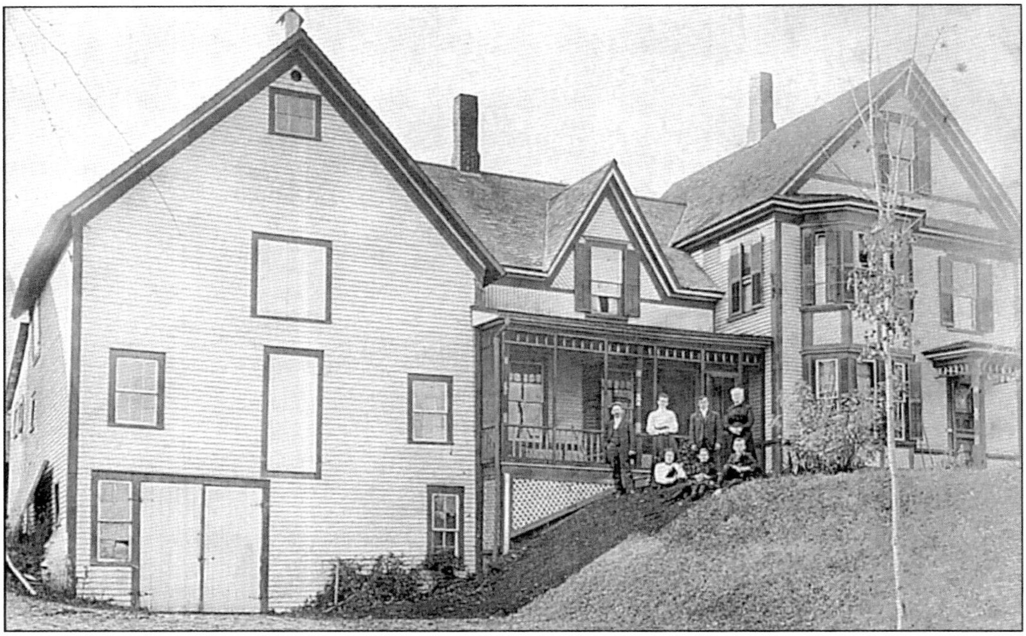

Bryon Curtis (1870–1931) and Augusta Curtis (1865–1920) are pictured on the back row at left in this photograph, along with their children, Justin and Jennie, in front. Today, the Curtis-Britch Funeral Home Inc. is under the direction of owner Roland N. Britch Jr., longtime friend and business partner of Frankie Curtis.

Justine Alonzo Curtis, born in 1899, was in the class of 1918 at Newport High School. He joined his father in 1927 in the family funeral home business. He married Frances (Frankie) Gates, who was born in 1911, the daughter of Richard and Laura Gates, in New York City. Mr. Richard Gates was a theatrical designer and artist of oil and water colors. Justine passed away in 1978, and his wife Frances in 1987.

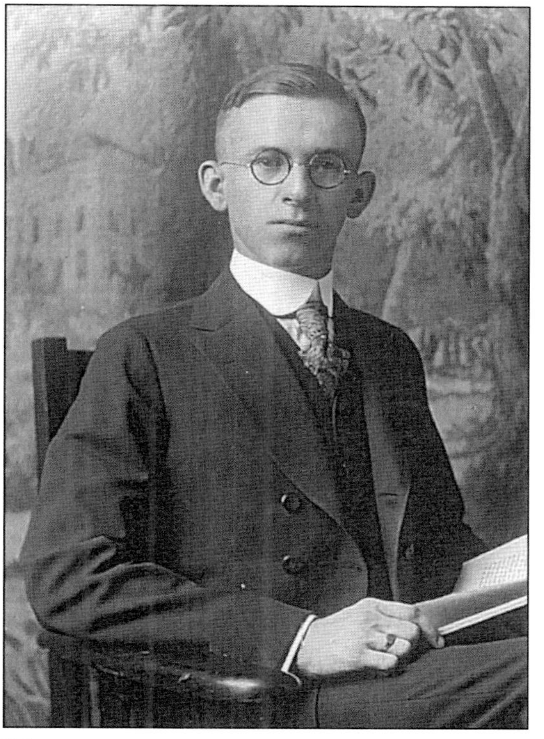

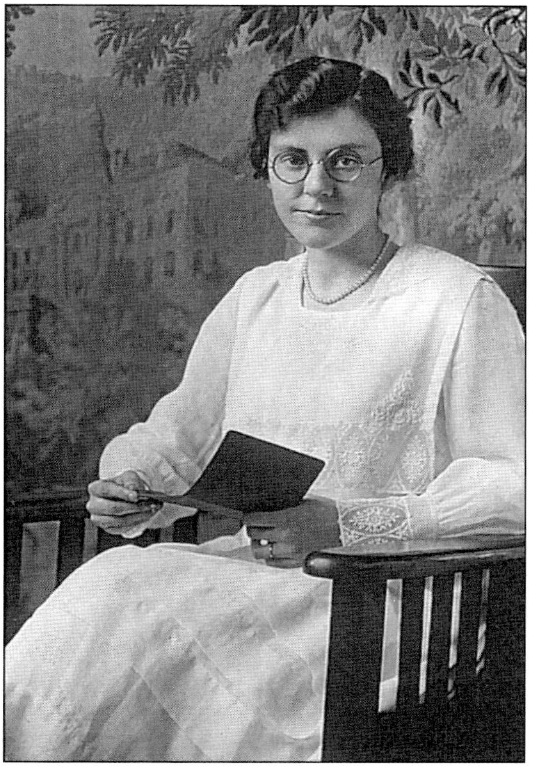

Jennie Curtis Dexter, born on May 2, 1901, graduated from Cornell University in 1924, married Milton Dexter, and had one child. She died in 1985. The Curtis family will long be remembered for their Christmas lighting displays that attracted large crowds. The railroad train would holt on the trestle bridge so that passengers could catch a glimpse of the Christmas scenes in the 1930s.

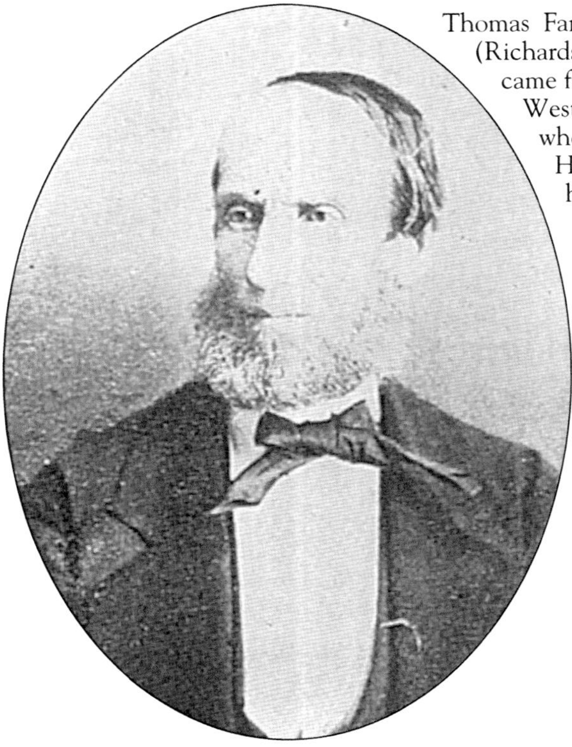

Thomas Farrant, born in 1820, and his wife Jane (Richards), were the parents of five children. They came from England in 1868 to Pender's Point in West Derby. Farrant was a market gardener who grew produce for the Memphremagog Hotel. In 1869, Farrant purchased a homestead of 50 acres on the west shore of Lake Memphremagog.

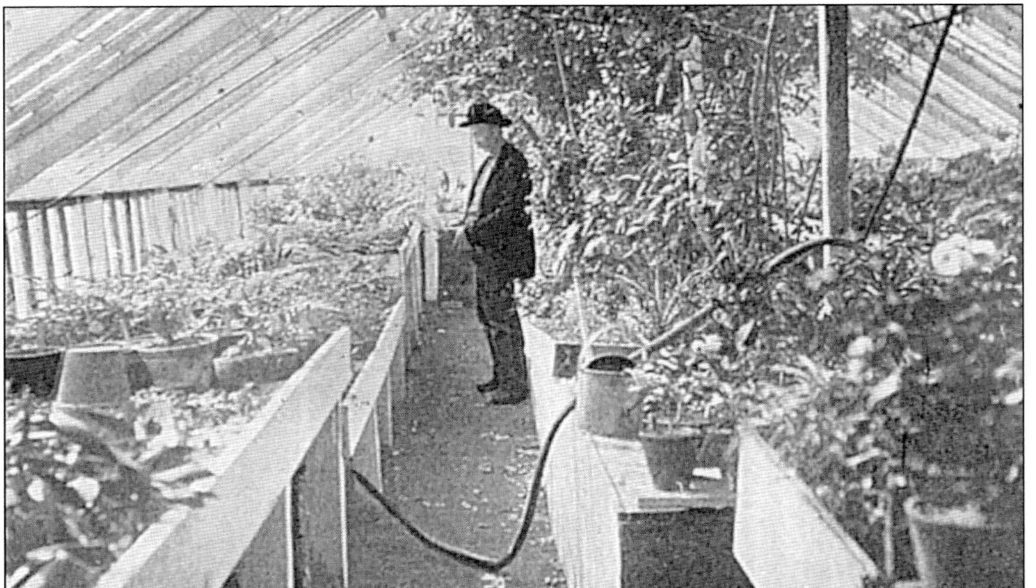

Farrant established one of the first greenhouses for growing vegetables and flowers in Northern Vermont. It was known as Vine Haven Fruit & Flower Farm. Thomas Farrant had mastered his business and was a pleasant man and a true English gentleman. He passed away in 1883, and his wife in 1904. Both are buried at the East Main Street cemetery.

John Farrant, son of Thomas and Jane Farrant, returned to the family greenhouse and florist business after the death of his father. A lover of flowers, John always planned for another season until his health began to fail him. He resided on Farrants Point for 75 years.

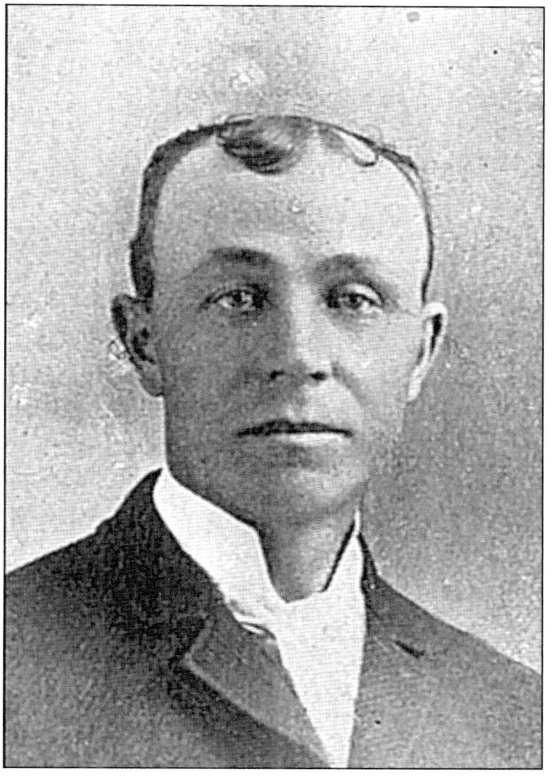

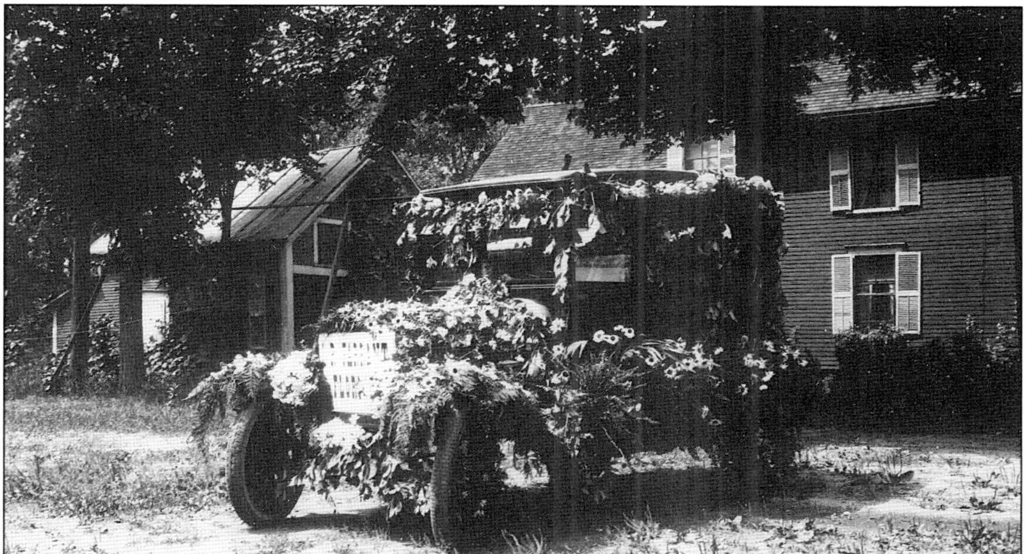

A year after his 82nd birthday, John passed away on January 22, 1946. He cultivated the public taste for the beauty in nature and art and was a true public benefactor. (Courtesy of Richardson Cartee Collection.)

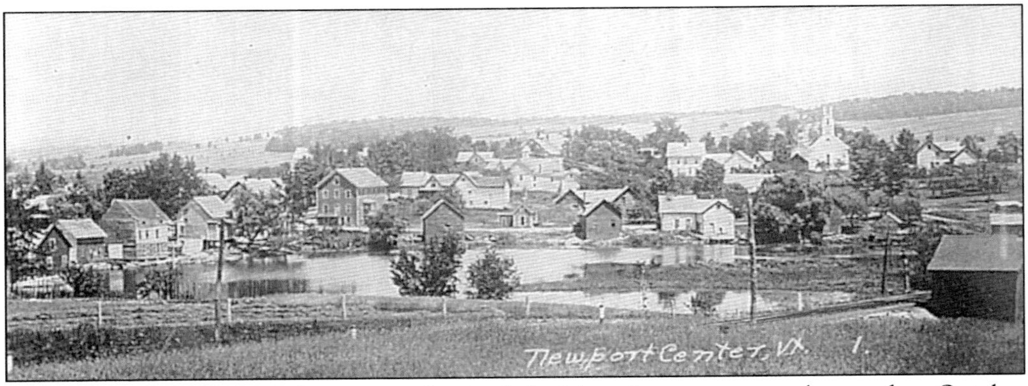

Newport Center Town, with one part sharing Lake Memphremagog, was chartered on October 30, 1802, up until including what is now Newport City. Mud Creek was also known as Sleeper Pond and named for George Little Sleeper, Esq., known as the father of Newport Center. When he came in the 1860s, there were only five houses. Sleeper laid out streets selling lots for $100, resulting in the rapid growth of the village.

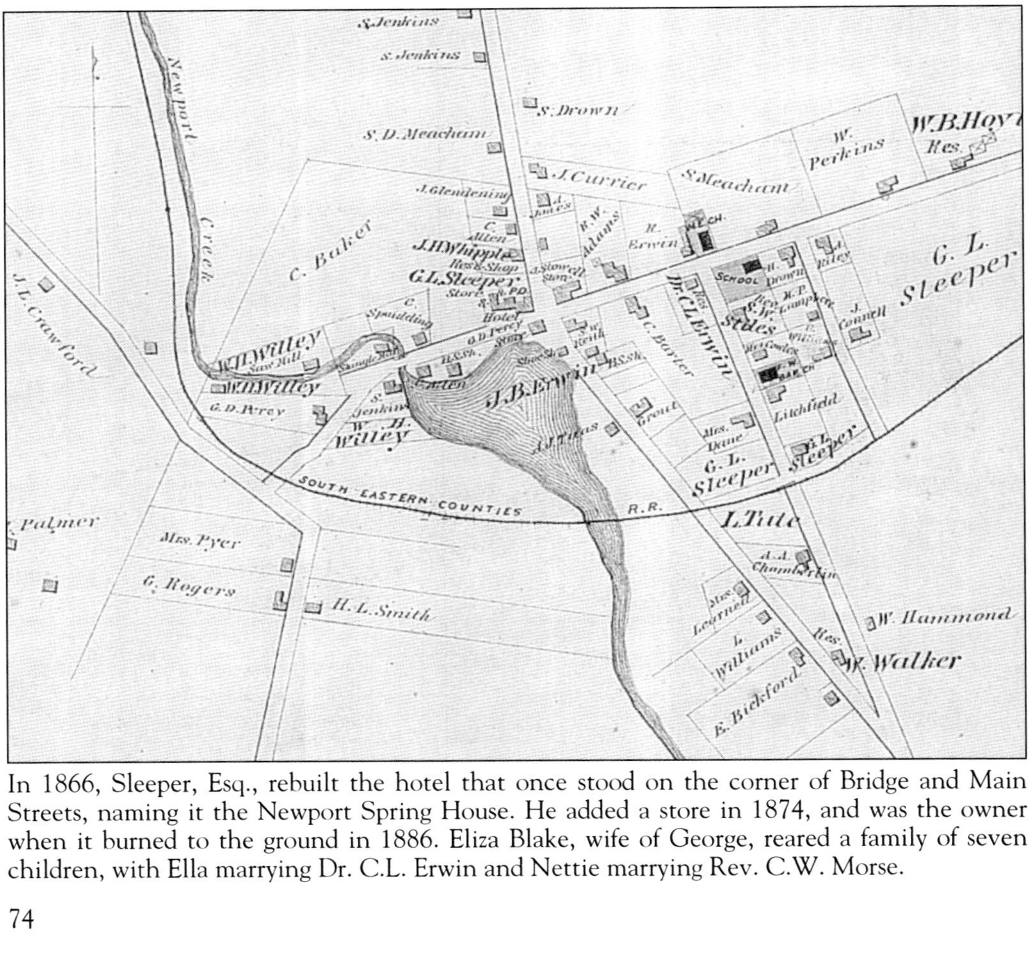

In 1866, Sleeper, Esq., rebuilt the hotel that once stood on the corner of Bridge and Main Streets, naming it the Newport Spring House. He added a store in 1874, and was the owner when it burned to the ground in 1886. Eliza Blake, wife of George, reared a family of seven children, with Ella marrying Dr. C.L. Erwin and Nettie marrying Rev. C.W. Morse.

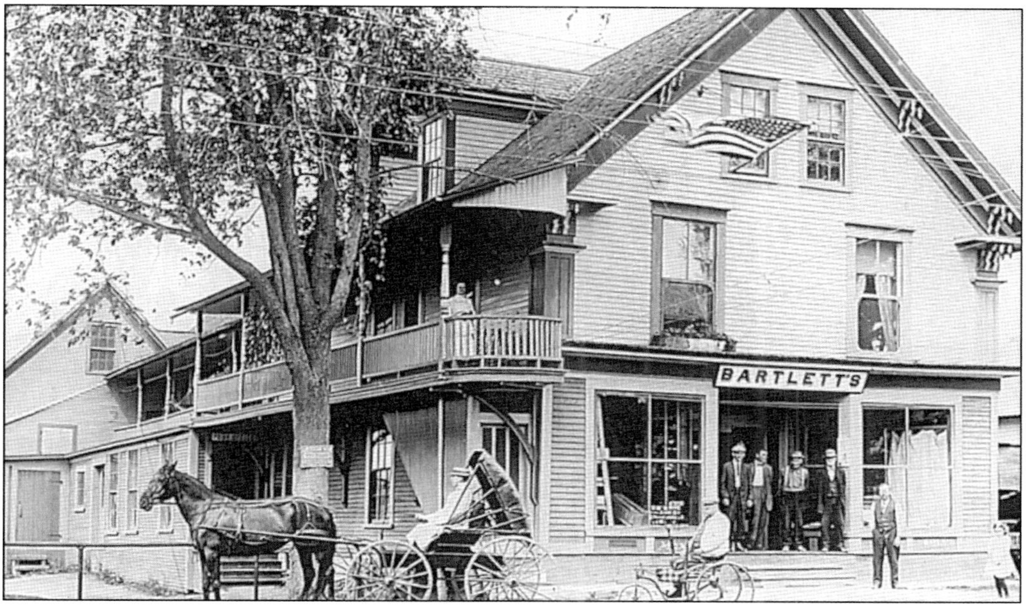

Bartlett's General Store, formerly known as Taylor's, had as proprietors Grandpa Bartlett, his son Herbert, and his grandson Guy, who ran the post office. Loretta Hilliker, born May 27, 1902, the daughter of Chancy and Mary Armstrong, remembers being asked to pose for this photograph in her carriage with her horse, Molly, the year she was married in 1920. On July 4, 1921, fire destroyed the general store when young boys were using explosives to usher in the Fourth of July.

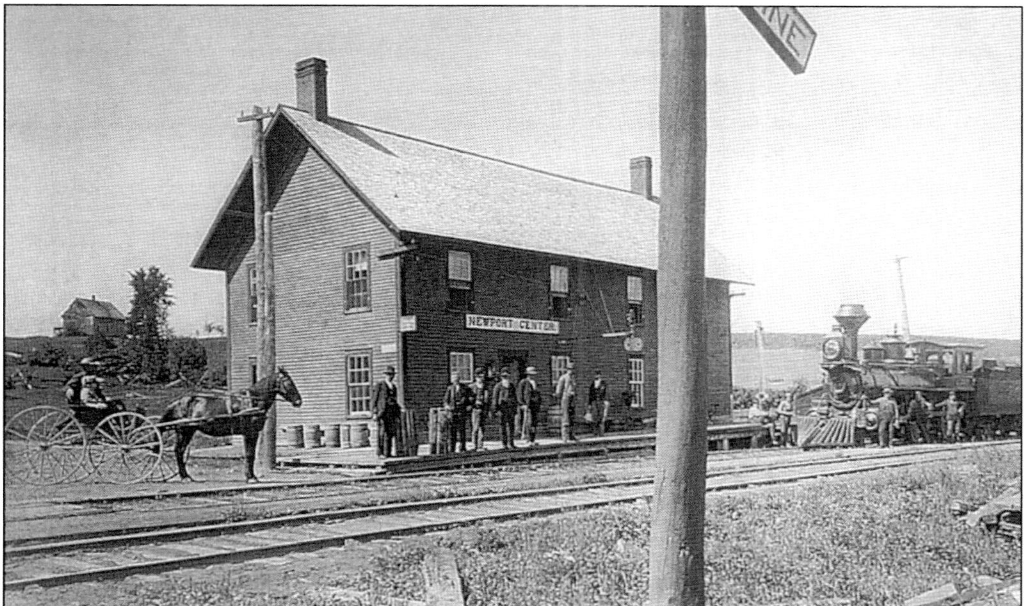

The first railroad station is seen by the covered bridge in this view looking up Bridge Street in the 1870s. Henry L. Smith became the Railroad Station Agent in 1879. Shipments of lumber, butter, and 90 carloads of hay were shipped in 1896.

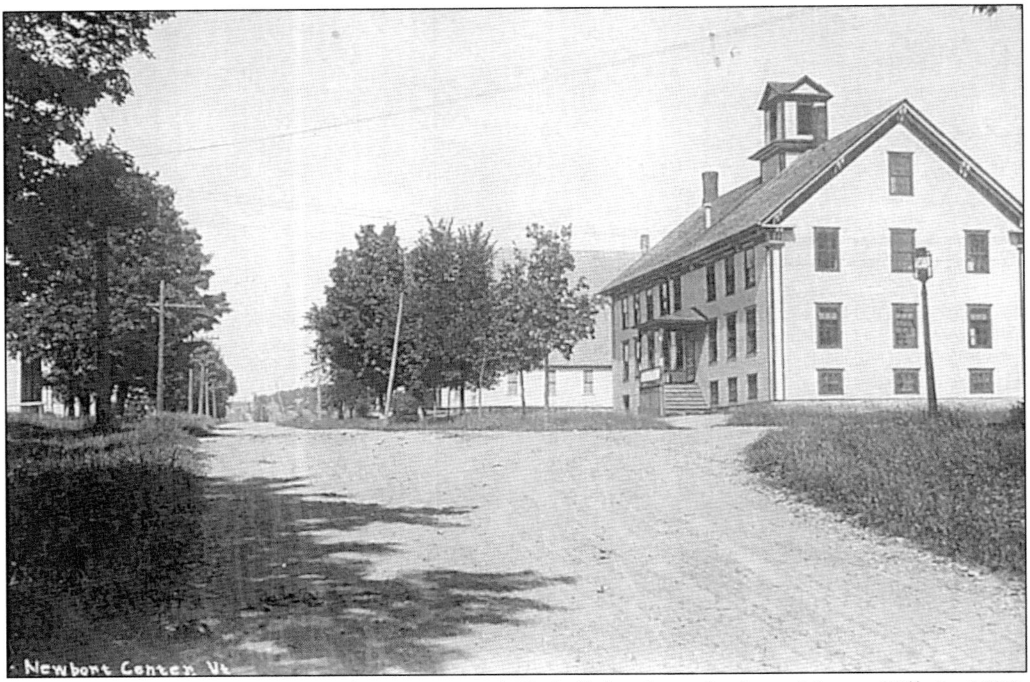

In 1901, the Newport Center Elementary and High School was built on Vance Hill. In 1979, the school succumbed to a wrecking crew, and the Town's Clerk building stands here today.

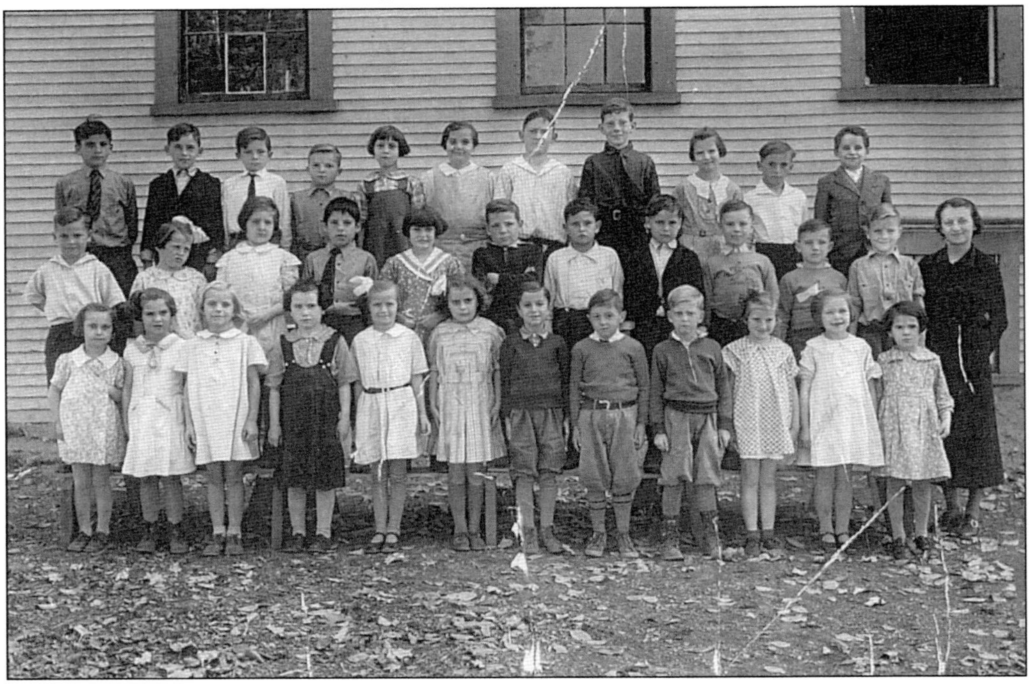
This grade school photograph shows the classmates of Lorraine Maloney, who is second row third from the left. Lorraine was the daughter of Herbert and Florence (Selby) Tute, both longtime postmasters of Newport Center.

Abail Abbott Adam's father, Deacon Martin Adams, one of the first pioneers of Duncansborough (Newport) in the late 1700s, built a log cabin on the Lake Road. Later, Martin moved his wife Mercy (Ryder) and family to Canada where Abail was born in 1802 in Hatley, Quebec. Brothers Abail and Hallet made the first clearing where Newport Center stands at the crossroads.

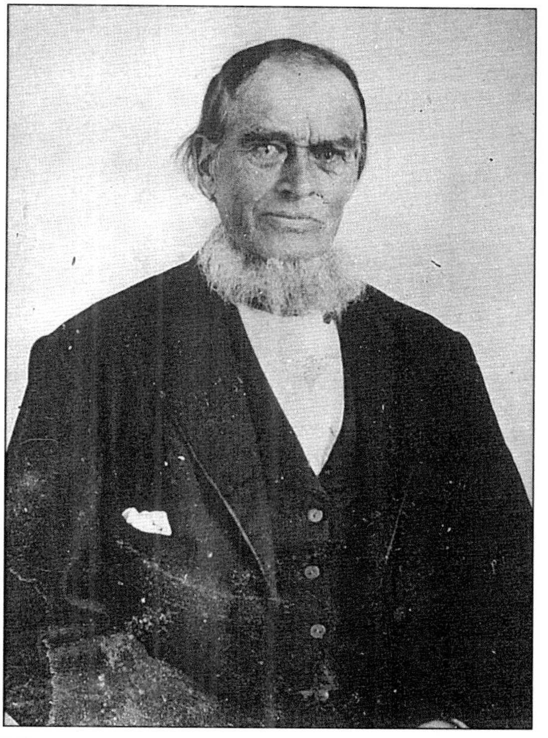

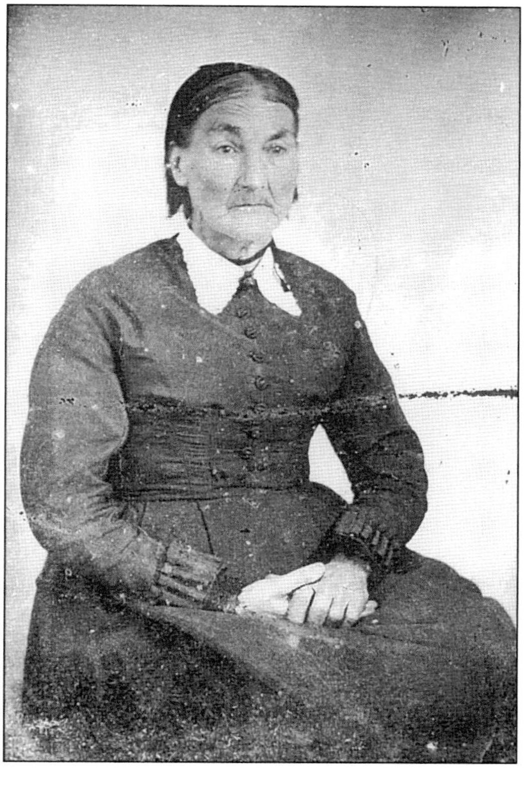

Irene (Gray) Adams, born in 1807, married Abail June 10, 1823, and had 14 children between 1824 and 1854. Their son, Ranson Willis Adams, was born in 1851 and owned Steven's Mills in Richford. His son, Dr. Ranson W. Adams, was born in 1886. Abail and Irene were both laid to rest at the Lake Road cemetery, with Abail dying July 7, 1881, and Irene on April 1, 1885.

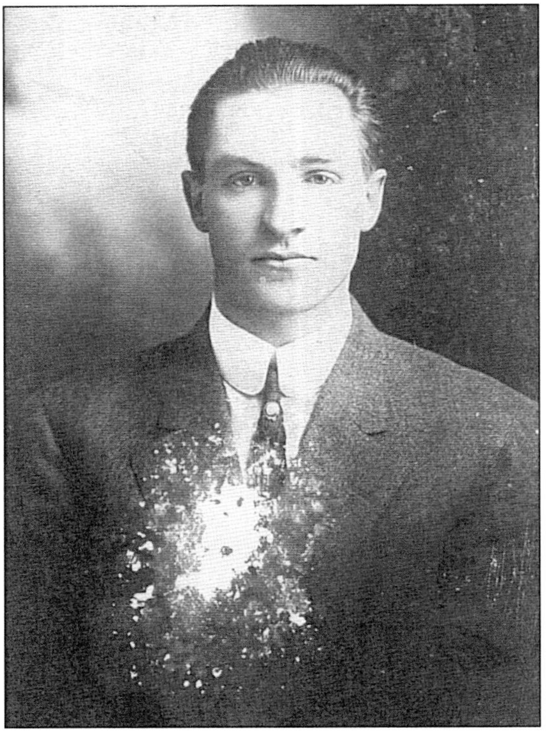

Dr. Ranson Willis Adams was a graduate of the University of Vermont Medical College. He and his wife Marie (Tynan) Adams came to Newport Center in 1912, where he set up his practice and raised three children: Elizabeth, Ranson (known today as Bill), and Rebecca.

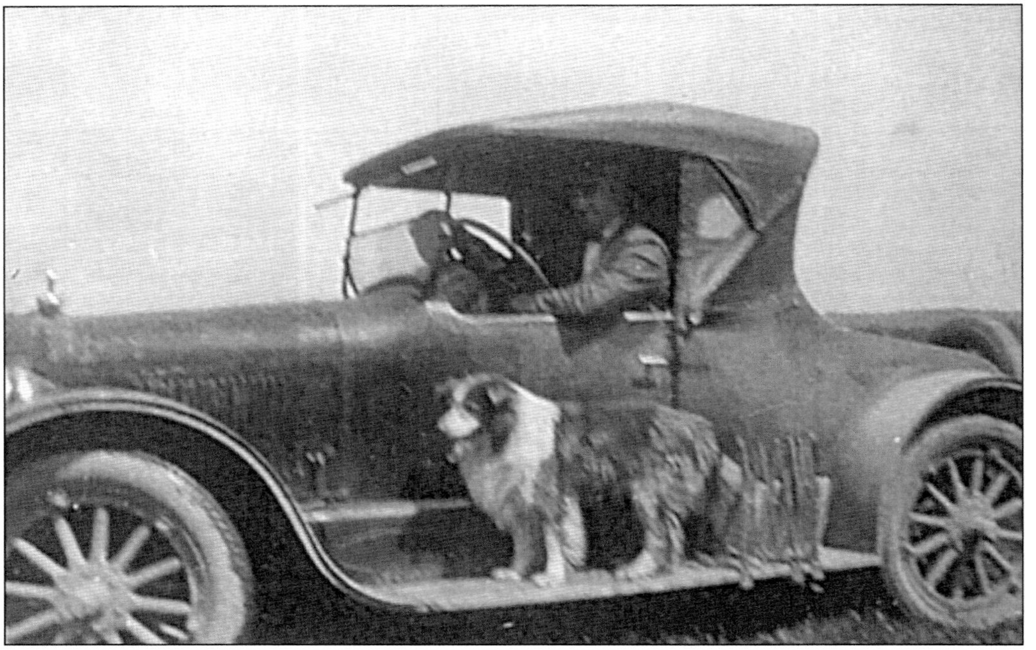

Abail Adams, grandfather to Dr. R.W. Adams, wrote in a letter, dated 1845: "He was commencing tomorrow on a house & shed but, I do not get much money it is scare here." Dr. Ranson W. Adams has left a family legacy in Newport Center where he was an old-fashioned country doctor who made house calls. He passed away in 1959.

Dr. Thomas H. Hoskins of Newport Center is credited with planting the very first McIntosh apple tree in the United States in 1868. He was a pioneer in testing new varieties, and focused on apples that could withstand the cold of Vermont. Born in 1828, Dr. Hoskins possessed a vigorous personality and was known as a writer on agriculture and horticulture topics.

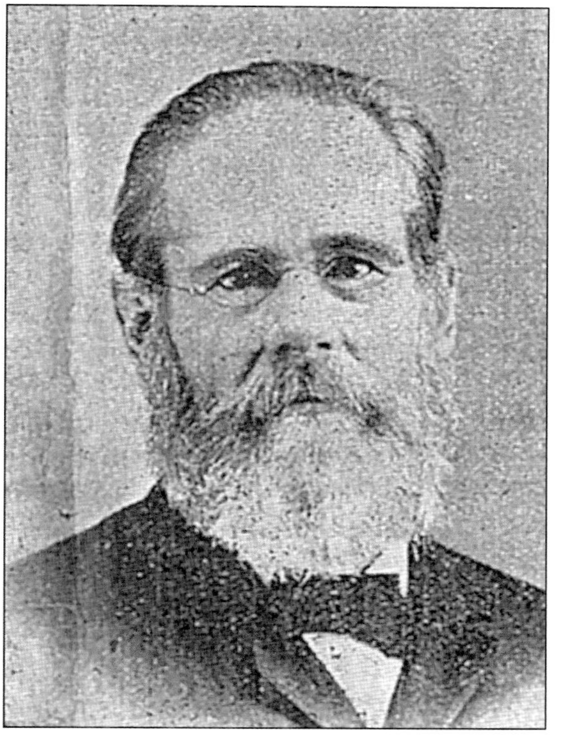

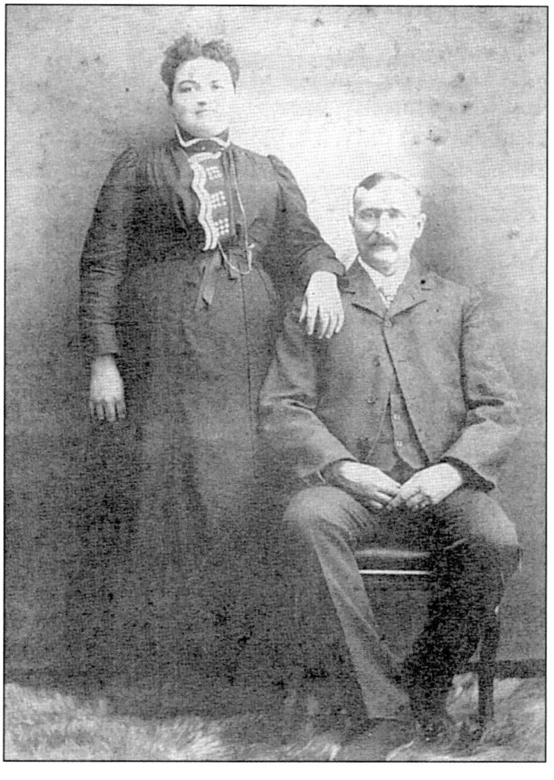

On Simon O. Whipple's farm in Newport Center Dr. Hoskins planted the first young seedling apple tree, obtaining it from the McIntosh family in Canada. The McIntosh family had American relatives who, in the 1870s, used barrels of these apples to help sell the trees by delivering them in a horse-drawn wagon. S.O. Whipple was born in 1828, and his wife, Finetti (Hildreth) Whipple, was born in 1827. Simon was a farmer and an agent for G.C. Barnard Photo Crome & India-Ink Portraits.

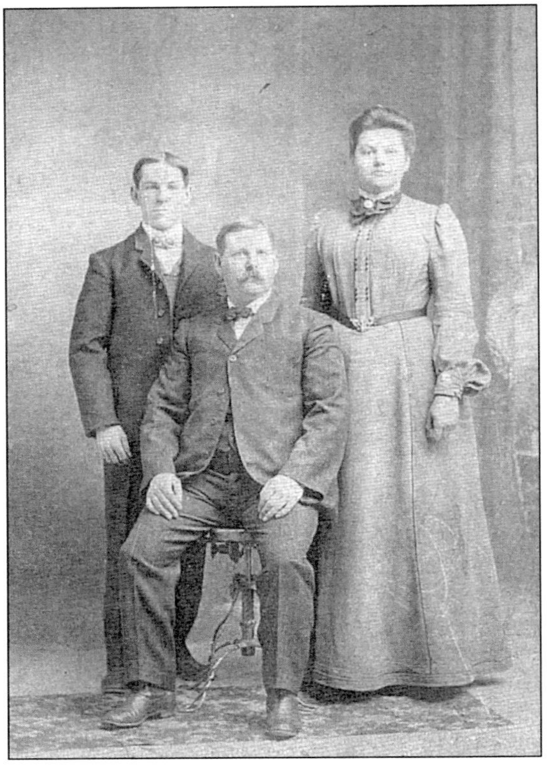

This family photo is of Calvin Whipple, born 1886, and his wife May (Kittridge), born 1871, with their only son Charles, who was born on the Whipple Farm in 1888. Calvin was the only son of Simon Whipple. Calvin purchased 85 acres of farm land from his father in 1890 for $2,500, 22 years after the first apple tree was planted in the United States. Charles died in 1959 and his wife Etta (Swett) in 1975. They were parents of Gilbert and Harry.

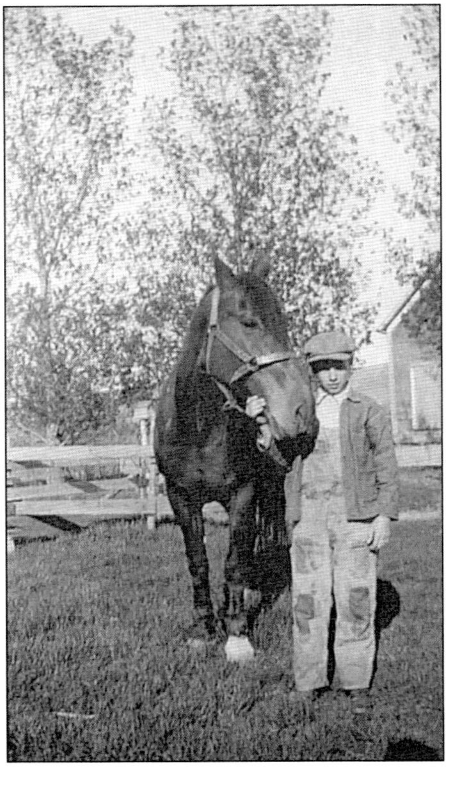

Gilbert Whipple was a young lad growing up on the family farm, the same farm his great-grandfather Simon Whipple farmed. On his farm today, Dr. Hoskins's original McIntosh apple tree still lives after 131 years. The apples have had phenomenal success surviving temperatures as low as 35 degrees below zero.

Two

West Derby and Derby Center, Vermont

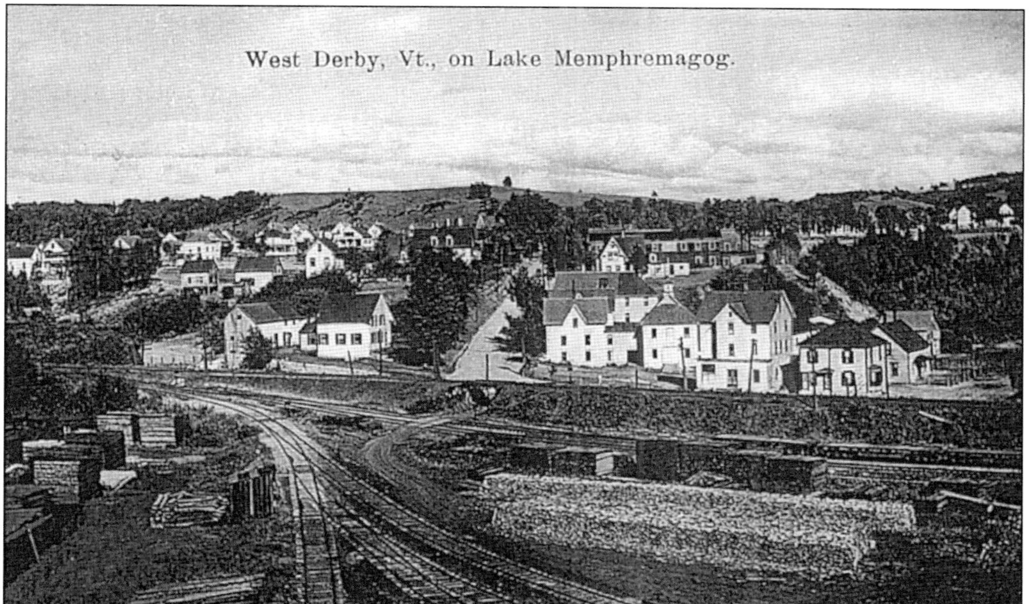

West Derby grew into a forceful industrial and residential area in the 1800s near the Clyde River. By the 1850s, the area now called the Causeway and the East Side had 2 log homes, 18 dwellings, 1 hotel, 2 stores, and 130 inhabitants. On March 5, 1918, West Derby incorporated and became part of the City of Newport.

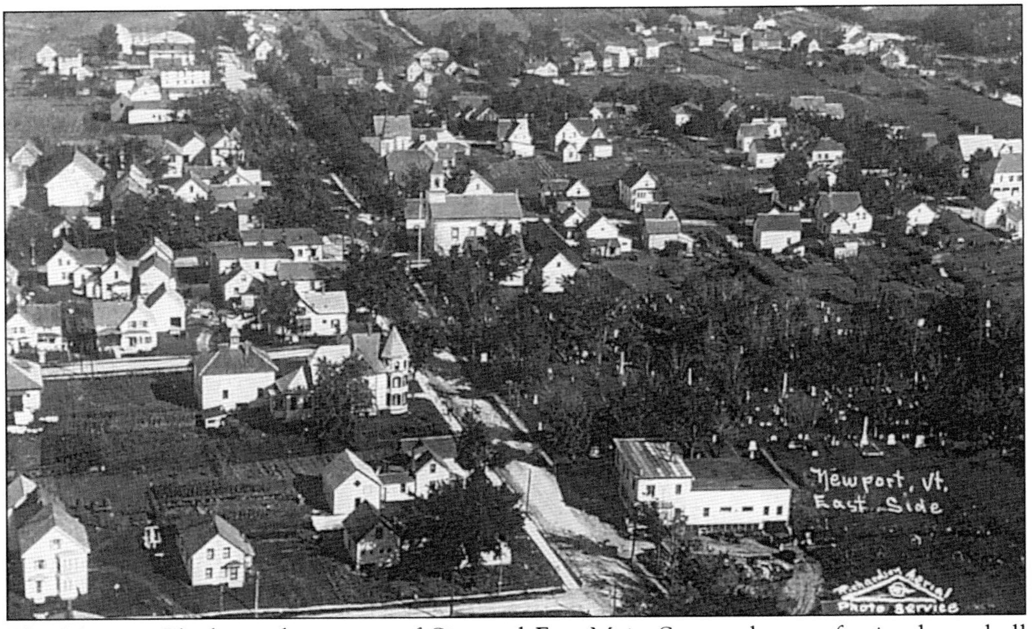

The Magoon Block on the corner of Sias and East Main Streets, known for its dance hall on the third floor, was built by Joseph Dane, a man responsible for much of West Derby's early prosperity.

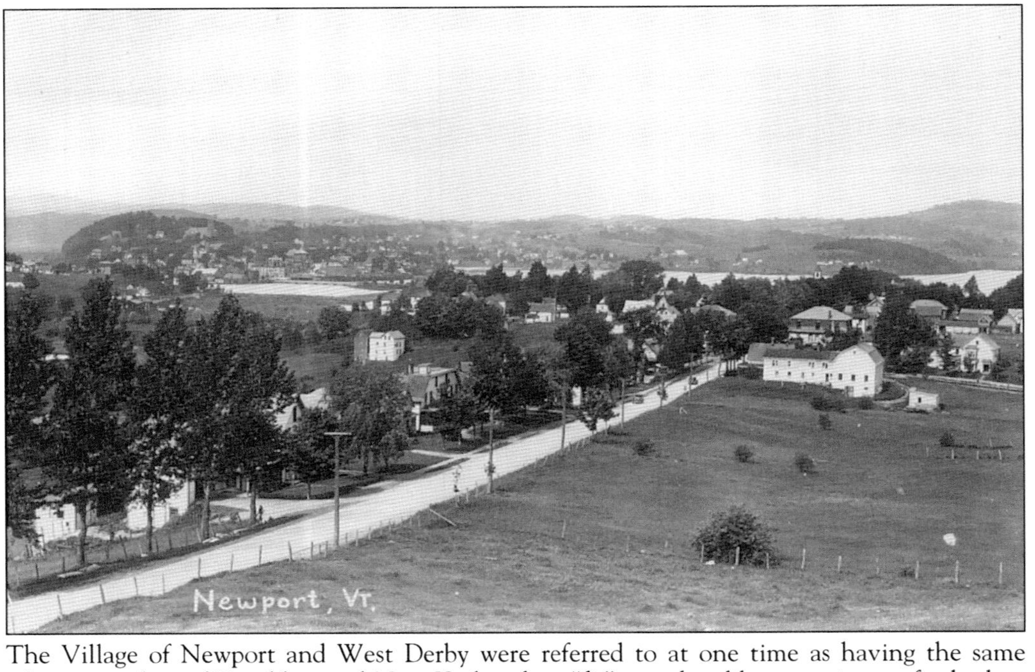

The Village of Newport and West Derby were referred to at one time as having the same relation to that of Brooklyn and New York—they "fit" together like two pieces of a broken saucer. (Courtesy of Richardson Cartee Collection.)

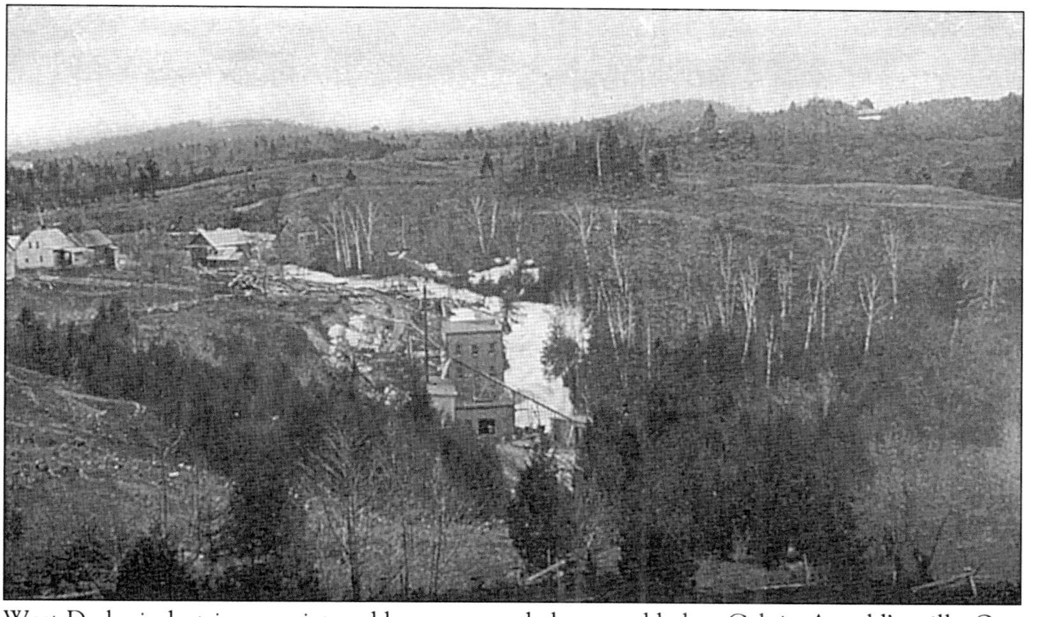

West Derby industries are pictured here centered above and below Calvin Arnold's mills. One of the old gristmills owned by Nelson Davis and sold to George Foster burned in 1914, with a loss of $7,000.

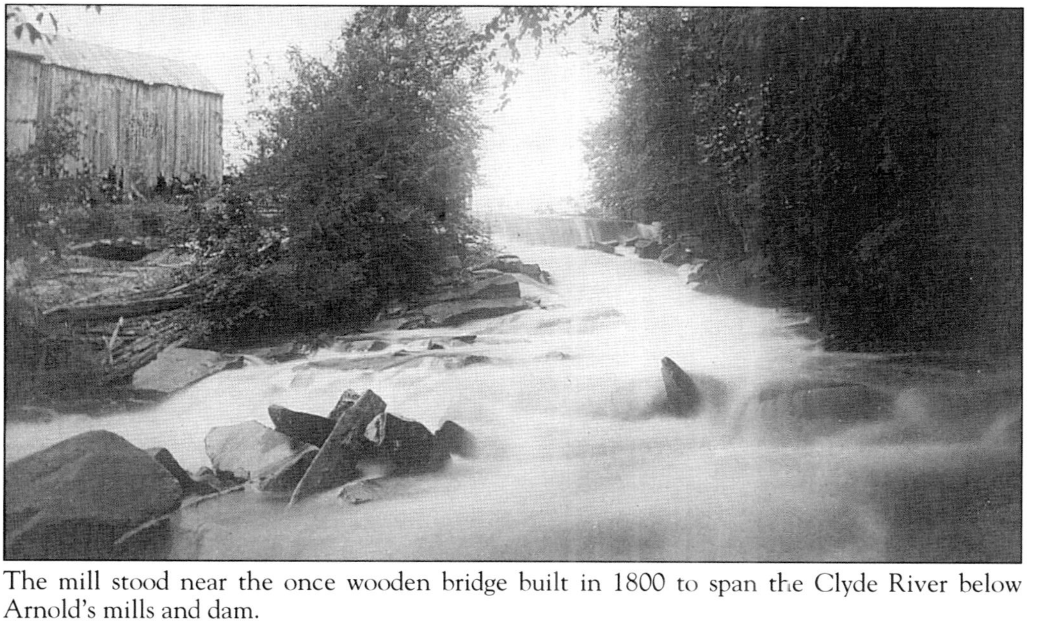

The mill stood near the once wooden bridge built in 1800 to span the Clyde River below Arnold's mills and dam.

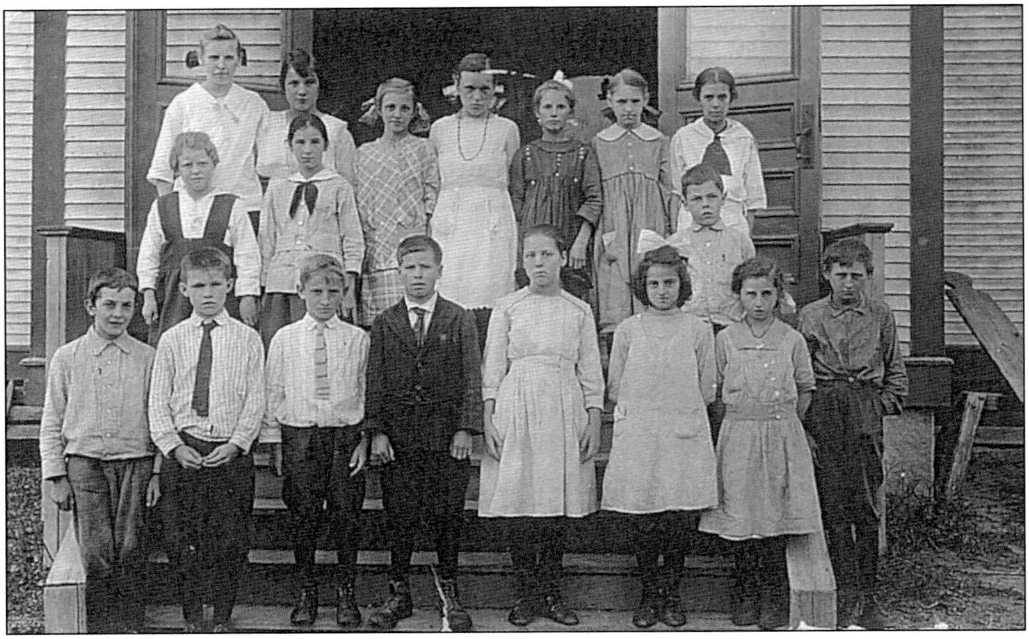

The West Derby School was built in 1899. Several generations of children received their early education here, such as the ones in this class photo of fifth and sixth grade students in 1921.

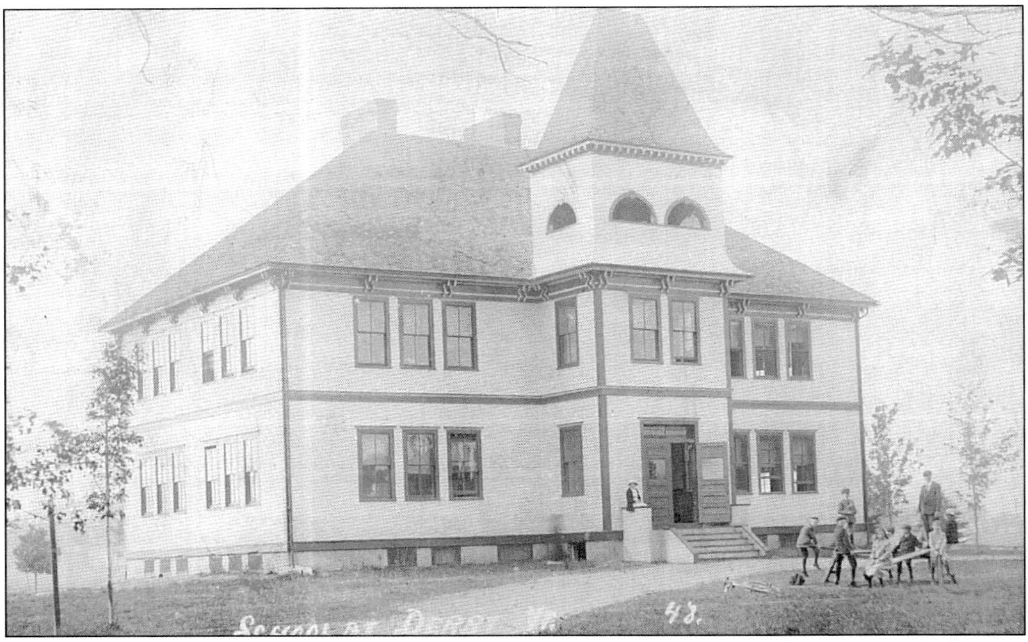

In 1961, this picturesque old structure fell victim to the wrecking ball with the school bell being preserved by the town. The new elementary school took the place of the east and south school buildings with the dedication taking place on September 16, 1962.

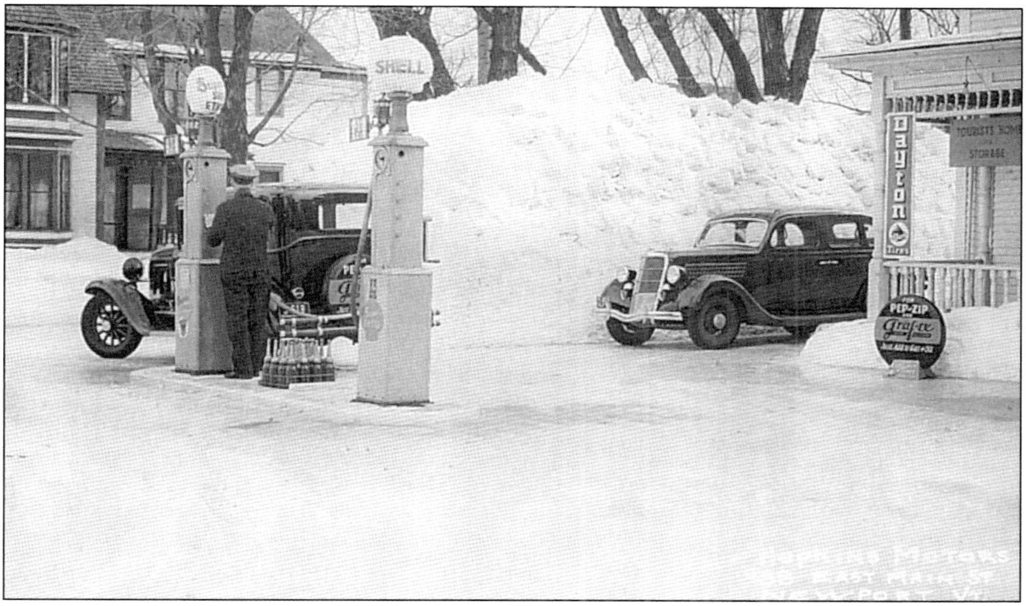

Warren Hopkins Motors & Filling Station once stood on the corner of Autumn and East Main Streets. It was used as a tourist home and service station.

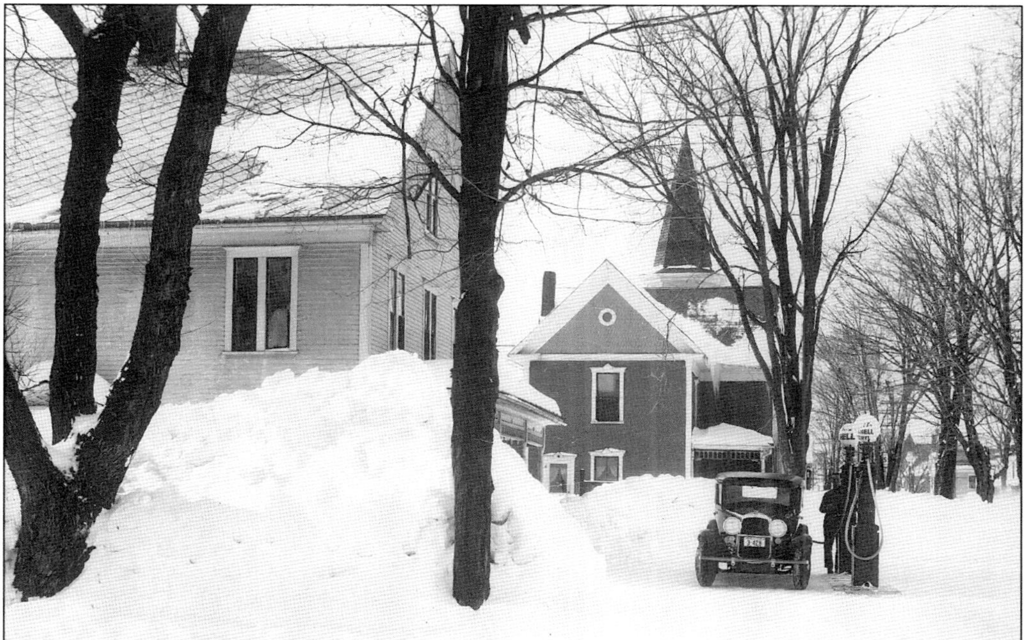

Next door to Warren Hopkins Motors & Filling Station was McCauley's old homestead, and farther west stands the Christian Science Church and steeple. (Courtesy of Richardson Cartee Collection.)

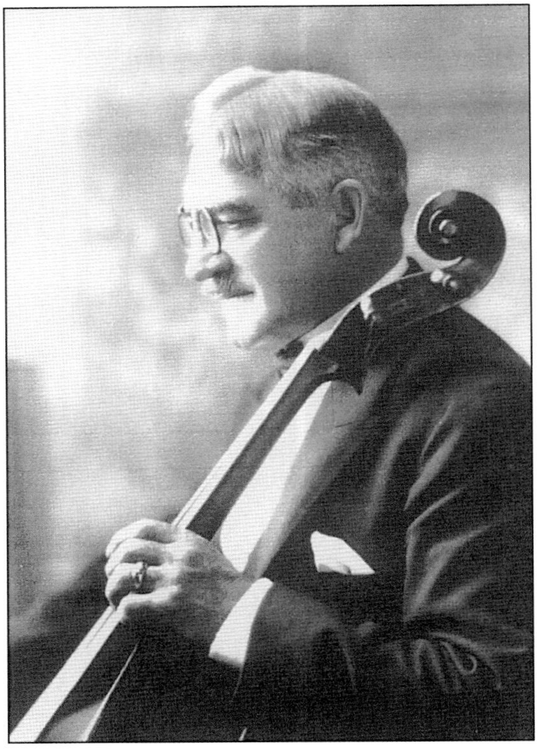

Charlie McCauley was a well-known music and piano dealer. His wife Rose gave music lessons and recitals for her students. The McCauleys were a musical family, known as the Charlie McCauley's Orchestra playing at dances and social gatherings.

Charlie and Rose McCauley's family home still stands today on East Main Street. Shown in this photograph c.1910, from left to right, are son Ted, with dog Trixie; Rose and daughter Gladys in horse-buggy; and Charlie and son Parker with family horse.

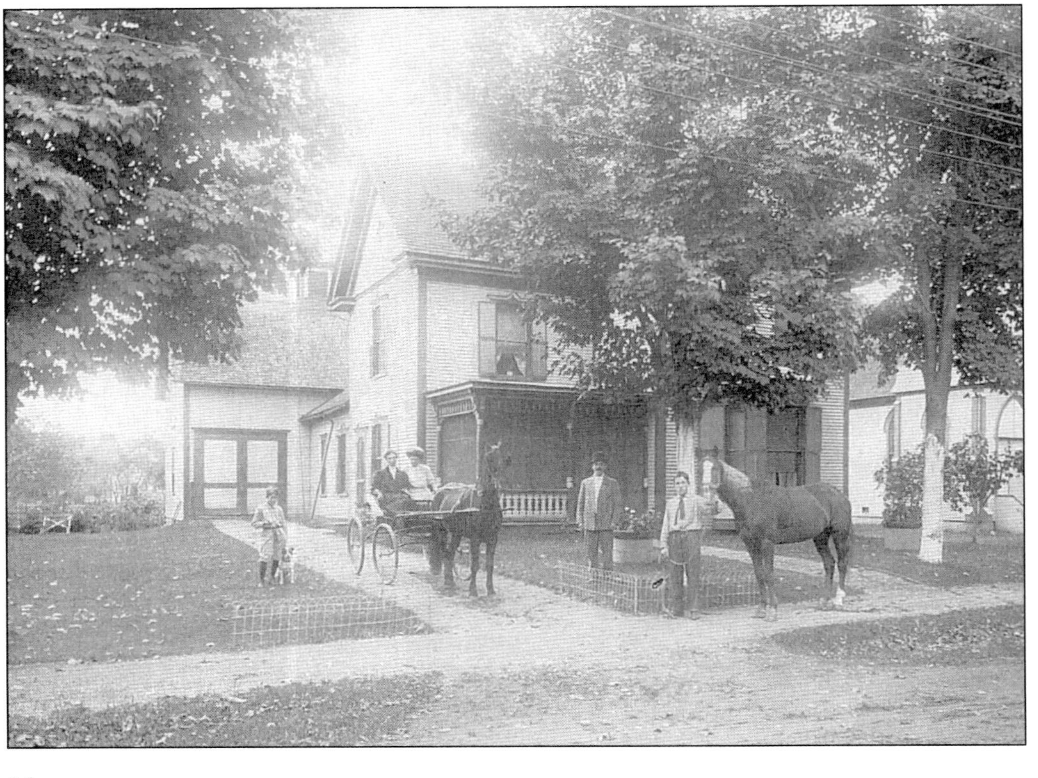

The East Main Street Baptist Church, the first church erected in West Derby, was constructed by George Boyton at age 24. In 1856, he did most of the work himself, finishing in 1859 when the church opened to all denominations. (Courtesy of Richardson Cartee Collection.)

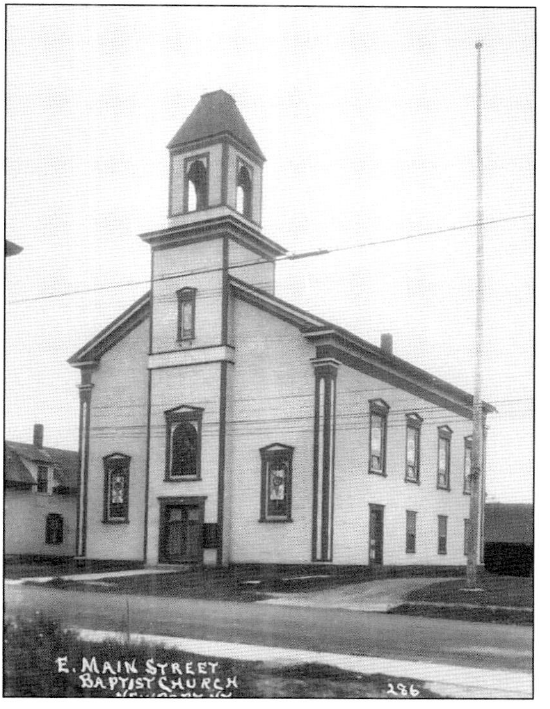

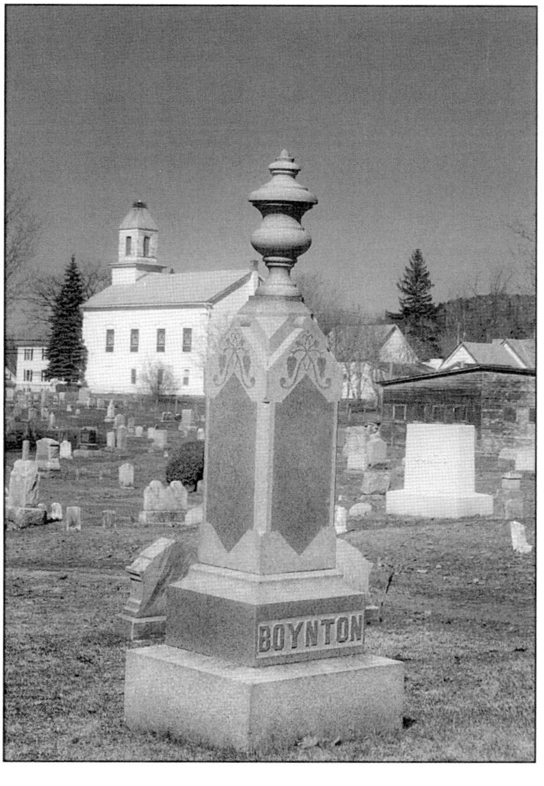

In 1870, next to his church at the West Derby cemetery, Boyton was buried "beneath the shadow of the temple dedicated to God," which was constructed by his own hands.

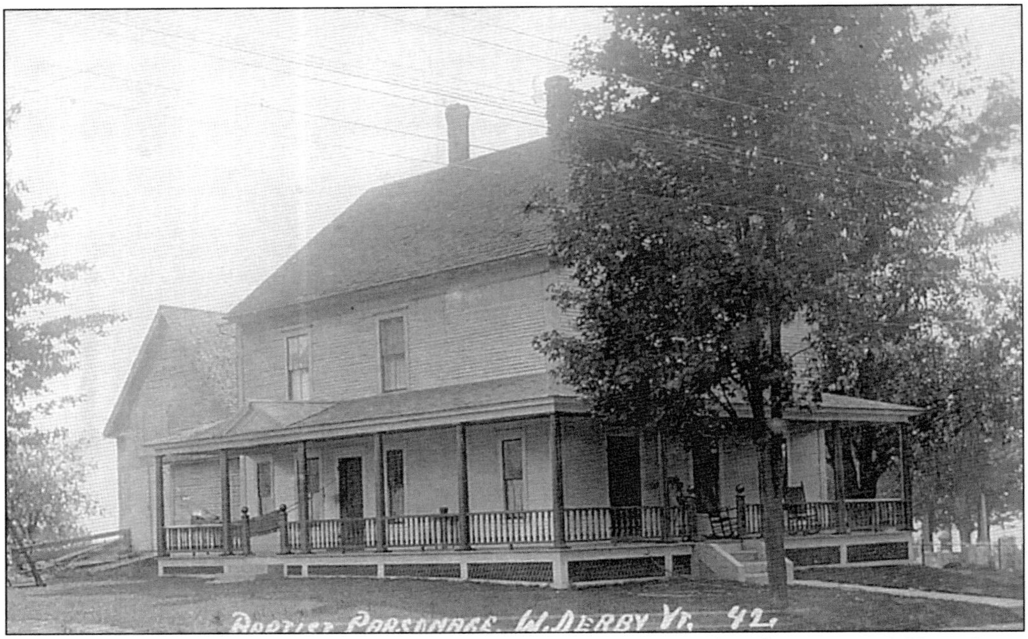

One of the first schools in West Derby stood west of the Baptist church prior to 1860, and was also used for religious services with the Reverend Isaac Blake as preacher. In 1856–57 Charles K. Adams taught at the school. He was born in Derby and later served as president of Cornell University. When the West Derby school was built in 1899, this school became the parsonage for the Baptist church.

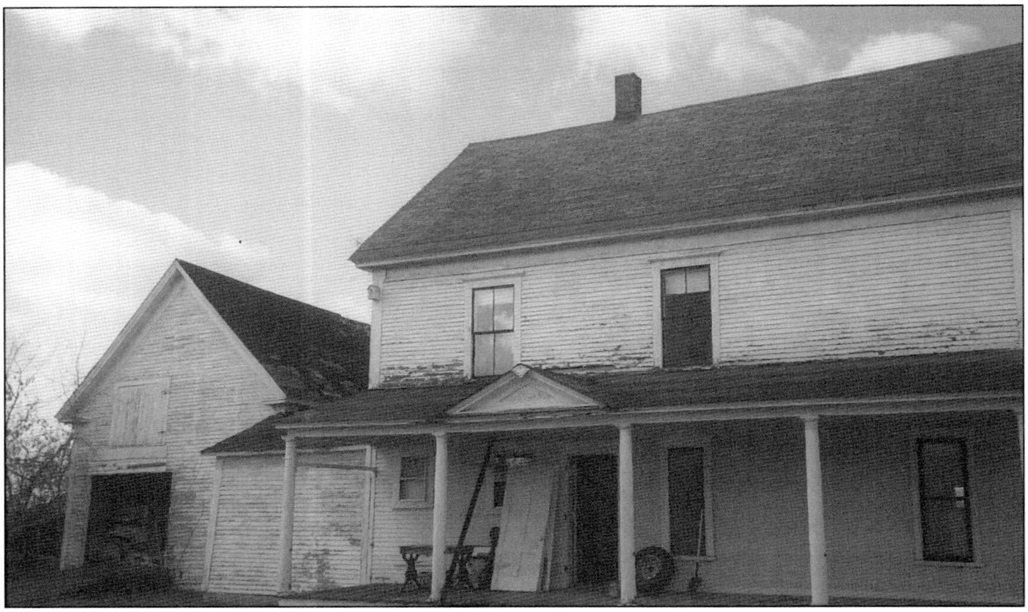

In November of 1997, this old West Derby landmark was torn down to make way for the East Main Street Baptist Church's new parking facility.

Walter H. Darling & Son Bottling Works was established in 1889 from the basement of Mr. Darling's residence. Business increased, and by 1893 he built a four-story structure with a 25-by-40-foot ell, with two stories on the Causeway. "Maggie Little," Newport Fisherwoman, gives a demonstration to the Anti-Saloon League around 1901 at the Darling Bottling Company that Newport Beer is nonalcoholic and is not unlawful to sell.

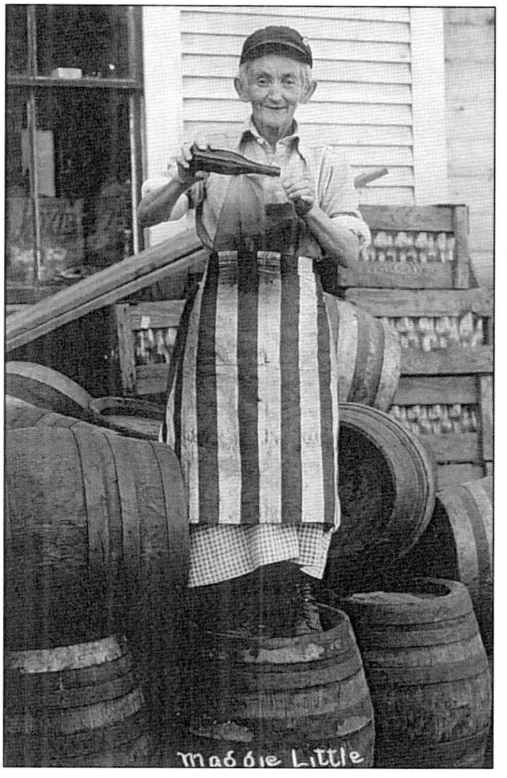

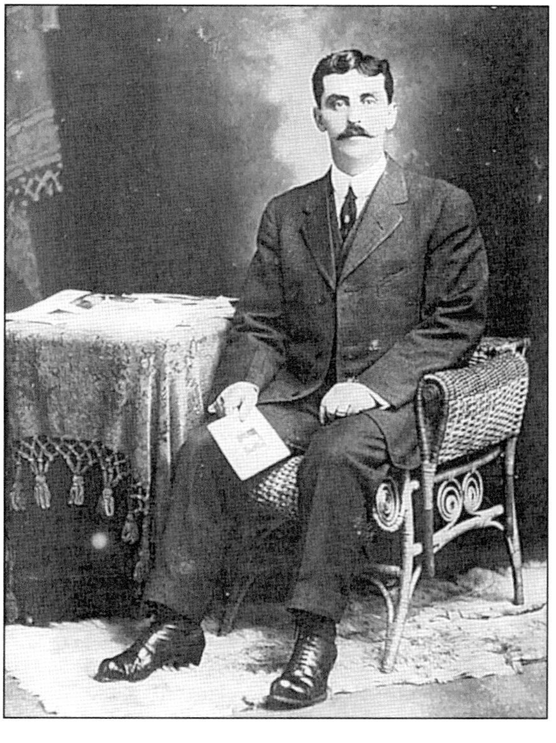

In 1910, the name of the business was changed to the Memphremagog Bottle Company, and in 1924 was sold to John T. Rocque. The Bottle Works plant operated by steam power in bottling nonalcoholic carbonated beverages. John Rocque passed away in 1955 and was buried at the Pine Grove cemetery.

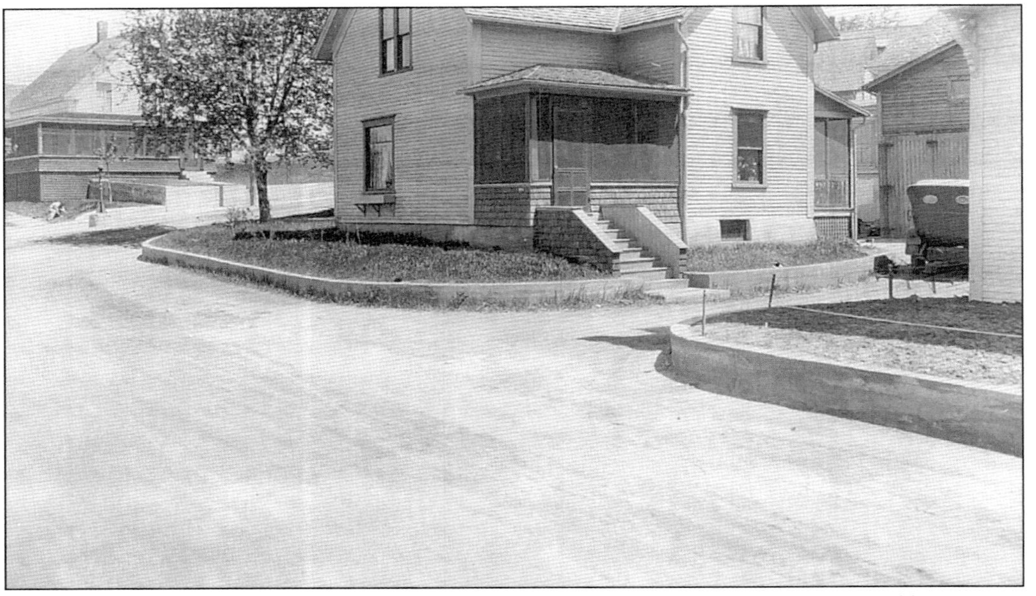

On the Causeway at the corner of East Main Street once stood a group of homes and businesses, such as the Memphremagog Bottle Company and Rice & Frawley's car dealership, along with a grocery store and gas pumps.

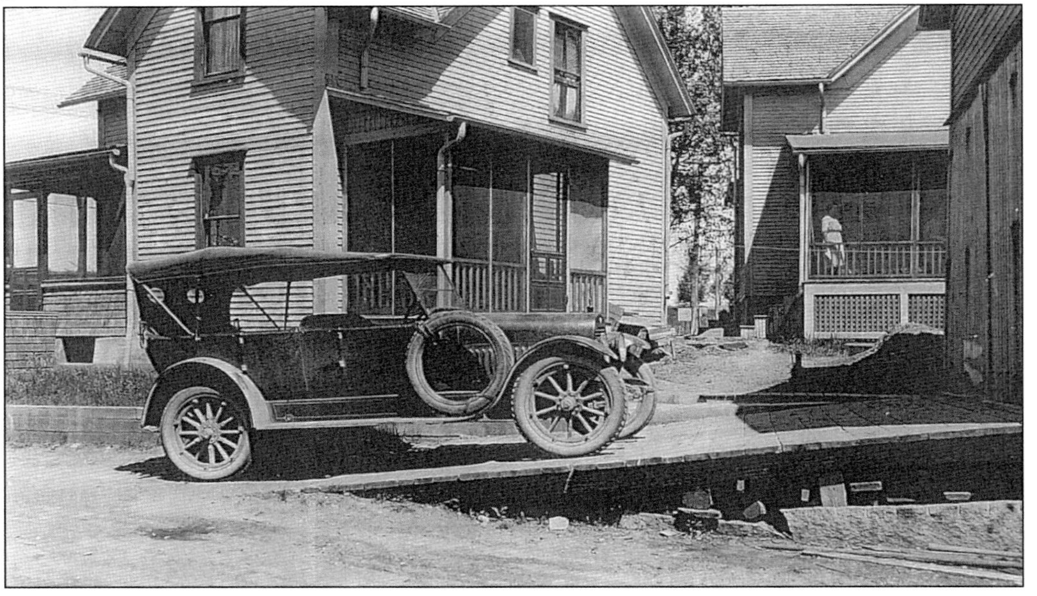

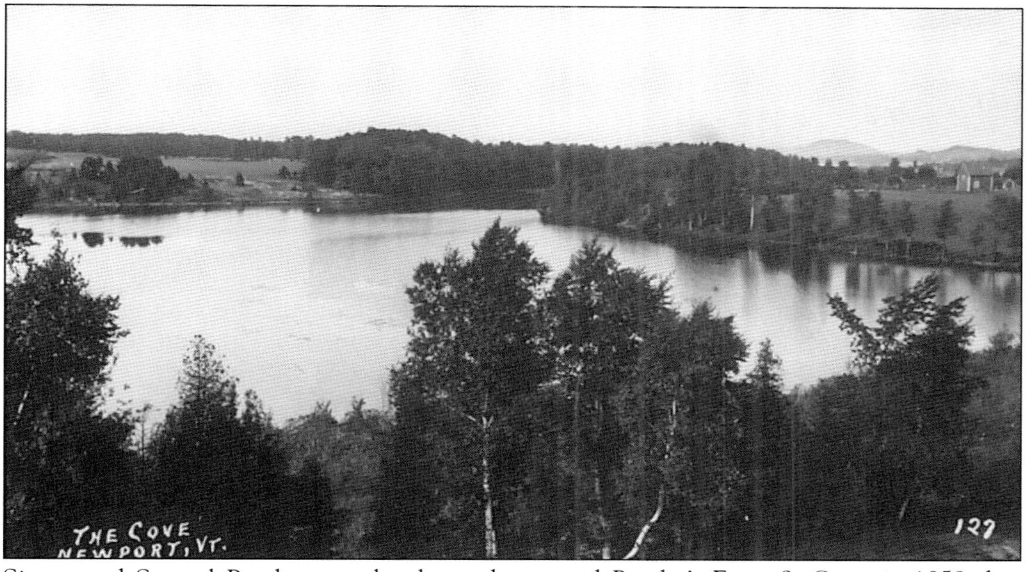

Simon and Samuel Pender were brothers who owned Pender's Farm & Cove in 1858 that bordered years later on Roeder's Bluff, later known as Prouty Beach. (Courtesy of Richardson Cartee Collection.)

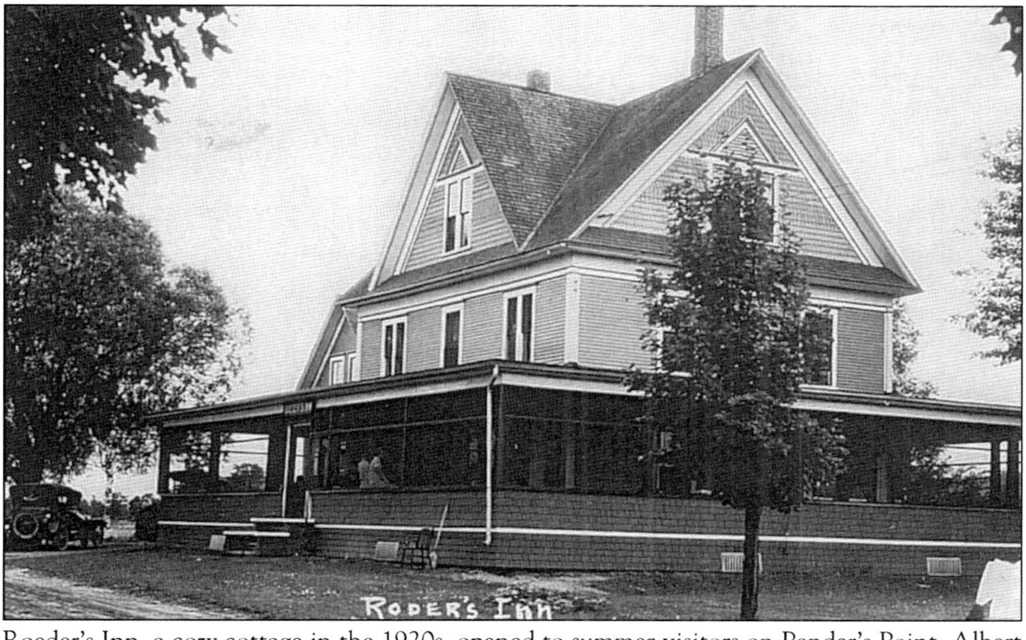

Roeder's Inn, a cozy cottage in the 1920s, opened to summer visitors on Pender's Point. Albert Roeder rebuilt the rustic bridge over the cove, as a shortcut to Indian Point and the Bluffs for the roaming pleasure of his guests.

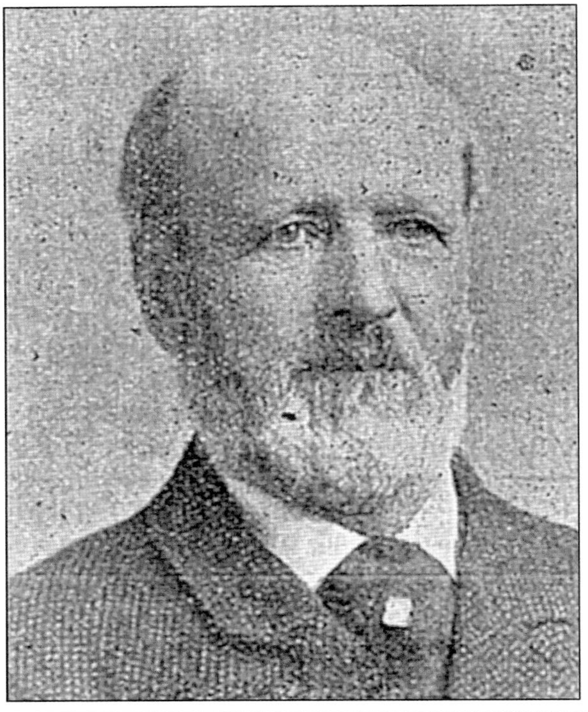

Nathaniel Ball, born in 1826, came from Massachusetts in 1868 and invested his small savings into the purchase of 75 acres of farm land known as Ball's Bluffs. Ball had kindly manners and a strict sense of honesty that won him many friends. He was a novice at farming, but with the help of his wife Isidora his first payment was made by the sale of potatoes at 11 1/2¢ per bushel.

Ball's family home is shown in this photograph taken on August 25, 1879, near the Cove. He raised four sons on his pioneer truck farm, a desirable location being only one mile from Newport. Ball owned a lookout point on Lake Memphremagog where he leased lake front lots for pretty summer cottages, later known as Camp Elizabeth.

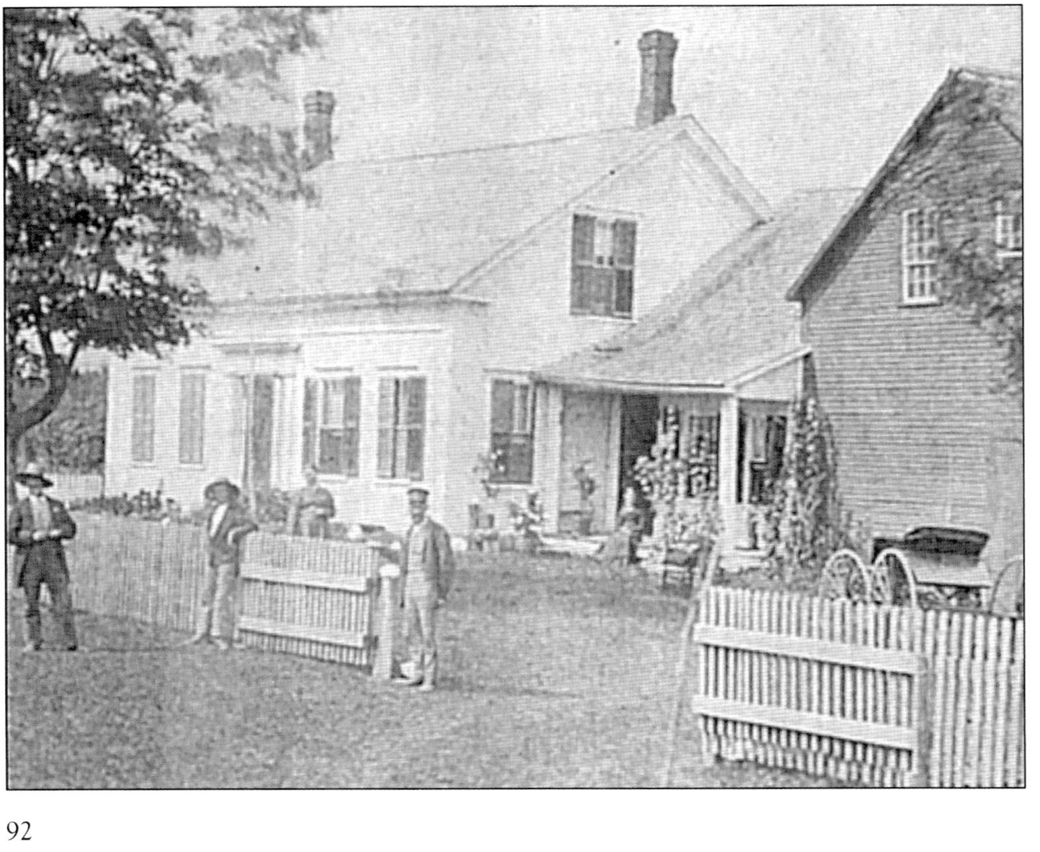

Eva Alberta Lockhart was born July 2, 1887, the daughter of Wm. George Lockhart and Effie Root Lockhart. Eva was once secretary for B.F. Moore & Company, and secretary and treasurer for Pine Grove Cemetery Association for 70 years.

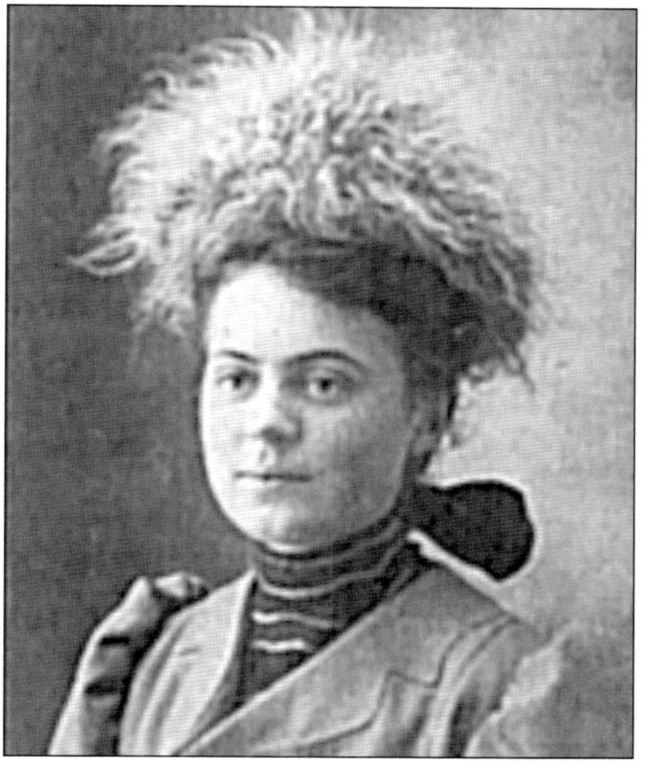

Newton Thomas Scott was born April 8, 1879, in Coaticock, Province of Quebec, the son of William and Augusta (Moulton) Scott. Newton graduated from Stanstead College and McGill University in Quebec, and attended Massachusetts General Hospital while studying to be a doctor. A childhood accident that left him with the loss of one eye caused him to change his profession to working as a male nurse.

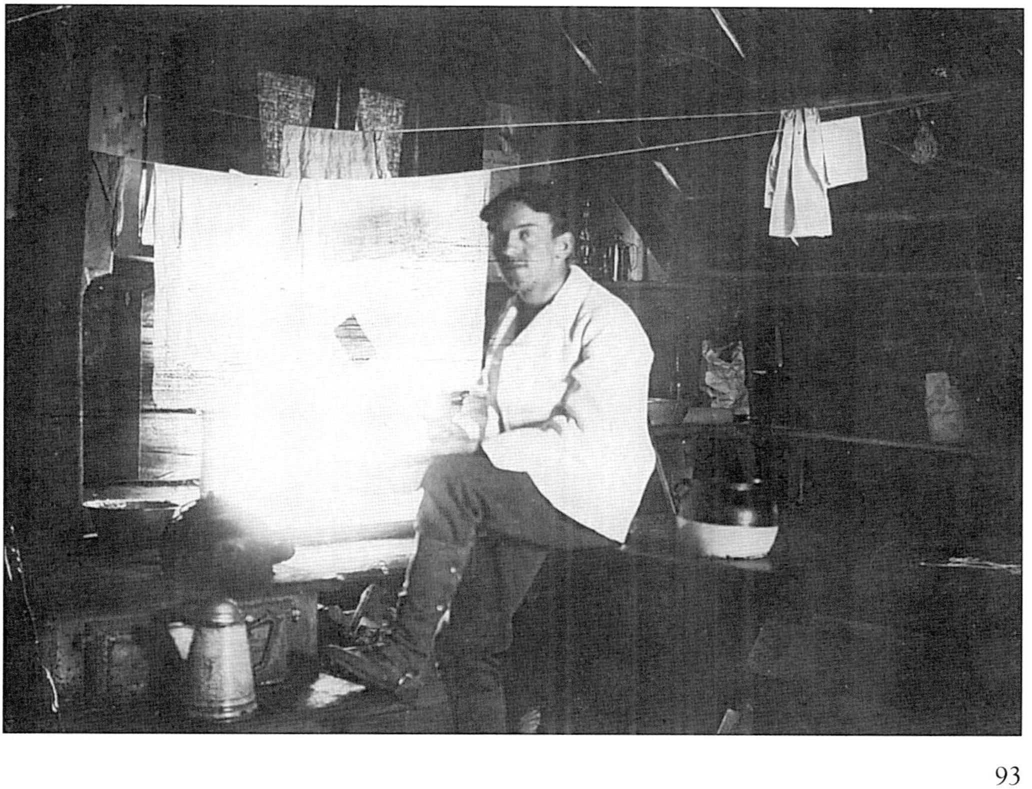

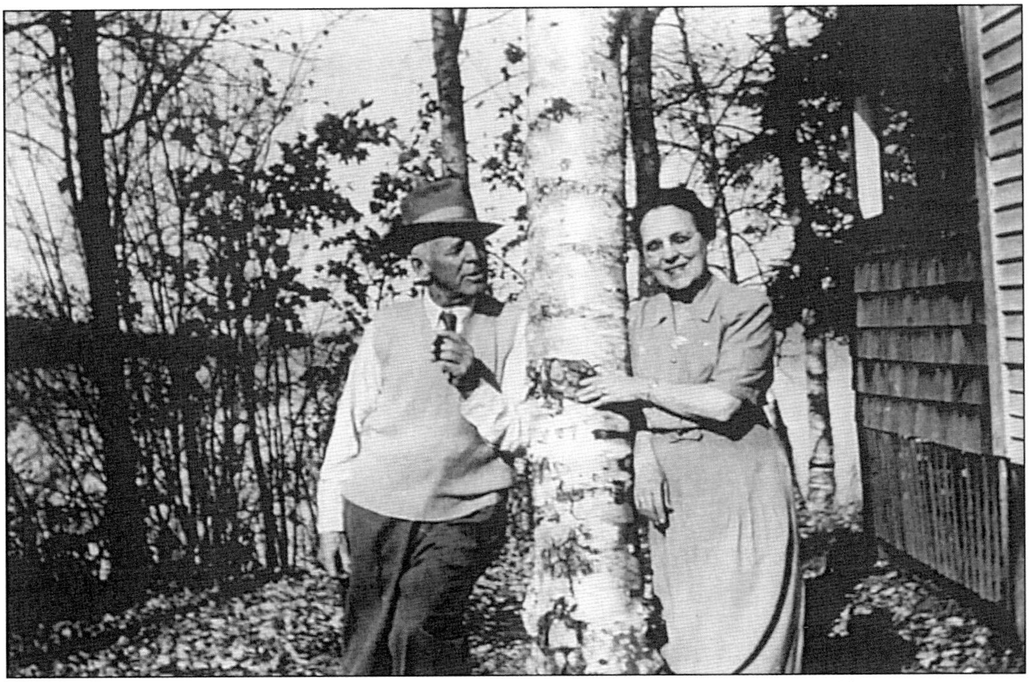

Bluffside Farms, on the old Ferry Road called The Bluffs, was purchased by William James Scott of Compton, Quebec, in 1906 from Charles F. Bigelow. Scott, born in Richmond, Province of Quebec, came to Vermont with his wife Augusta and raised three sons, George, Ernest, and Newton, along with three daughters, Elizabeth, Beatrice, and Grace.

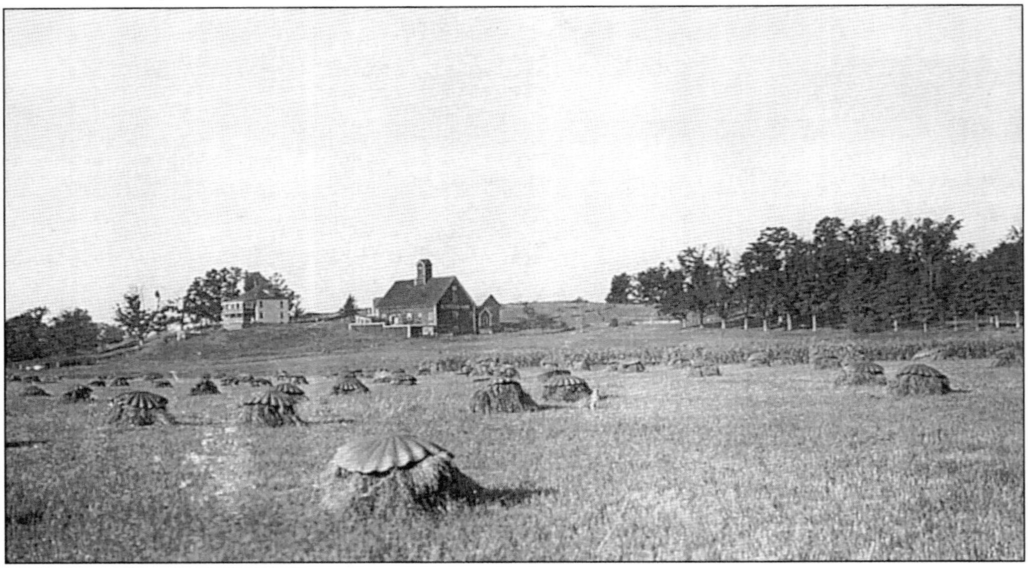

Newton T. Scott, along with his wife Eva, announced that his Bluffside Bathing Beach and Recreation grounds, later known as Prouty Beach, would open to the public on Memorial Day in the early 1900s. Across the cove in 1915, plans were made for the Indian Point Golf Club. A location near the Bluffs was selected for the golf greens. Fences were removed and the greens were constructed.

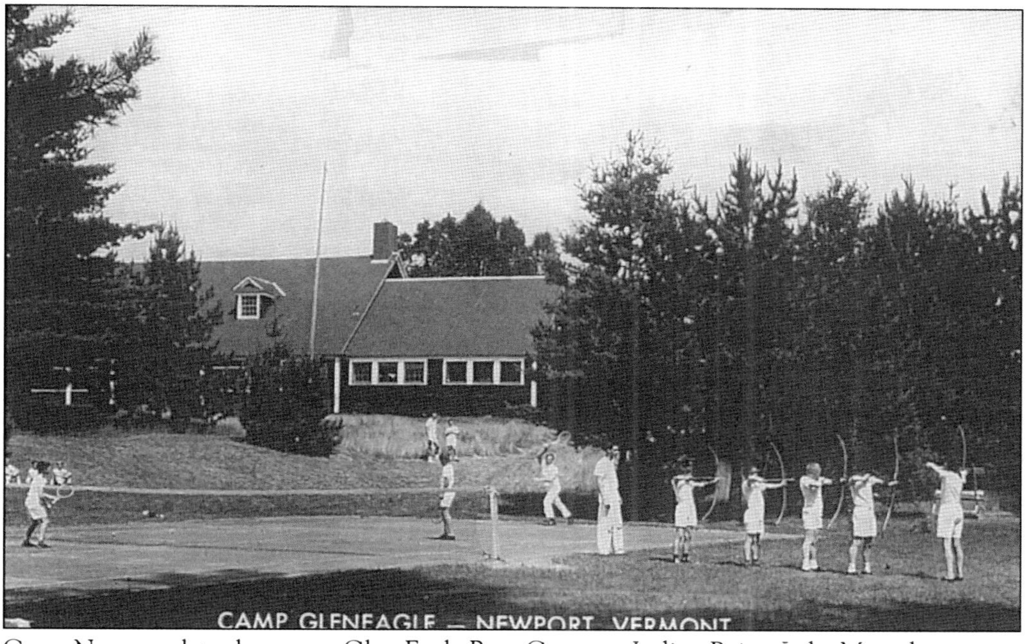

Camp Neperan, later known as Glen Eagle Boys Camp on Indian Point, Lake Memphremagog, was built in the late 1920s. Frank Beauregard constructed it for Dr. John Miner of Connecticut. The camp included four buildings, a main lodge, infirmary, dormitory, and dinning halls. The boys camp later was the scene of many summer concerts by music students at Seuffert's Music Camp.

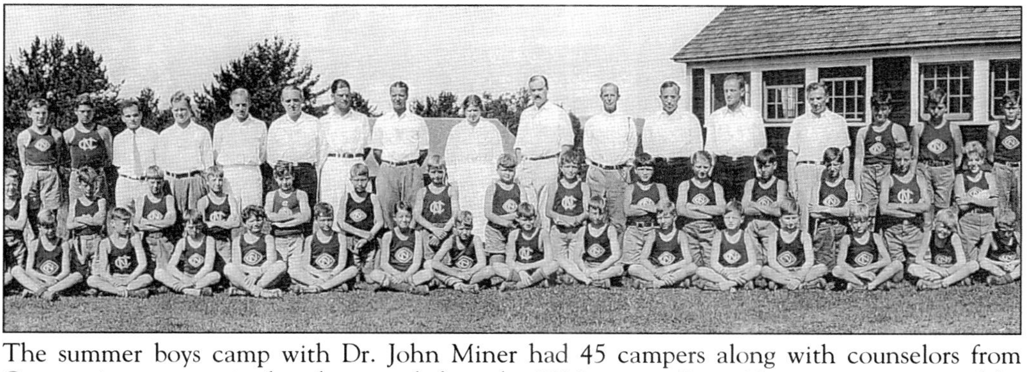

The summer boys camp with Dr. John Miner had 45 campers along with counselors from Connecticut, as seen in this photograph from the 1930 season. Camp Neperan was equipped for outdoor sports with a fleet of row boats, canoes, and two sail boats.

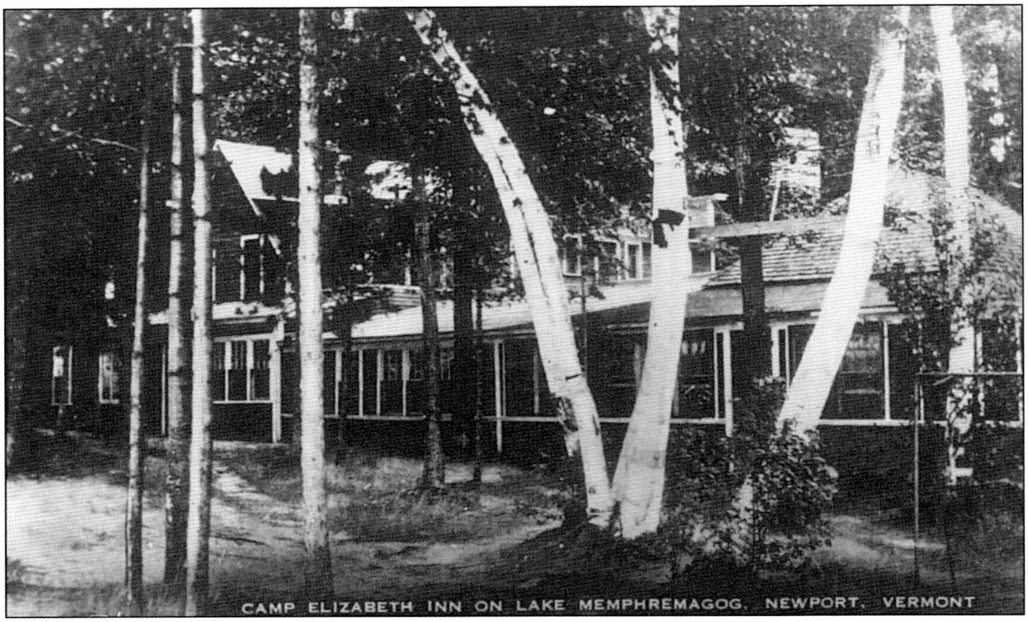

Camp Elizabeth, a summer resort on The Bluffs, was named after Frank and Minnie Flint's daughter who died young. The popular resort in the early 1920s could accommodate 100 guests at a time and had large verandas, cherry fireplaces, and cushioned chairs and nooks. In January of 1933, there was a disastrous fire to the entire structure, and the reflection in the sky guided the firemen to the summer resort. (Courtesy of Richardson Cartee Collection.)

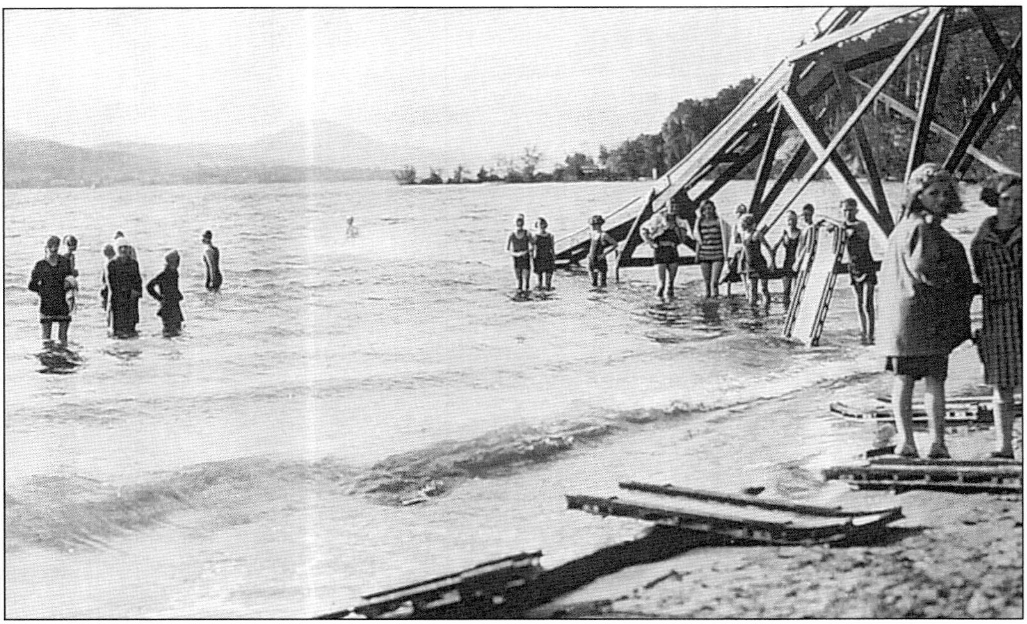

In May of 1933, Camp Elizabeth rebuilt on a smaller scale and offered small private cottages to the summer tourists. Children enjoyed one of the first "water slides" by coasting down from the top of the hill on a "rail-sled" into the water below.

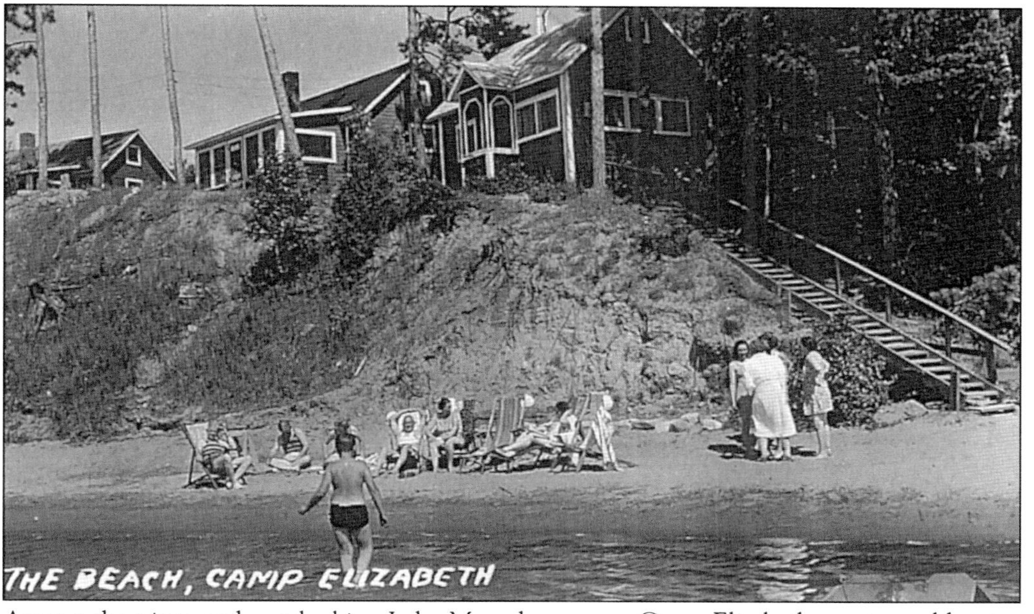

Among the pines and overlooking Lake Memphremagog, Camp Elizabeth guests could enjoy tennis, boating, or the splendid bathing on the beaches.

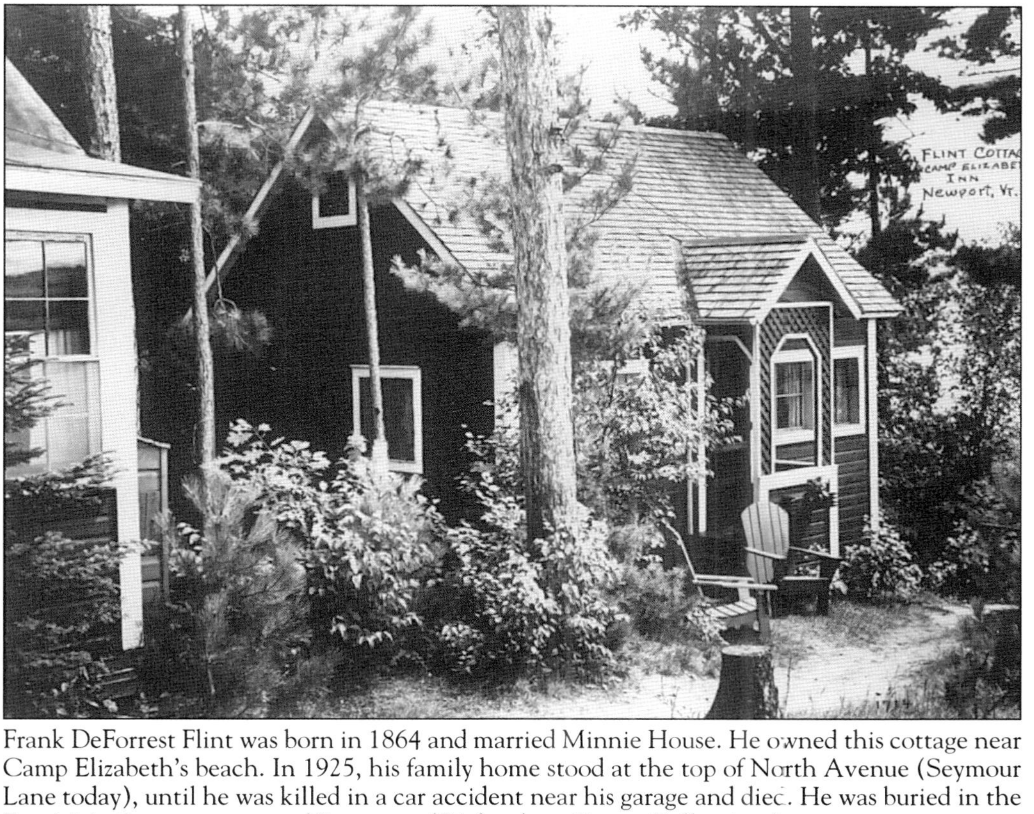

Frank DeForrest Flint was born in 1864 and married Minnie House. He owned this cottage near Camp Elizabeth's beach. In 1925, his family home stood at the top of North Avenue (Seymour Lane today), until he was killed in a car accident near his garage and died. He was buried in the East Main Street cemetery. (Courtesy of Richardson Cartee Collection.)

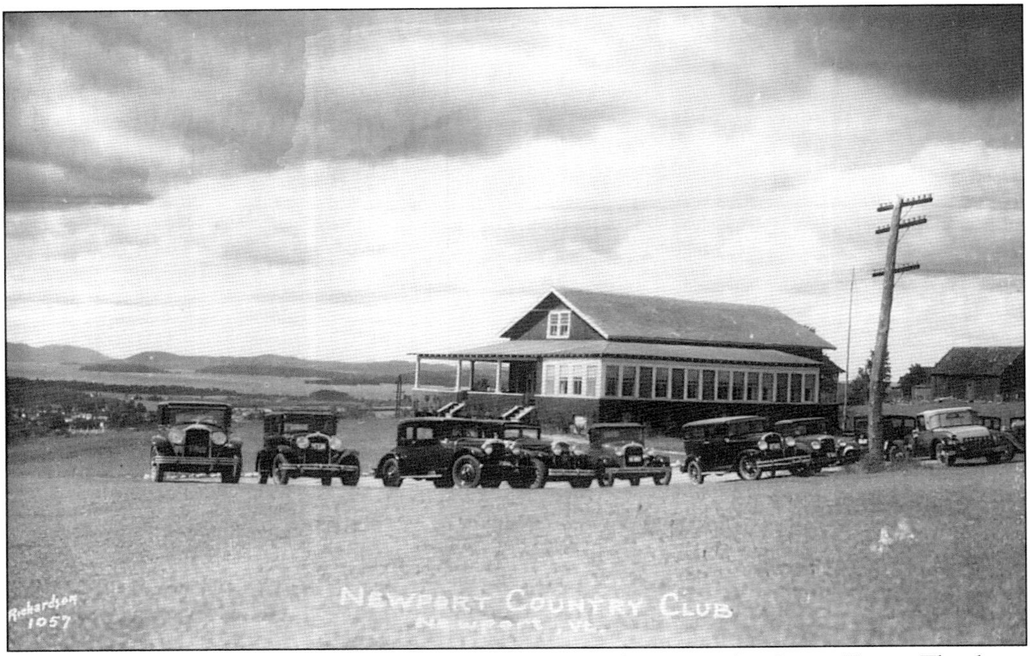

The Newport Country Club in 1921 had a five-year lease on the Percy Farm. The lease included 115 acres on Pine Hill overlooking Newport and Lake Memphremagog, and the club had already procured 35 memberships. By 1931, the old Club House was moved to the present site and yearly dues were $15. A member was also required to purchase one share of stock at a value of $125. The first officers of the club were: George Frost, president; P.O. Miller, vice president; Aubrey Akin, secretary; and Rudolph Bigelow, treasurer. (Courtesy of Richardson Cartee Collection.)

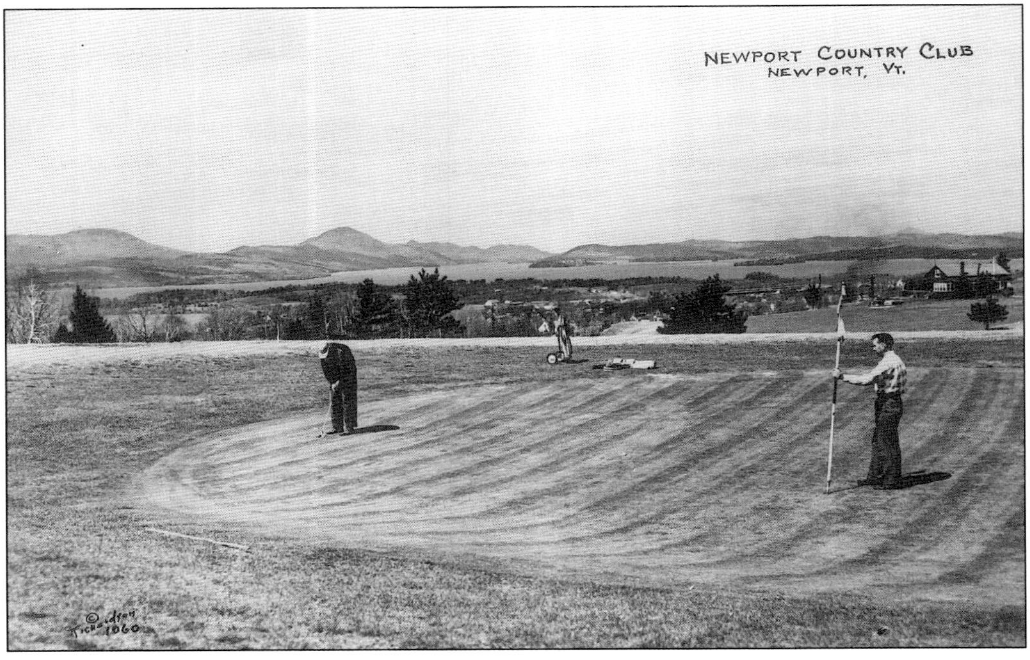

John Parker Lindsay, son of John and Pleuma (Ball) Lindsay, was born in 1829 and married Julia Atwater Manvel in 1863. Lindsay spent his business life in Connecticut and New York City, inventing and placing his patents on the market. He patented the safety pin in 1877, along with the paper clip, buttons, and loop fasteners.

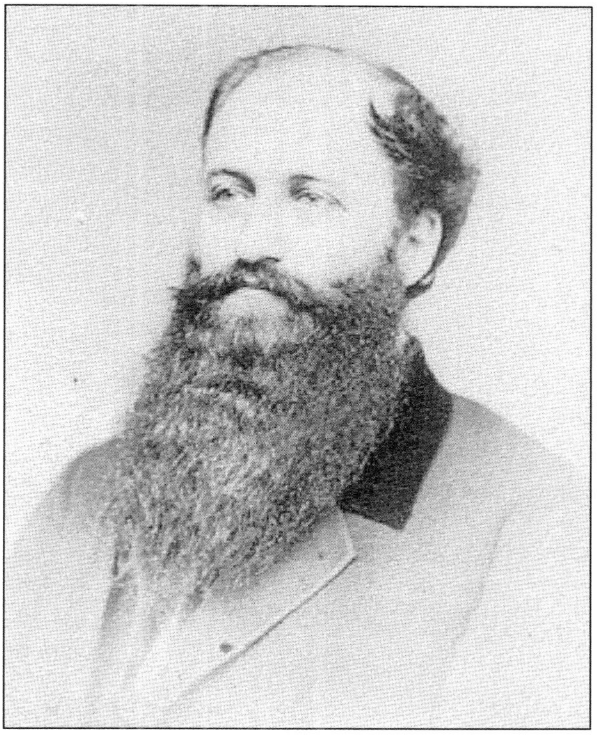

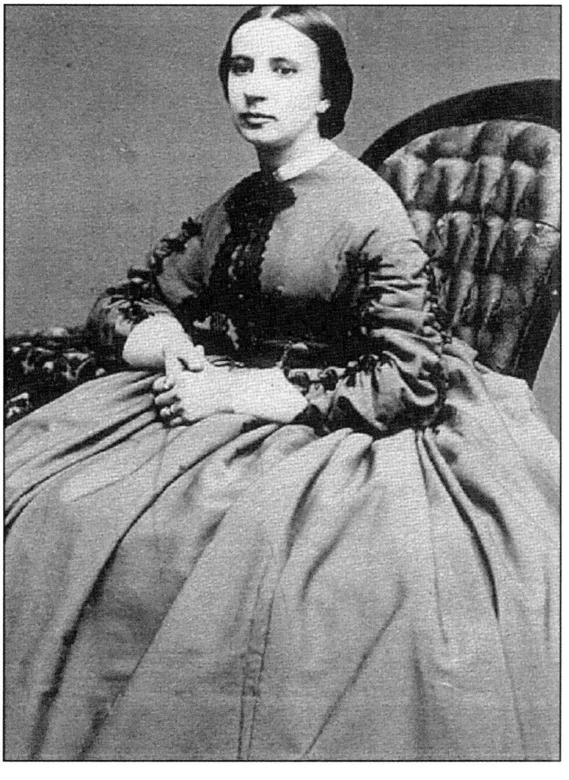

Julia Lindsay, shown in this photograph, had five children: John, Howard, twins William and Walter, and Adelaide. John Lindsay purchased the original old farm in Derby that dates back to the 1700s, including shore line property on Lake Memphremagog. He was of Scotch ancestry, and characterized by caution, courage, and endurance. He died in 1892, and Julia in 1917.

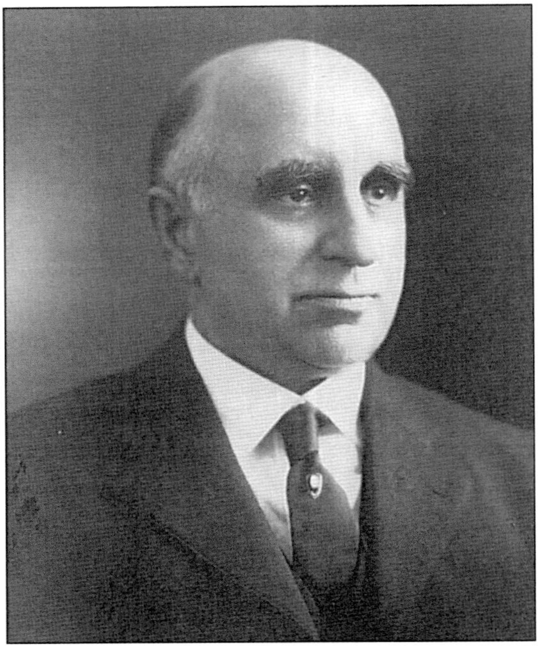

William Culter (Will) Lindsay was born August 21, 1867, remained single, and was employed as an attorney. He was a longtime resident and prominent businessman of both Newport and Derby. He was elected mayor of the City of Newport for the years 1922 to1925. Lindsay's last years were spent at his home on Sunset Terrace, exercising and racing his horses around the "circle" and back to his stables. He died in 1939 at the age of 71 years.

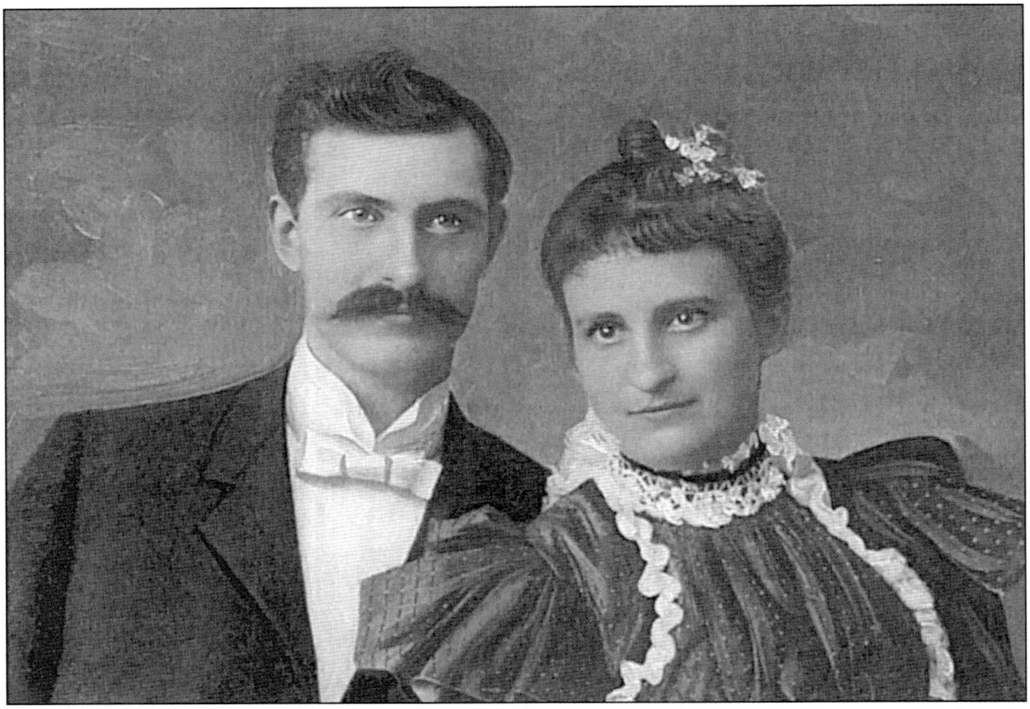

Malhon Henry Brown was born 1870 in Westfield to Cyrus and Hannah. He married Adelaide (Lindsay), born 1869 in NYC, in 1887. Malhon worked for the Railroad Postal Service and had three children: Lindsay, 1898; Elma, 1901; and Dayton, 1904. A granddaughter remembers Adelaide telling her how she would tie her father Lindsay to a "lamp post" in Newport while she gave painting and music lessons.

Lindsay Lodge at Lindsay Beach was opened in the 1940s by Alice Lindsay after her husband Howard died, and continued until the 1960s. Alice (Chase) Lindsay was born in 1879, the daughter of John and Nellie (Hall) Chase. She married Howard Lindsay, a U.S. Customs Inspector, and had two children: Dorothy, born in 1898, and John Parker, born in 1900. Dorothy became the bride of Frederick Bray in 1922 at the Lindsays' summer home.

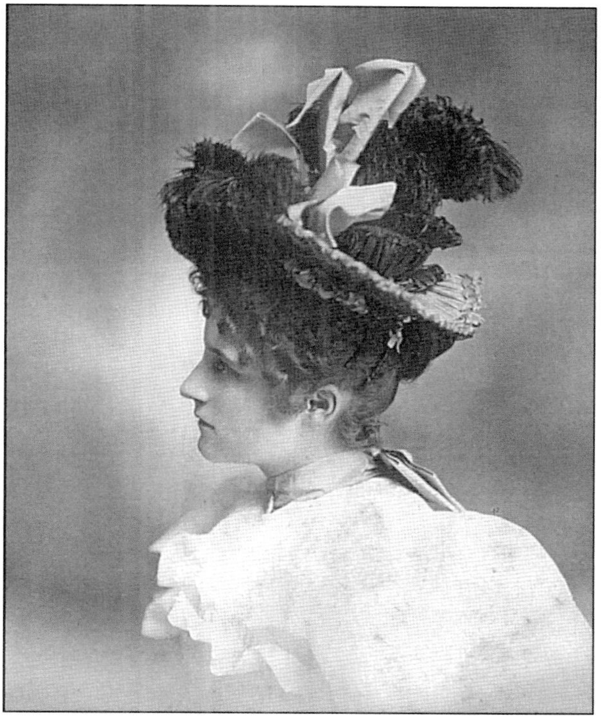

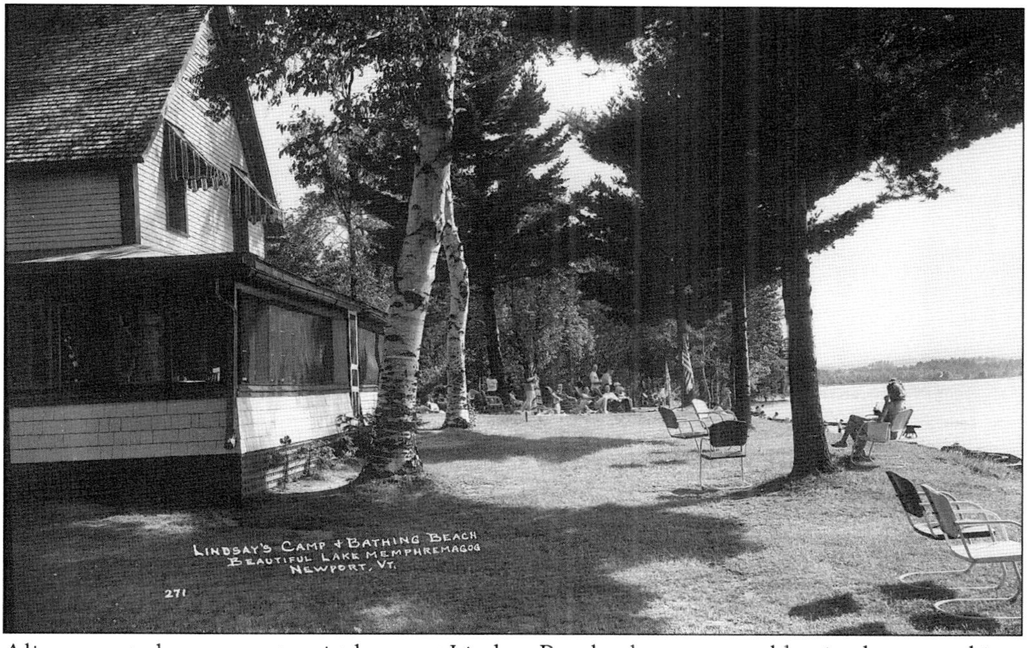

Alice operated a summer tourist home at Lindsay Beach where one could enjoy home cooking. Local folks enjoyed picnics and swimming at the beach on Lake Memphremagog, at a cost of 25¢ per person. John Parker Lindsay's Homestead was sold in 1981, and it remains in private ownership with the lake front property being enjoyed by the ancestors of John and Julia Lindsay for many generations to come. (Courtesy of Richardson Cartee Collection.)

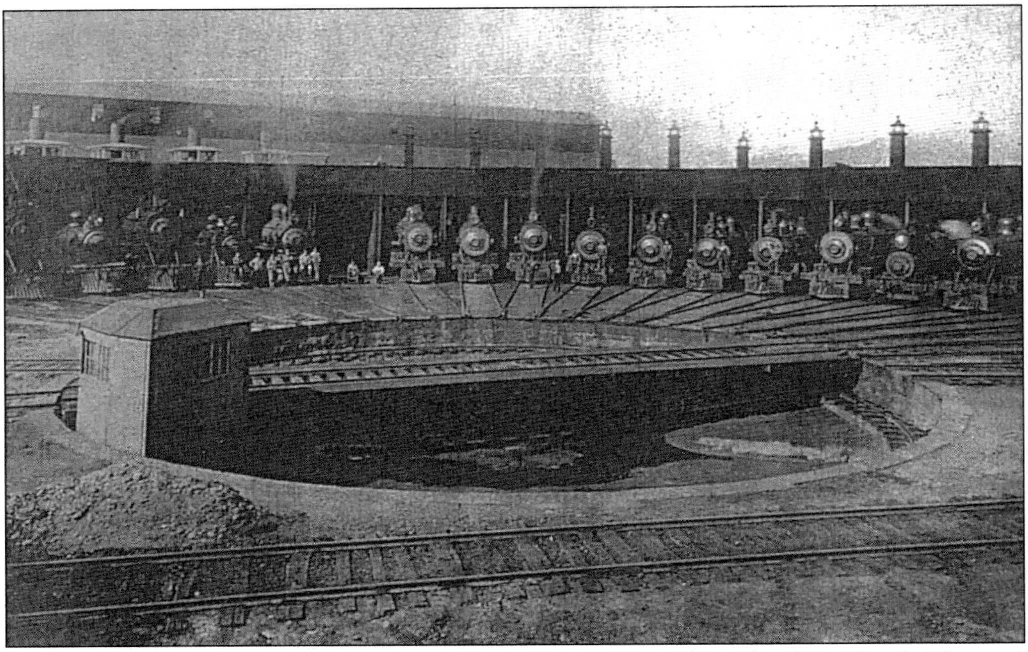

The roundhouse and coal shutes were once at the south yard on the Glen Road. The coal shutes were a long block of wooden buildings 300 feet long and 120 feet high. In 1909, the roundhouse was a large semi-circular brick structure divided into 21 stables for the Boston & Maine locomotives, and nine for the Canadian Pacific.

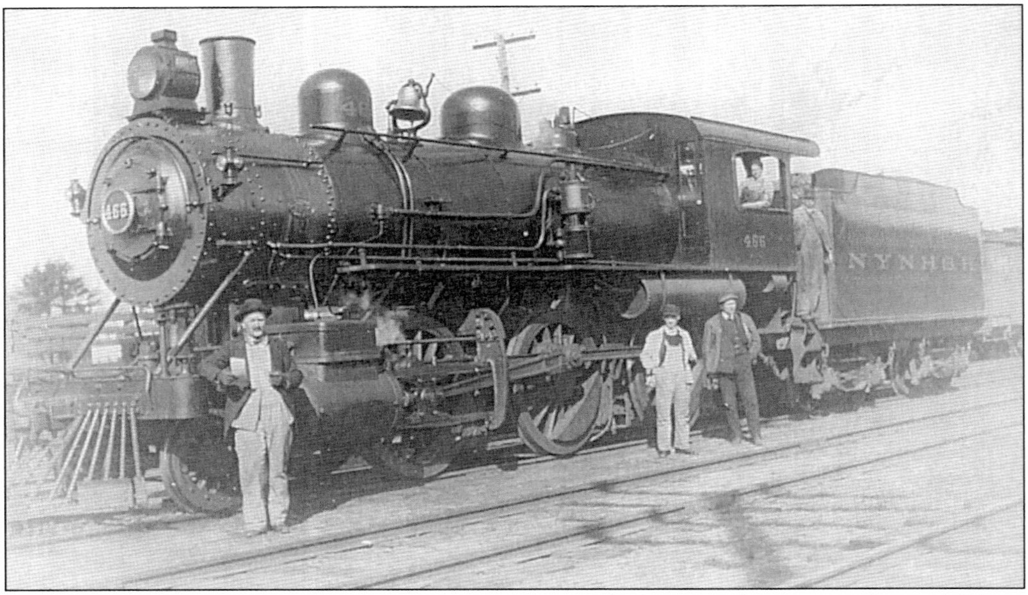

George W. Foster began his railroad career in 1890 with the Canadian & Pacific, Red Wing, and Allouette. During 41 years of service, he took only one vacation. He pulled freight and passenger trains, free of accidents, starting in Lyndonville, White River Junction, back to Newport, and then to Lyndonville, offering the engine cars no rest. These trips were known locally as "The Round the World Run."

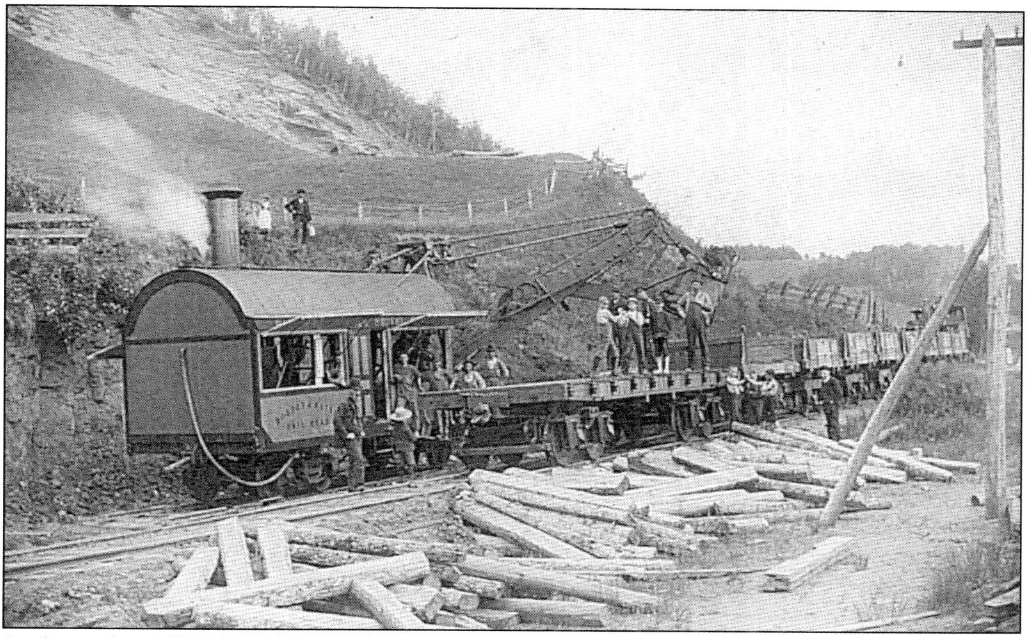

In the early 1860s, the Glen Road railroad tracks were laid. By 1863, the one-track South Bay trestle bridge was built over Lake Memphremagog, bringing the first passenger train into the Village of Newport.

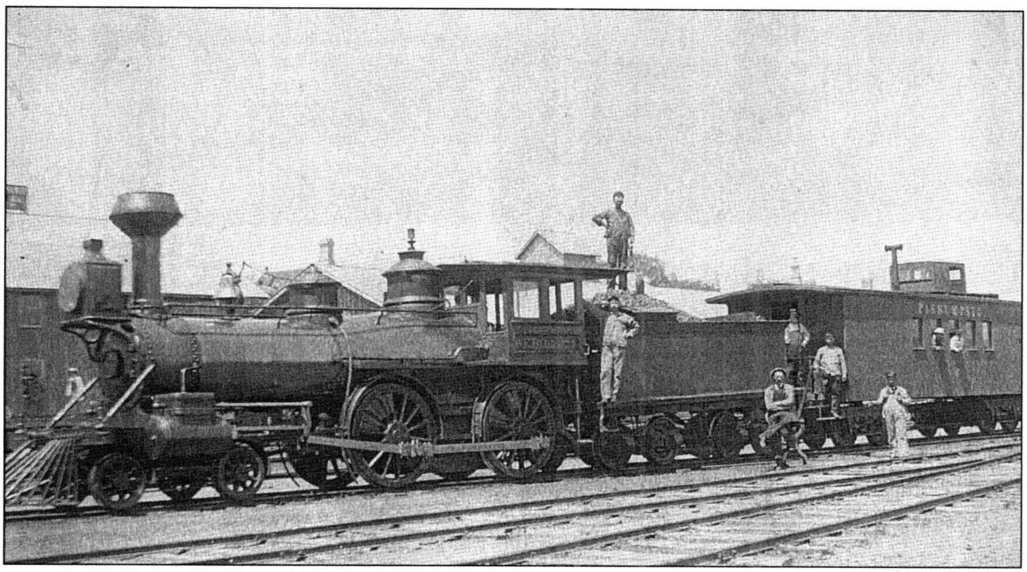

Pictured in this photograph are William George Lockhart as conductor, Charles Tarlton as engineer, and the train crew. Charles Tarlton began his railroad career at the age of 14 and in 1872 was promoted to engineer. He kept his own engine brass blazing by using his idle moments to polish the brass. In 1930, Tarlton received recognition of 50 years of service with the Boston & Maine Railroad.

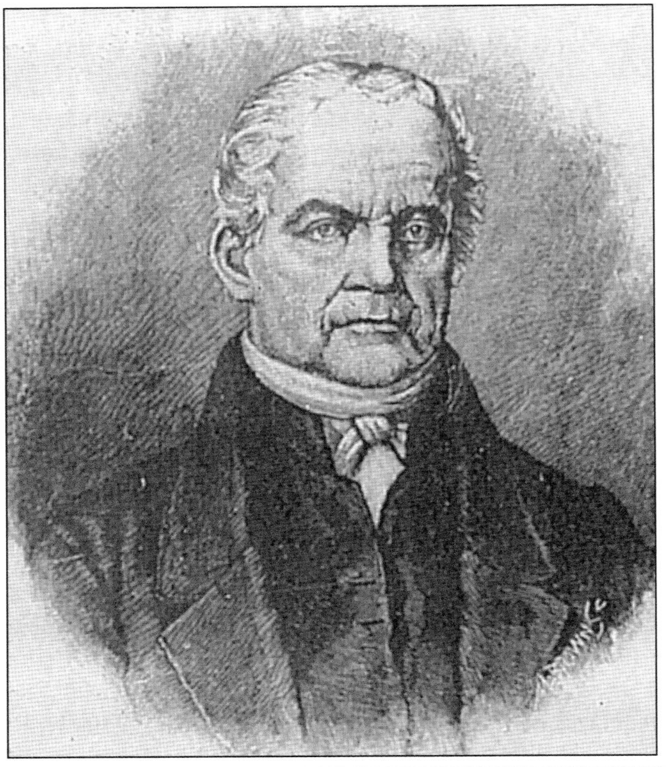

Captain Timothy Hinman was born in Connecticut, the son of Adam and Sarah Porter Hinman. A veteran of the Revolutionary War, Hinman was a true pioneer and established the first permanent settlement in Derby in the 1790s. At the Derby Center cemetery grounds near Hinman/Derby Pond, Capt. Hinman was buried in 1850.

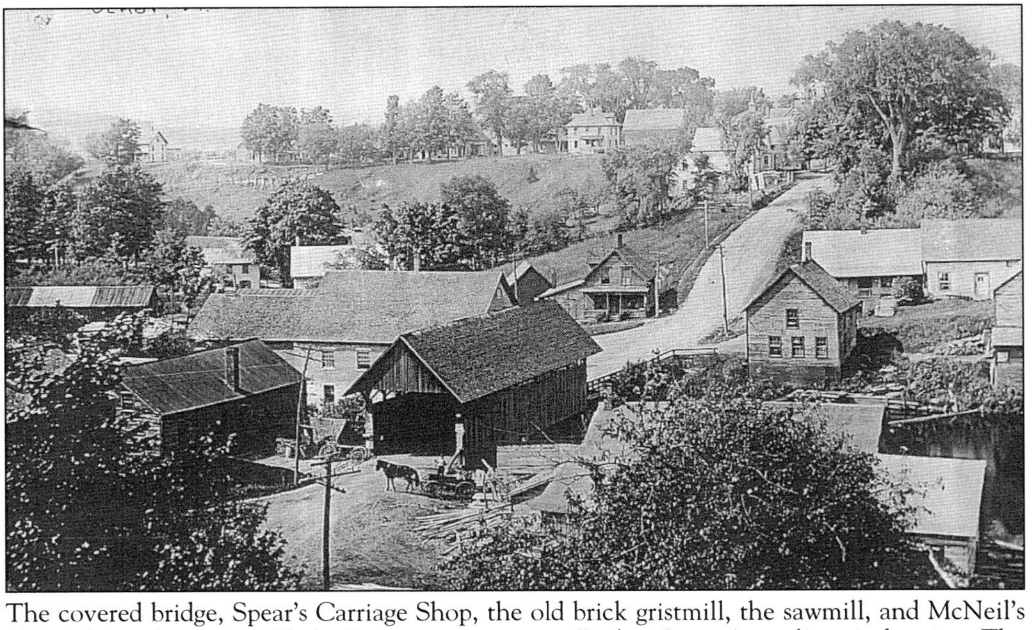

The covered bridge, Spear's Carriage Shop, the old brick gristmill, the sawmill, and McNeil's Shoe shop along the Clyde River were among Derby Center's earliest industries. The wooden covered bridge, built in 1800, spanned the river between the mills and Kilborn Hill. By 1840, eight sawmills, two gristmills, a tannery, and blacksmith shop centered around the old covered bridge.

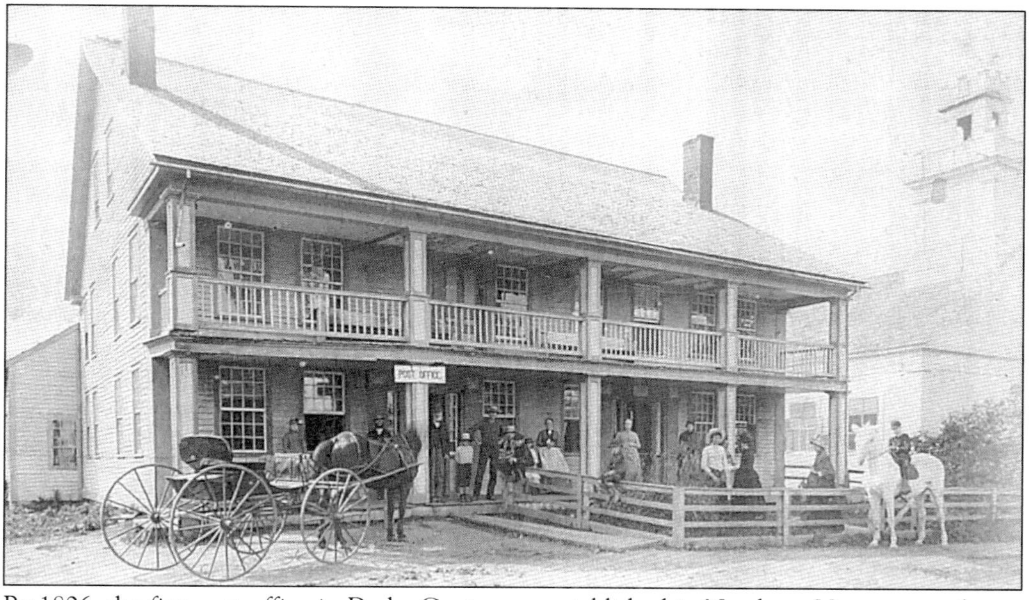

By 1806, the first post office in Derby Center was established in Northern Vermont, and over the years occupied many different locations. The post office in 1849 was located in John Kelley's store when he was appointed postmaster. From 1886 to 1889, the post office was in a large building constructed for a hotel that once stood opposite the Derby Academy on Main Street. A fire in 1930 destroyed the building.

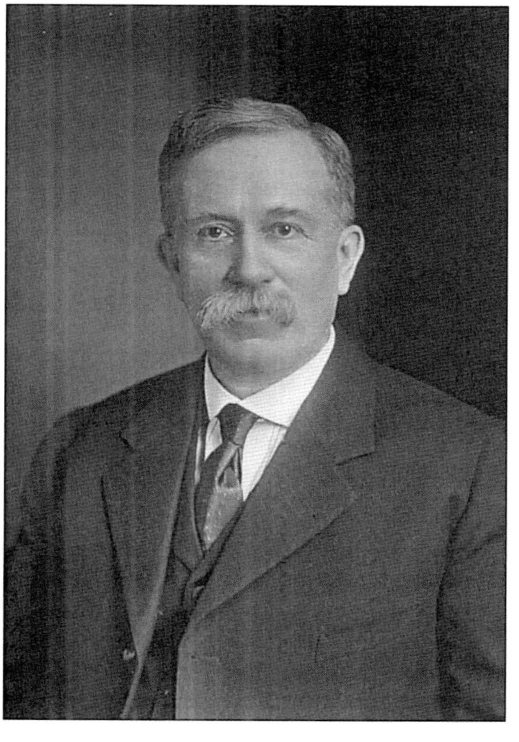

Wilbur M. Taylor was born in 1858, the son of Ira & Emily (Griggs) Taylor. He married Flora Chandler, who was born in 1860, the daughter of Daniel and Maria Chandler. W.M. Taylor was employed by Elisha Lane as a young lad in Derby Center.

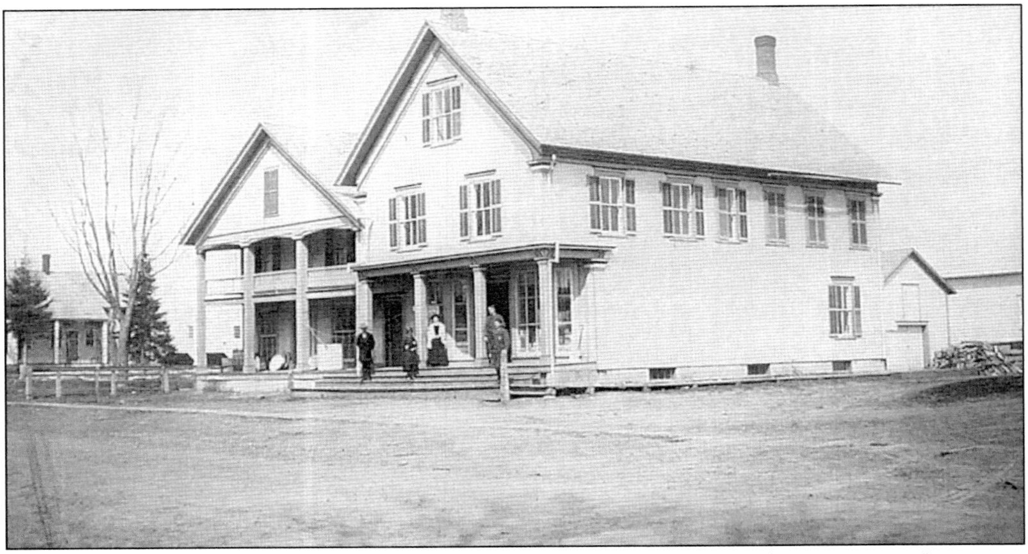

Elisha Lane was born in 1835, the son of Seymour Lane. He owned a commercial store in 1864 on the Clyde River in West Derby before he bought the Derby Center Store in 1879 on Main Street.

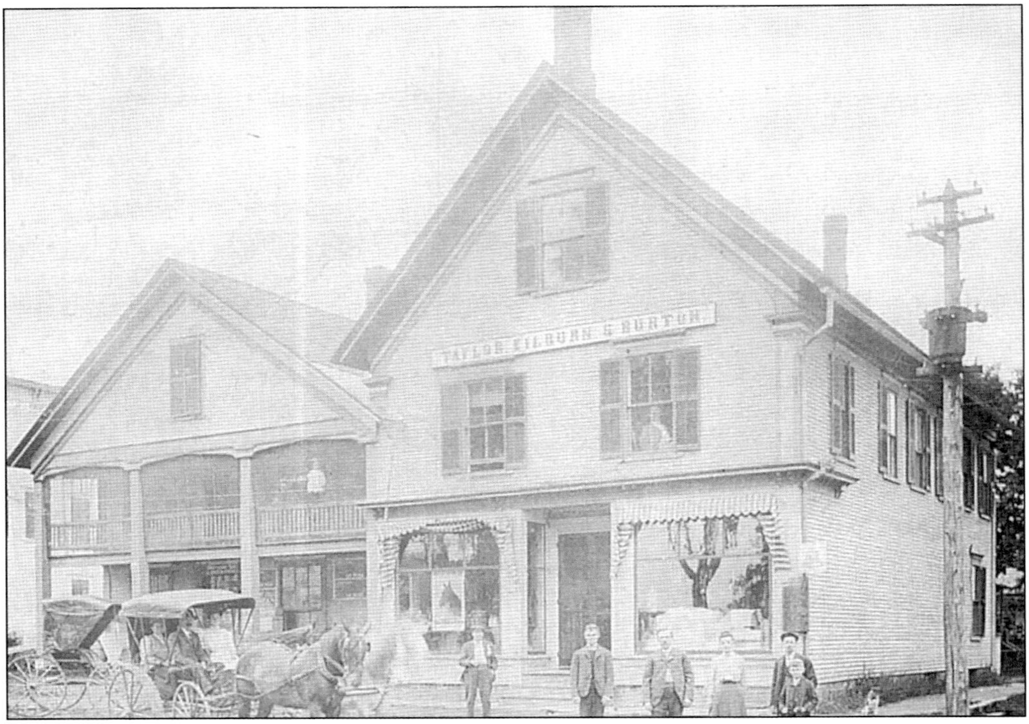

Taylor and his two business partners, Kilburn and Burton, purchased Elisha Lane's Store. By 1912, Taylor bought the interest of the others while his son Harold joined the business. His son Frederick joined later, and they were proprietors of the country store until they sold it in 1961.

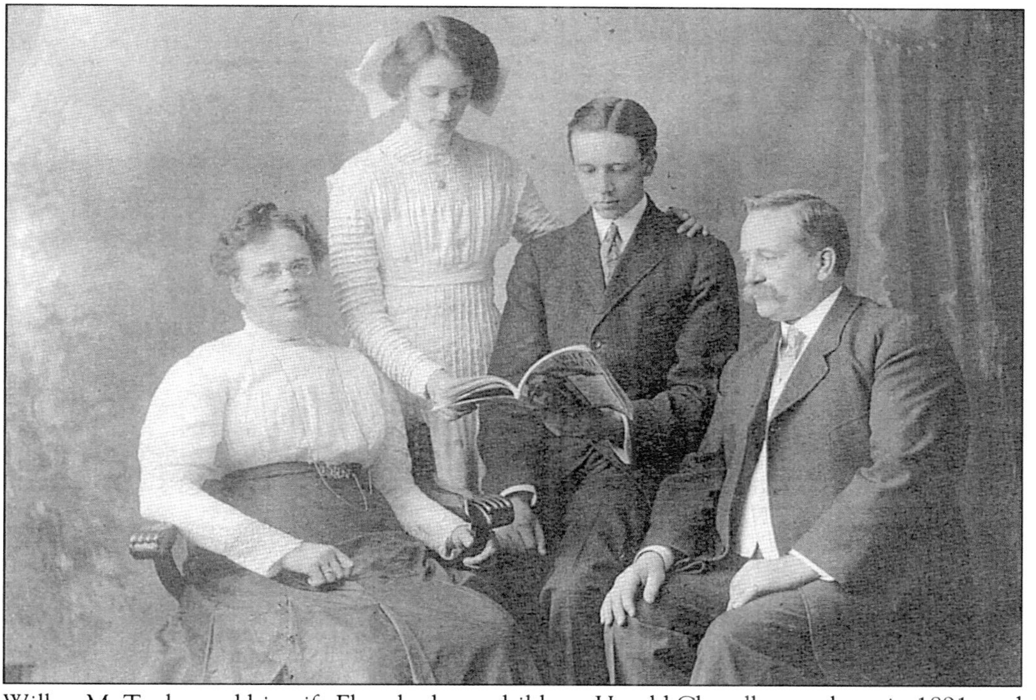

Wilbur M. Taylor and his wife Flora had two children. Harold Chandler was born in 1891, and his son Frederick was born in 1916. Emilie L. (Taylor) Hall was born in 1895, and became the mother of Richard and Blaine Hall.

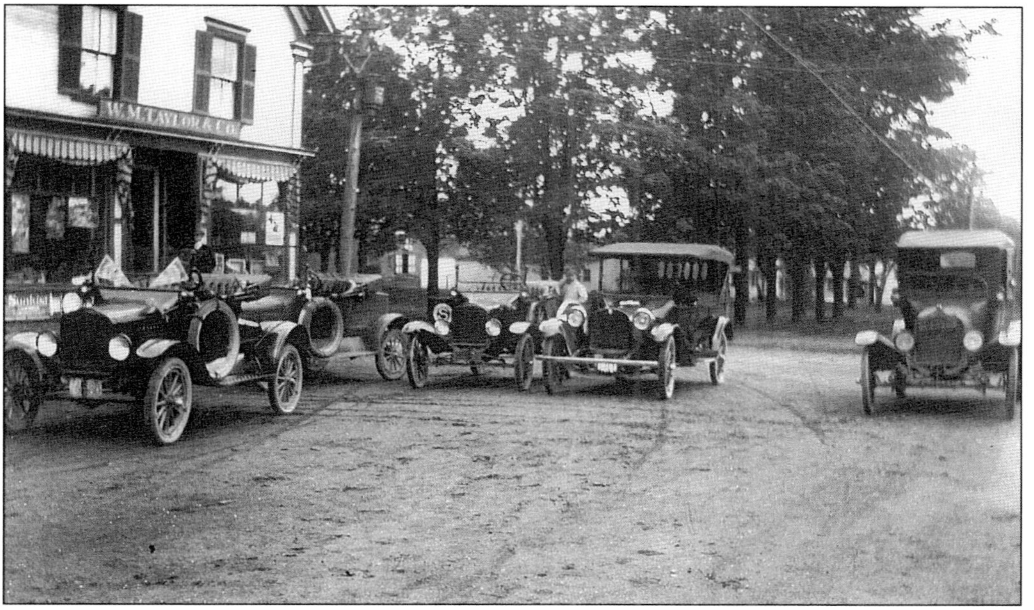

Harold Taylor along with his only son, Frederick, Frederick's wife and daughter all lived over the family-owned country store in a large apartment. In 1961, the store was sold and the Taylors had to empty 16 rooms of "stuff." They discarded ancient rolls of wallpaper, dusty smelly hats, and old boots—the collective memories of a past era.

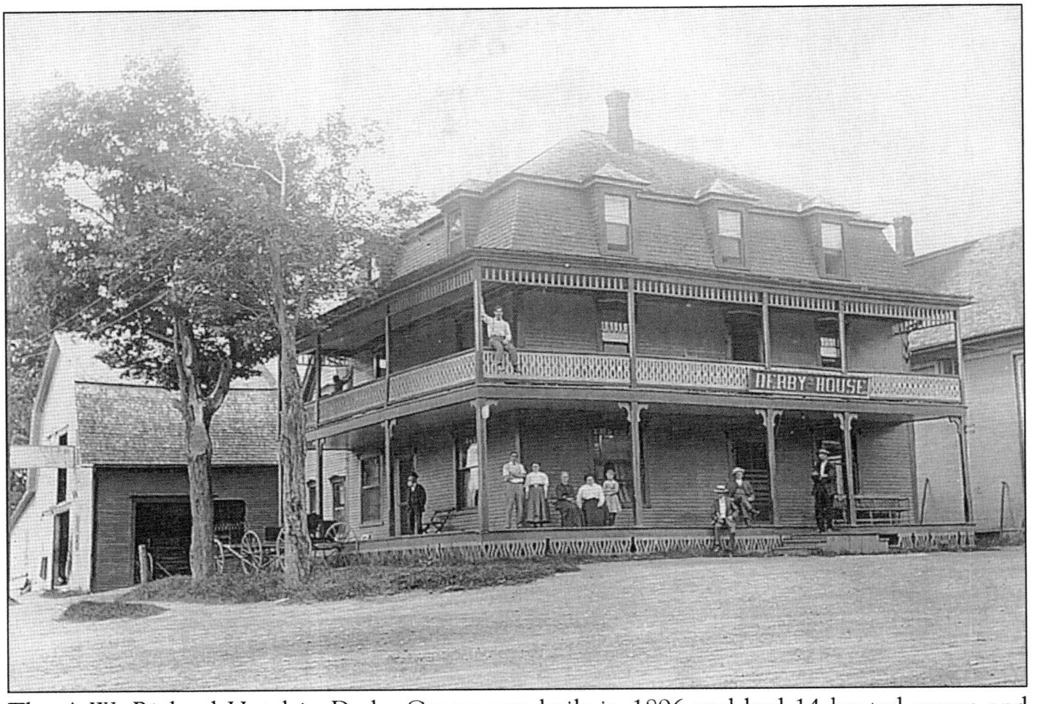

The A.W. Rickard Hotel in Derby Center was built in 1896 and had 14 heated rooms and a good livery stable. Harry M. Rickard was the proprietor and looked after the needs of his customers in a splendid manner.

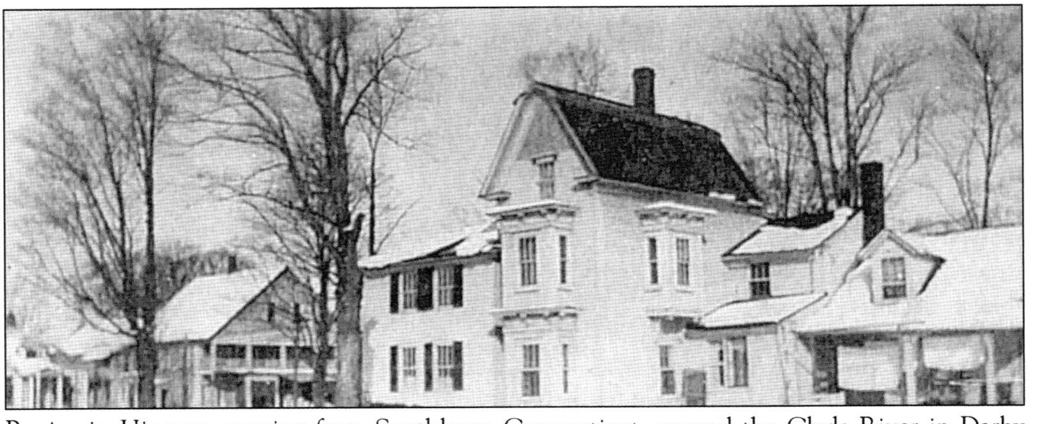

Benjamin Hinman, coming from Southbury, Connecticut, crossed the Clyde River in Derby and in 1816 commenced the construction of his home at Derby Center, named Clydeside. His daughter Harriet, born in 1842, married Major and later Governor Josiah Grout Jr. in 1868 and lived on the Hinman Homestead. Herbert H. Blake in 1916 bought the Hinman/Grout Homestead and Stock Farm, shown in this photograph dated November 6, 1919.

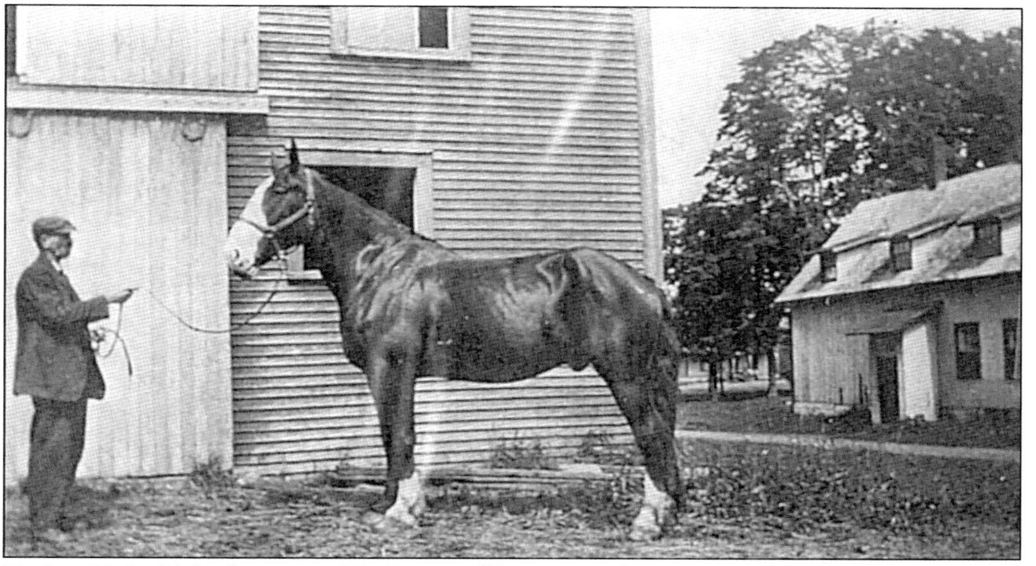

Herbert Hylas Blake, born in 1872, the son of Freeman and Mary (Beebe) Blake, is shown in this photograph with his prize horse. In 1895, Herbert married Marcia Fuller, daughter of George and Sarah Fuller, and raised two children to adulthood, Hazel Mae and Raymond. Herbert, a respected and prosperous farmer of Derby Village, passed away in 1929 and his wife in 1943. They were buried at Derby cemetery.

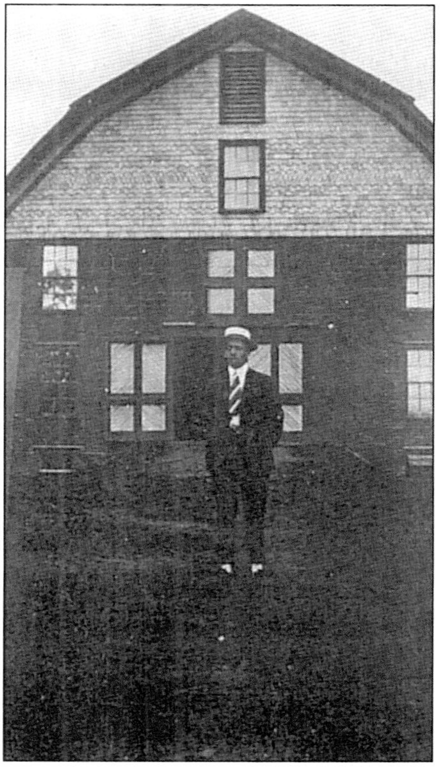

Born in 1896 to H.H. and Marcia Blake, Raymond Eliphalet Blake married Julia Leavens on June 12, 1918. They raised six children: Lucille, Marion, Herbert, Hazel, Mary Jean, and Charles. In 1929, Raymond moved his family on to the farm called "Clydeside." In 1938, he sold the farm, moved to Newport, and continued his political career until he retired in the 1970s. He is shown here in front of his barn.

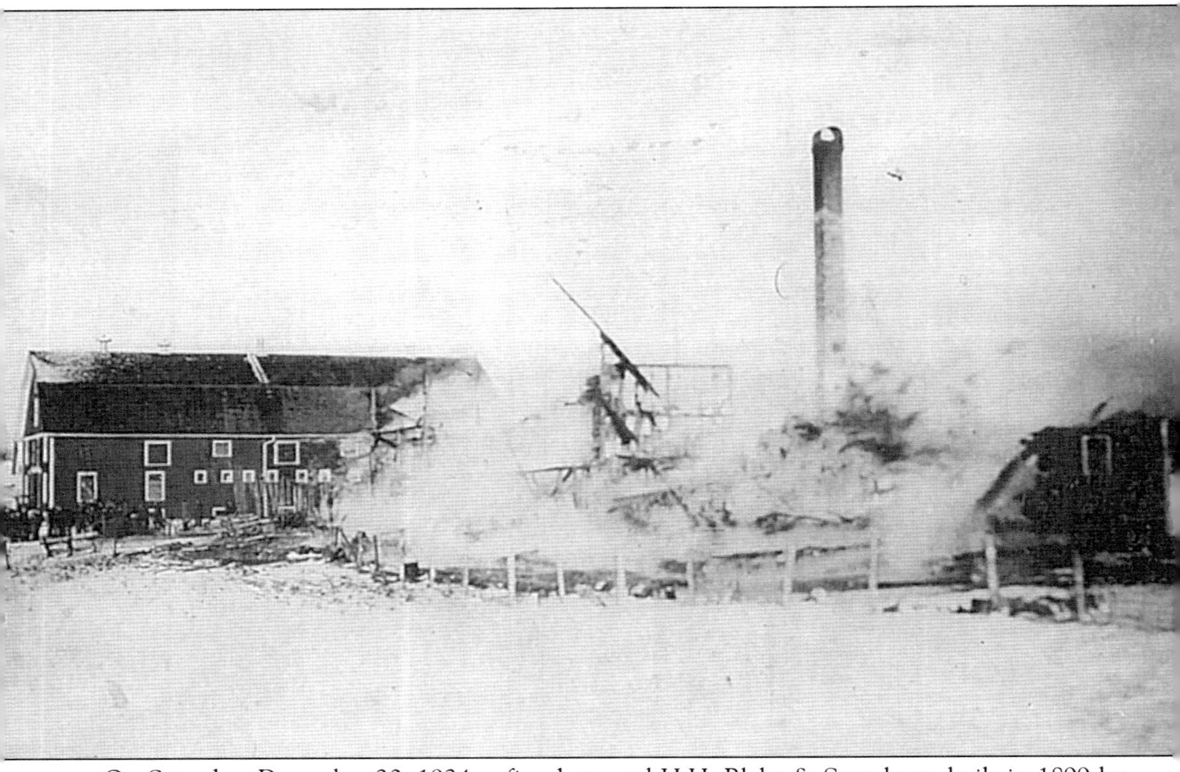

On Saturday, December 20, 1924, a fire destroyed H.H. Blake & Sons barn, built in 1899 by Major Grout. The barn used 100,000 feet of lumber and was 220 by 60 feet wide. Fire was started when a tractor moving out of the barn backfired and set a blaze resulting in a $50,000 loss. The wind to the west and northwest was all that saved Derby Center Village from being swept away by fire.

Three

Derby Line, Beebe, and North Derby, Vermont

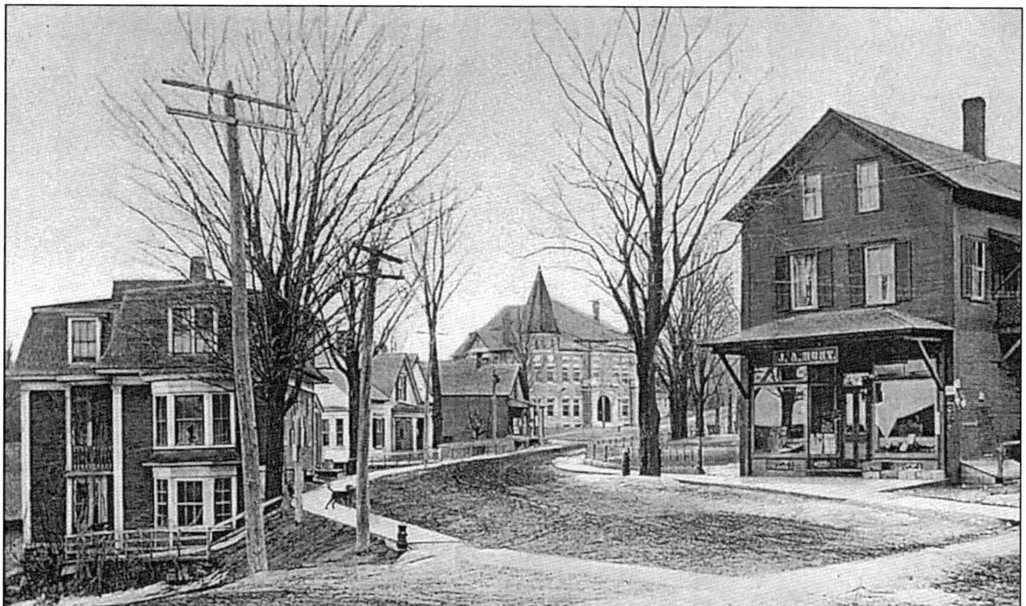

In 1901, Jerry A. Hunt opened a fancy new grocery store located at Liberty Square in Derby Line, Vermont. Hunt was born March 26, 1871, the son of Mitchell and Henrietta (Porter) Hunt. In 1896, he married Julia Ferry and reared two sons, Porter and Milton.

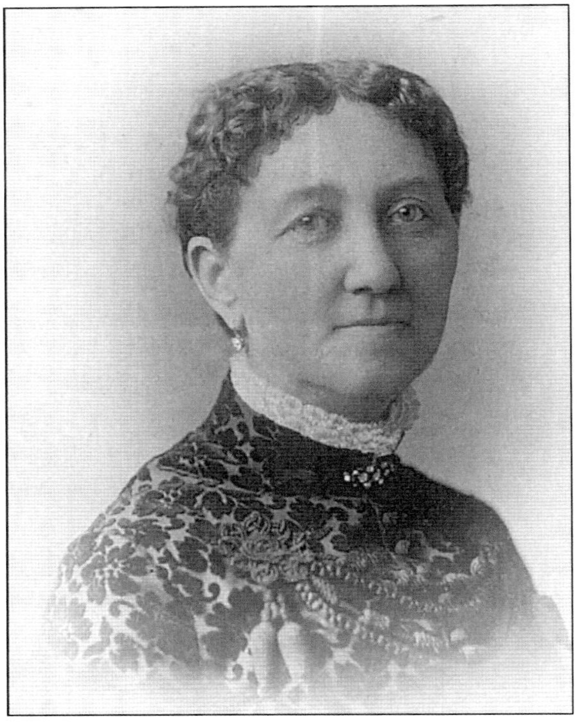

Martha (Stewart) Haskell was born April 28, 1831, the daughter of Horace Stewart and Catherine (Hinman) Stewart of Beebe Plain, Quebec. Martha's father was one of the wealthiest men in the country. Martha married Carlos Haskell in 1851 and, through both her parents and her husband's estates, became a wealthy woman. Her net worth at the time of her death in 1906 was in excess of $130,000.

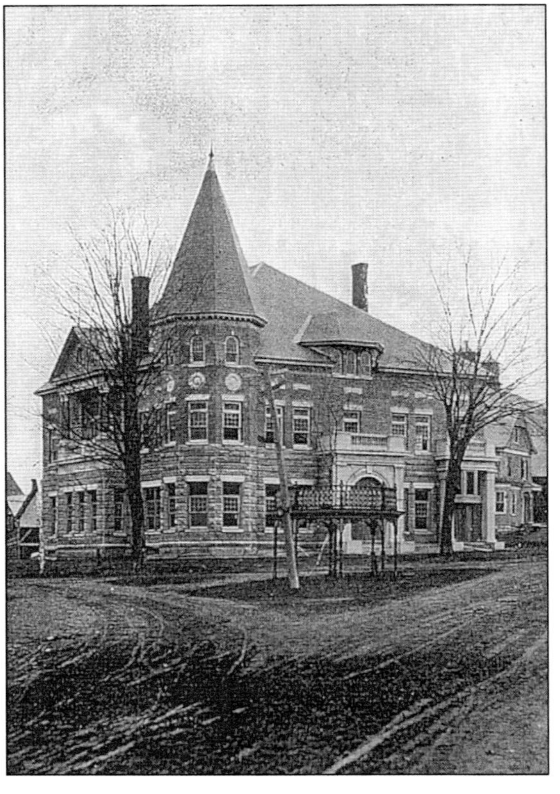

As a gift to Derby Line and Rock Island, Martha (Stewart) Haskell, together with her son Horace, erected in 1901 the magnificent Haskell Free Library and Opera House in memory of her late husband, Carlos. This world-famous institution straddles the Canadian-American border, and provides the border communities with a center of learning and culture.

Horace Stewart Haskell was born in Derby Line on August 9, 1860, the only child of Carlos and Martha. Horace received his formal education at the Derby Academy and was 18 years old in this 1878 photograph.

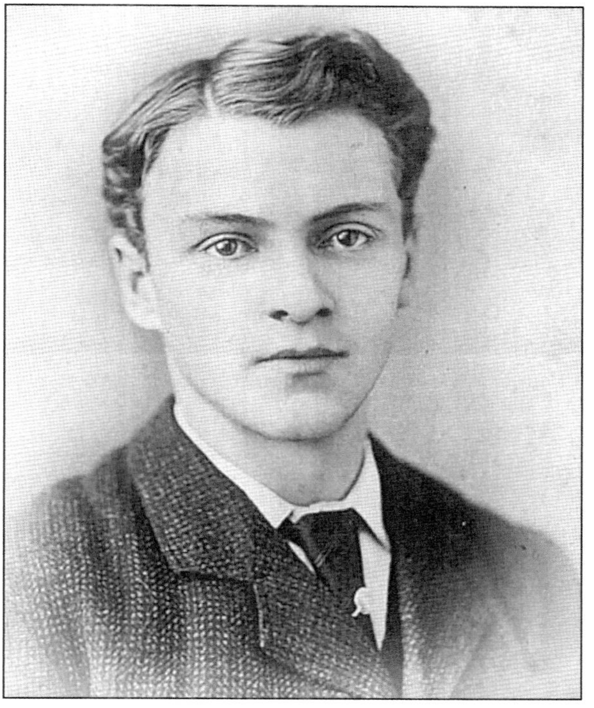

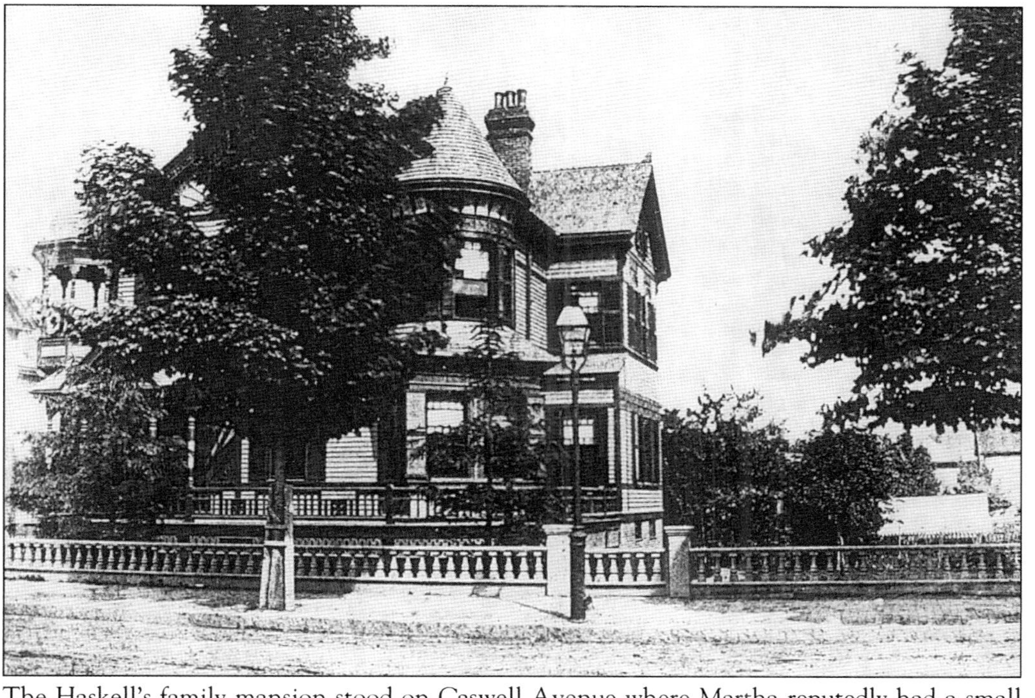

The Haskell's family mansion stood on Caswell Avenue where Martha reputedly had a small theatre on the third floor where she hosted plays and readings for her friends. Carlos Freeman Haskell, born in 1824 in Rock Island, Province of Quebec, inherited his father's business interests, which made him one of the wealthiest men on the border. He died in 1865.

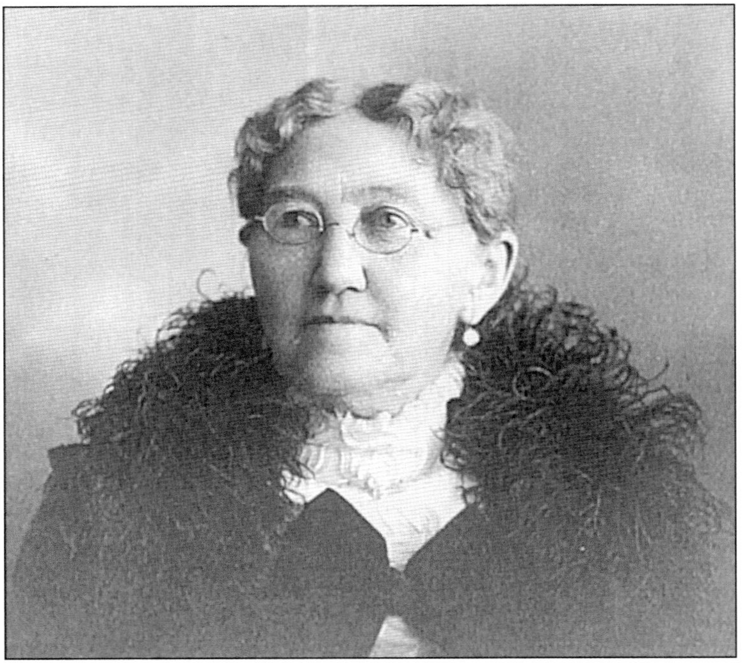

Martha (Stewart) Haskell lived to see this memorial to her late husband completed. An old-fashioned minstrel show took place, starring the late Eugene Cowles, composer of the song, "Forgotten," at the Dedication Ceremonies in 1904. Martha passed away on August 22, 1906.

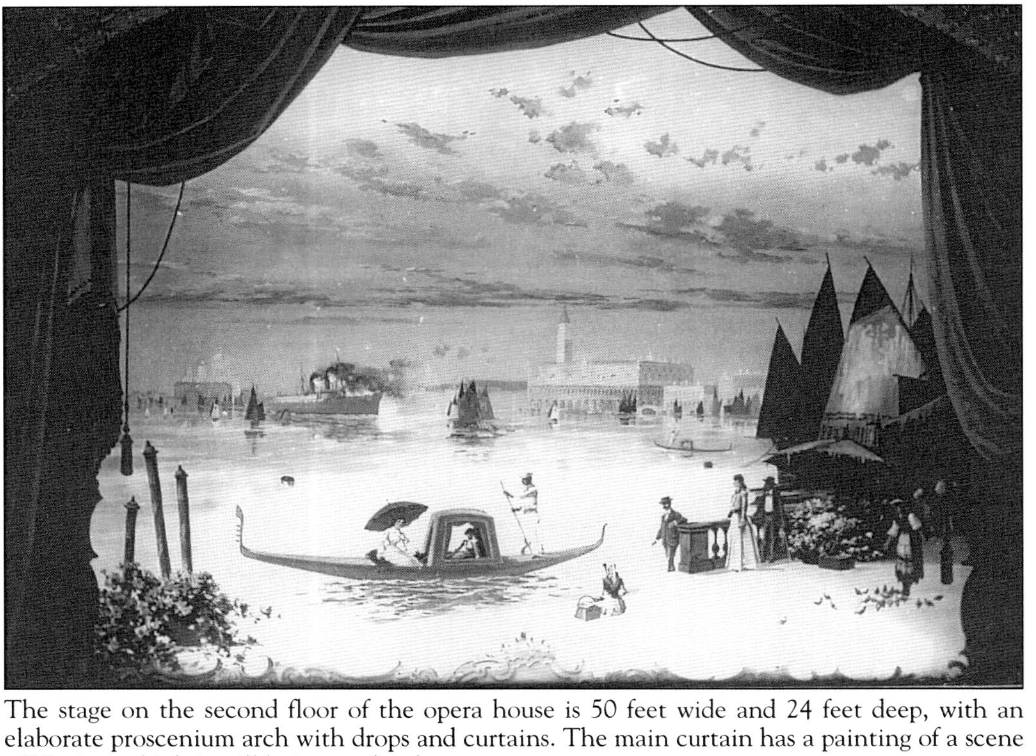

The stage on the second floor of the opera house is 50 feet wide and 24 feet deep, with an elaborate proscenium arch with drops and curtains. The main curtain has a painting of a scene of Venice, which is still being used today.

Colonel Horace Stewart Haskell in 1896 was made an aid-de-camp to Vermont governor Josiah Grout. He received the rank of Colonel, which he retained for the rest of his life. Haskell's first of three marriages was to Margaret Haven Sheafe, and they had a son, Tracey, born in1885. Colonel Haskell, shown in this 1896 photograph, died at Ocean Park, California, on September 29, 1940.

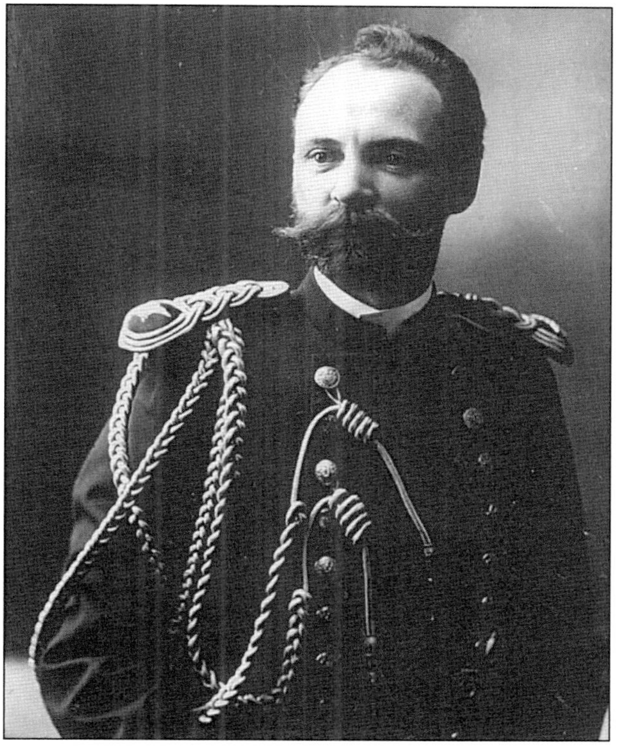

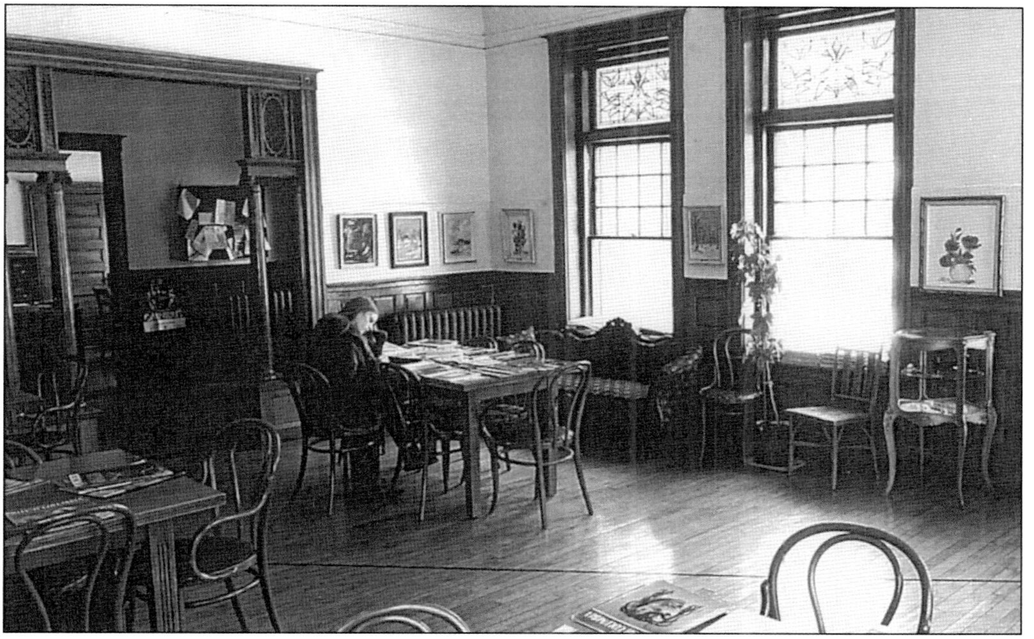

On the first floor of the Haskell Library, Ora M. Carpenter (1861–1932), the first librarian, once stood behind the desk, which is in Canada. In the reading room, the dividing line between Canada and the United States is marked by a block line on the floor—the building was constructed along the Quebec/Vermont Border.

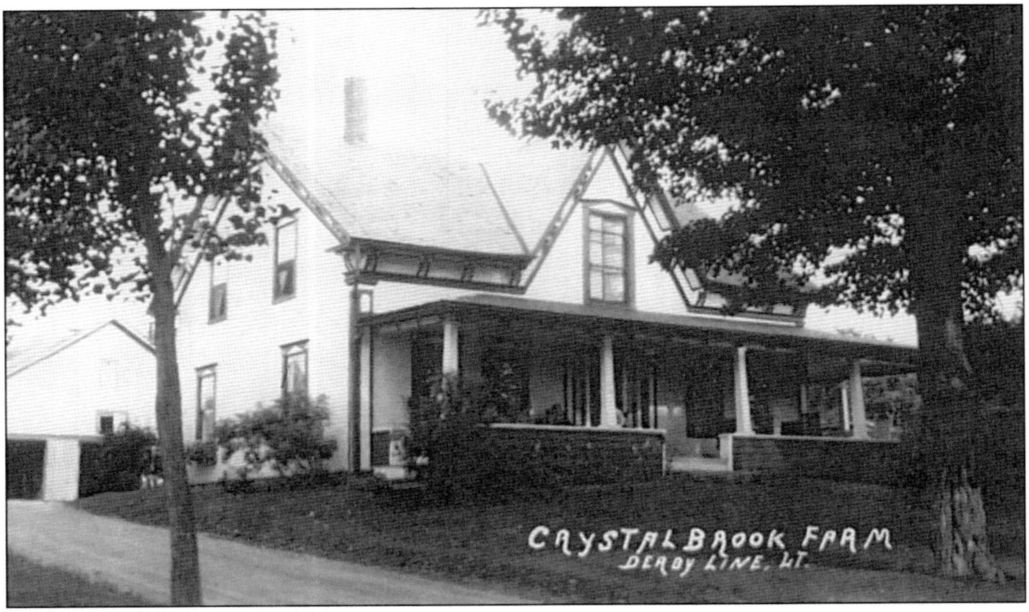

Crystal Brook Farm and Home could accommodate 15 guests with airy sleeping rooms, two porches, and shade trees. These were a few of the attractions where guests became friends. Clarence B. Kelly, Derby born, bought this 700-acre farm in 1916 with 100 milk and beef cattle. Kelly sold sandwiches and ice cream to tourists from his gas station on the main road.

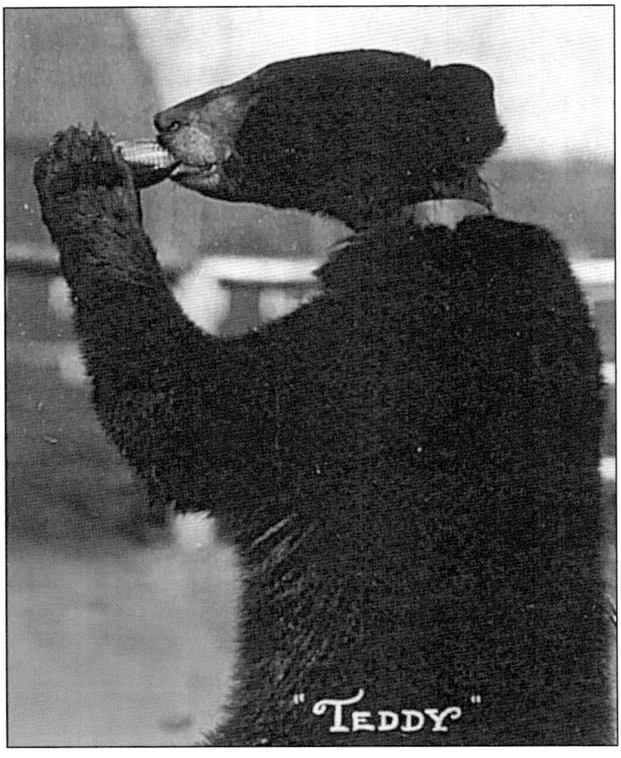

By 1925, Crystal Brook Farm was a popular tourist resort with a miniature zoo of monkeys, deer, and a black bear named "Teddy." Crowds of people enjoyed Sunday drives to Derby Line to see "Teddy," the zoo's main attraction. Today's grown-up children remember saving their nickels so they could buy a soft drink for "Teddy."

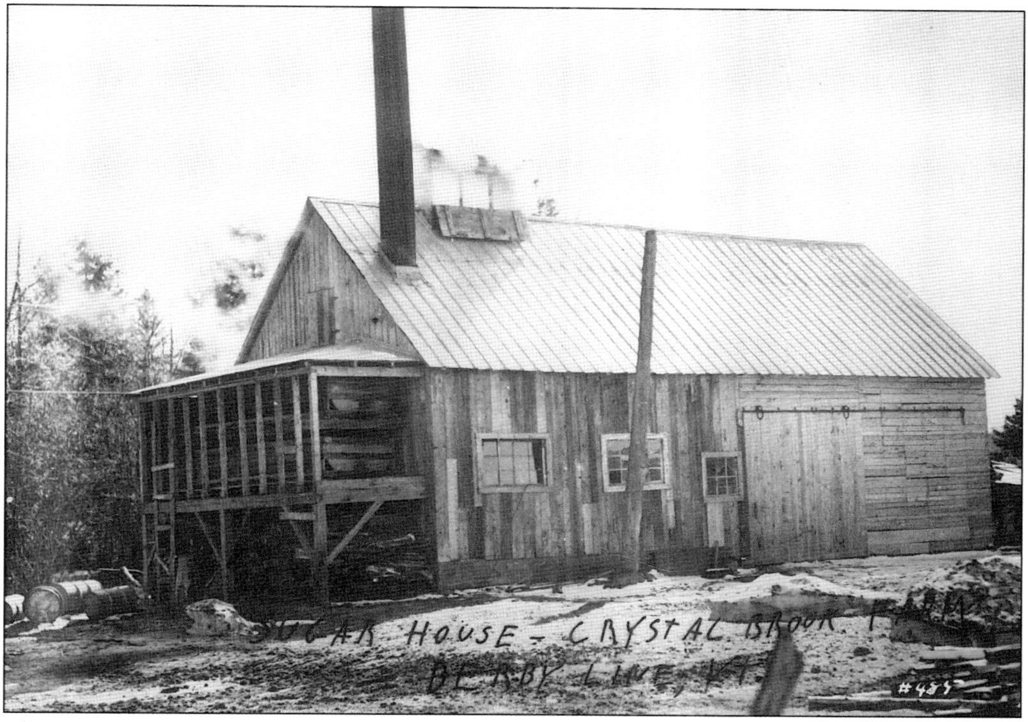

The Crystal Brook Farms maple syrup was gathered by a horse-drawn wooden sled in the spring and boiled down at the Farms sugar house in the woods. (Courtesy of Richardson Cartee Collection.)

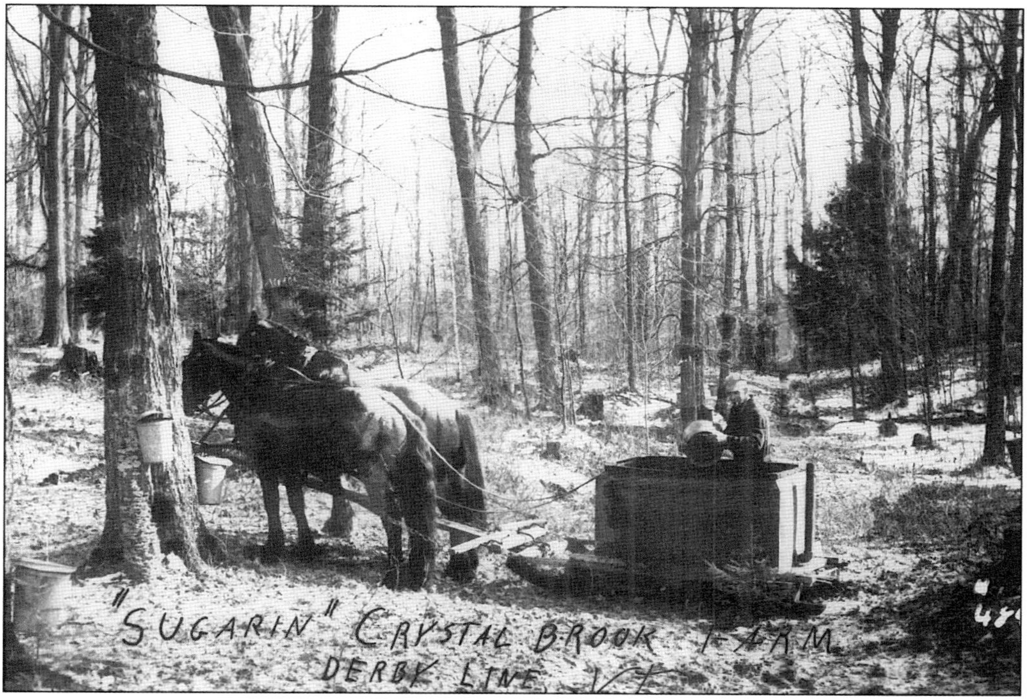

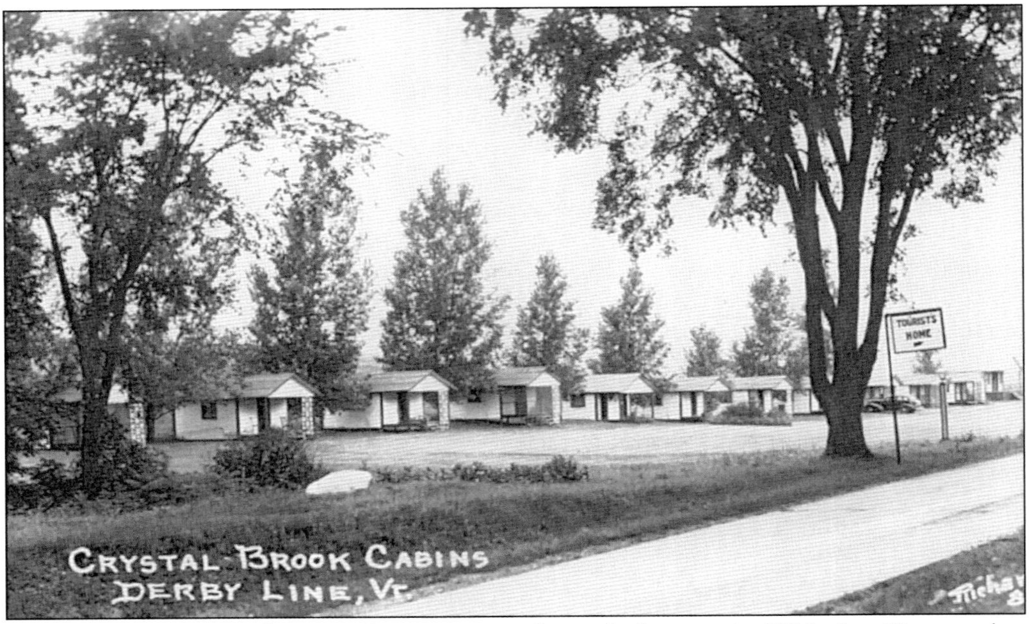

Crystal Brook Farm and Motor Court came to the end of an era in 1975 after 50 years that included saddle riding, fly and bait fishing, and freedom to roam the farm. An auction saw the disposal of the cabins where C.B. Kelly and his three sons, Lawrence, Prescott, and Winston, provided farm fresh milk, eggs, and maple syrup for those who sought the quiet, healthy atmosphere of the country.

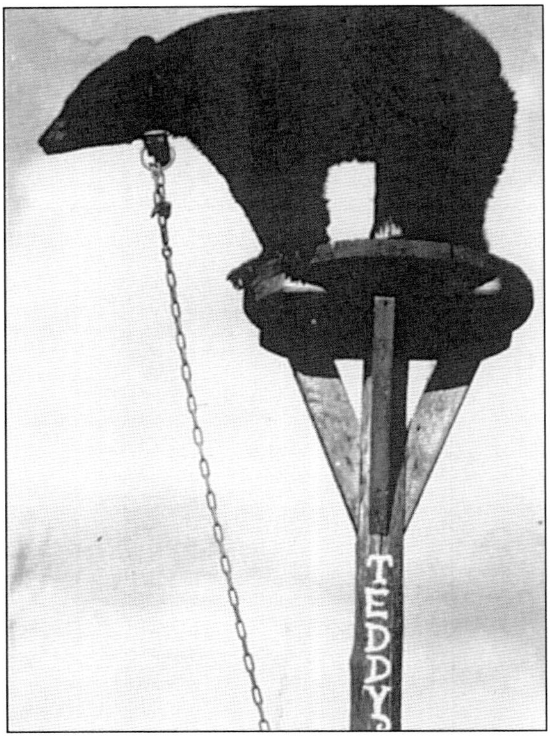

"Teddy" the big black bear would entertain the crowds as he would climb up and down his stand and perch on the top of his pole to gain attraction. Loved by several generations of children and adults on the Kelly's farm, "Teddy" died on May 31, 1935.

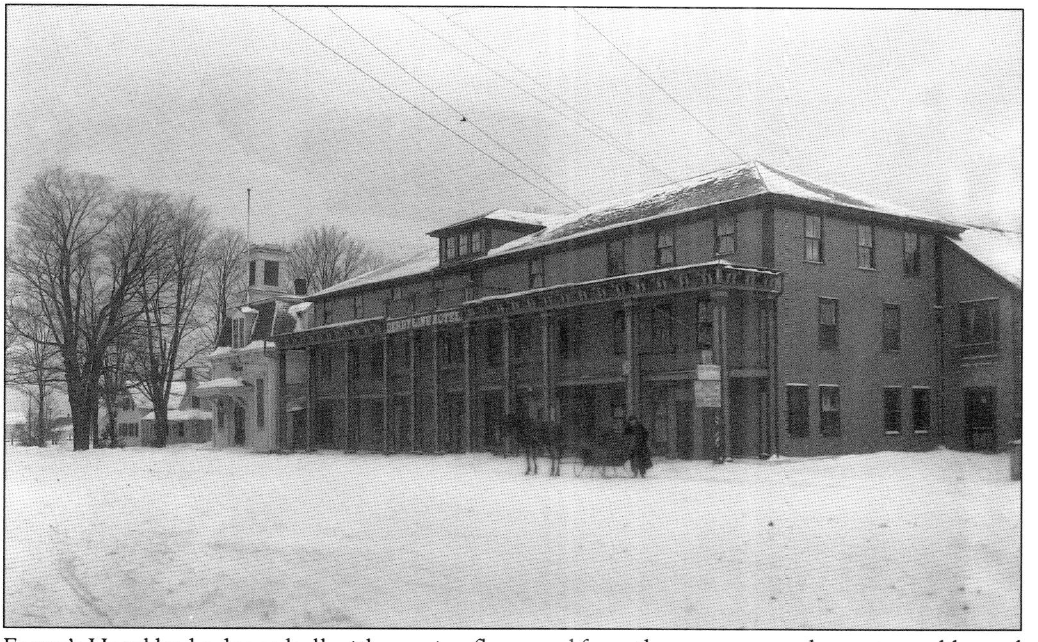

Foster's Hotel had a dance hall with a spring floor, and from the upper verandas orators addressed crowds and viewed parades. The People's Bank, founded in 1851, known today as Community National Bank, was located in this hotel for years.

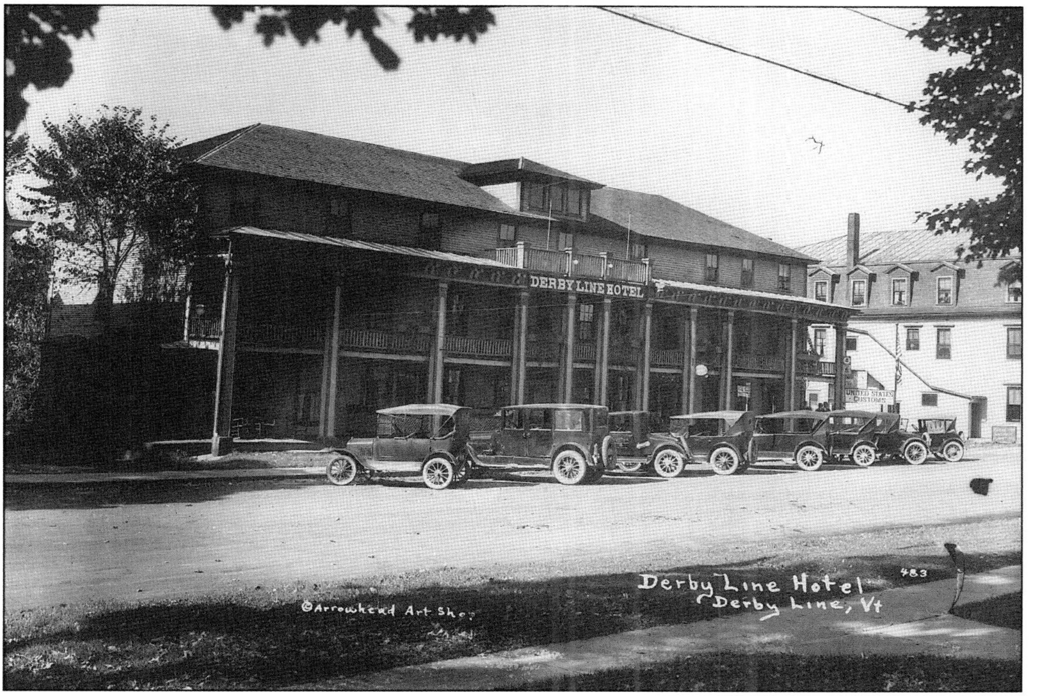

On July 4, 1789, President George Washington, in order to raise funds to operate the government, established the United States Customs Service, which celebrated its 200 years in 1989. (Courtesy of Richardson Cartee Collection.)

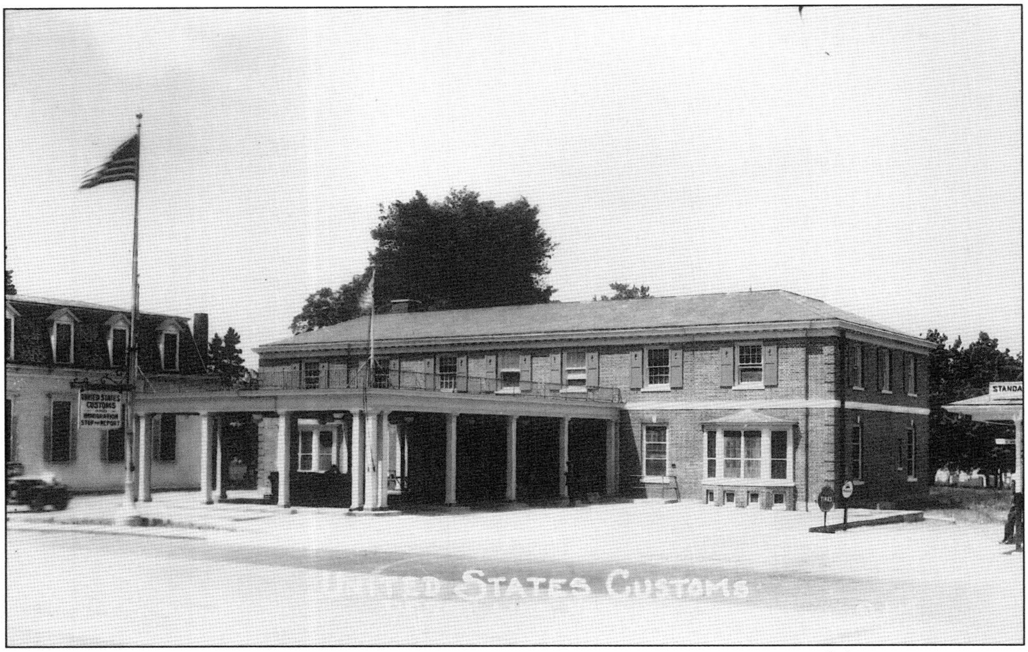

Captain Foster's Hotel, a historic landmark, once occupied the present site of the U.S. Customs and Immigration Inspection building in Derby Line, just over the border from Canada. (Courtesy of Richardson Cartee Collection.)

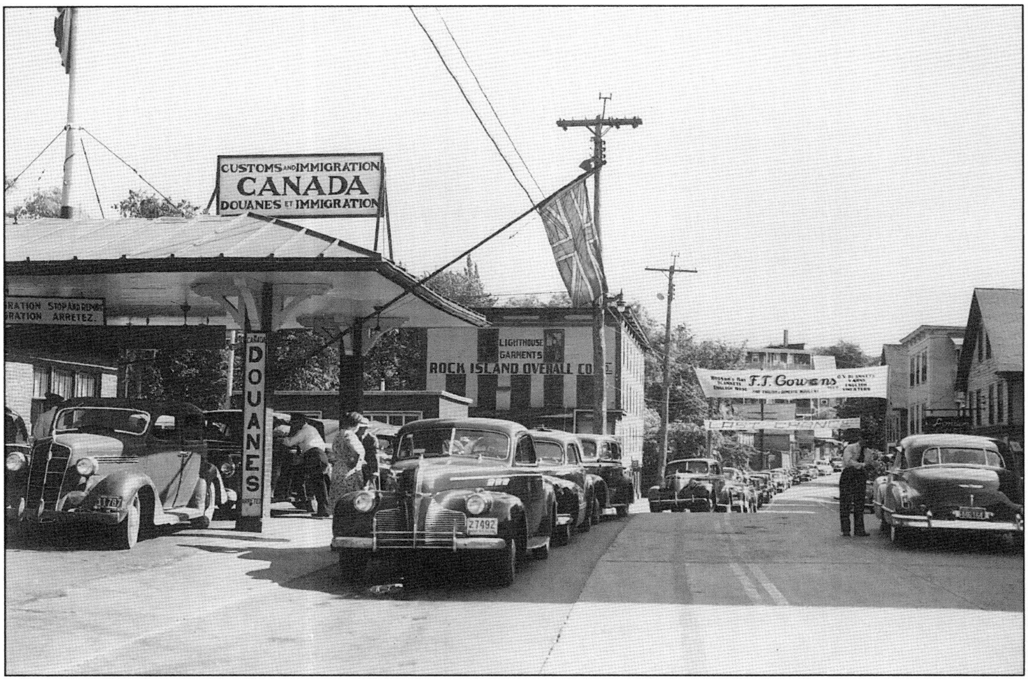

The old hotel was sold to the United States government and demolished in 1931. A new and modern building was built for the U.S. Customs and Immigration Office. (Courtesy of Richardson Cartee Collection.)

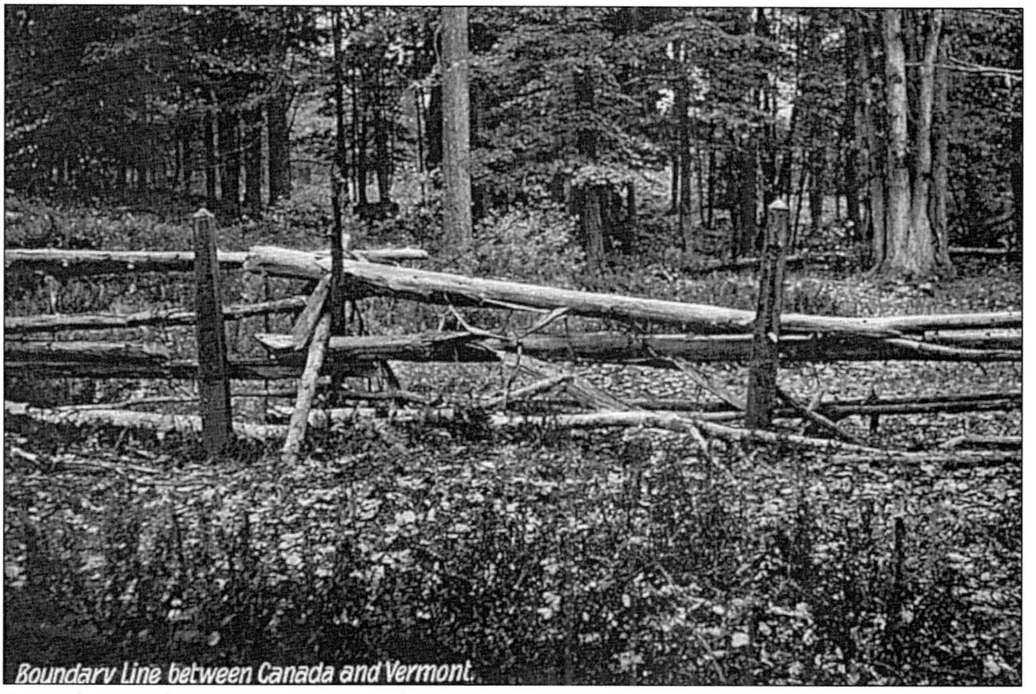

Smuggling, a favorite pastime on the Vermont-Canadian border, became a profitable and respected way of life in the 1800s. Stolen goods were left in the woods or cattle crossed the borders following a path of grain. Smuggling got its start as a result of the Embargo Act, designed to stop trade with the British. The smugglers found humor in the fact that the word "embargo" spelled backwards reads "O-grab-me."

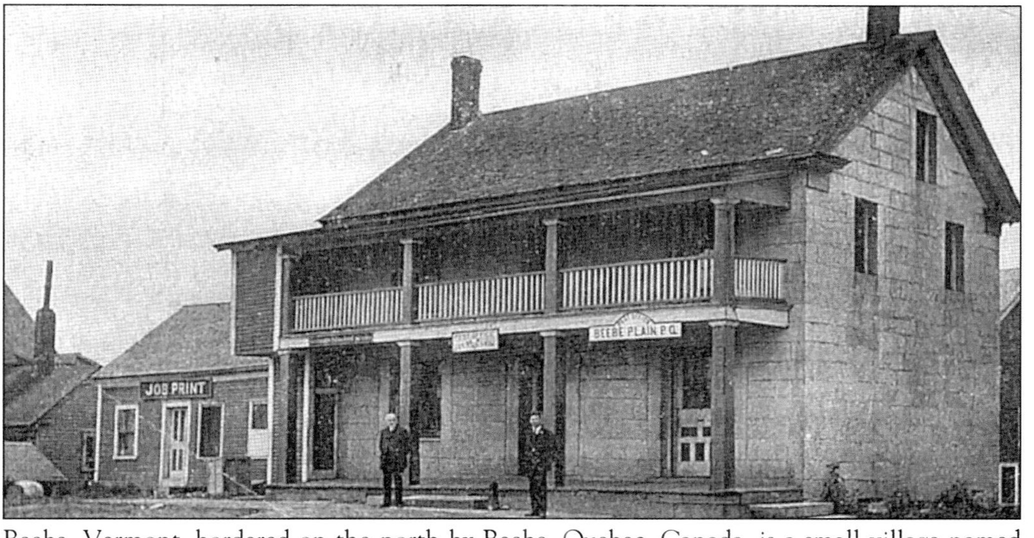

Beebe, Vermont, bordered on the north by Beebe, Quebec, Canada, is a small village named after its first settler, Zebulon Beebe, in 1796. The International Post Office of Beebe, Vermont, and Beebe, Quebec, were joined together in one building constructed of granite. Can-USA Street starts here with Beebe, Vermont, and Beebe, Quebec's border running in the center of the street, known as the friendliest "unguarded" border in the world.

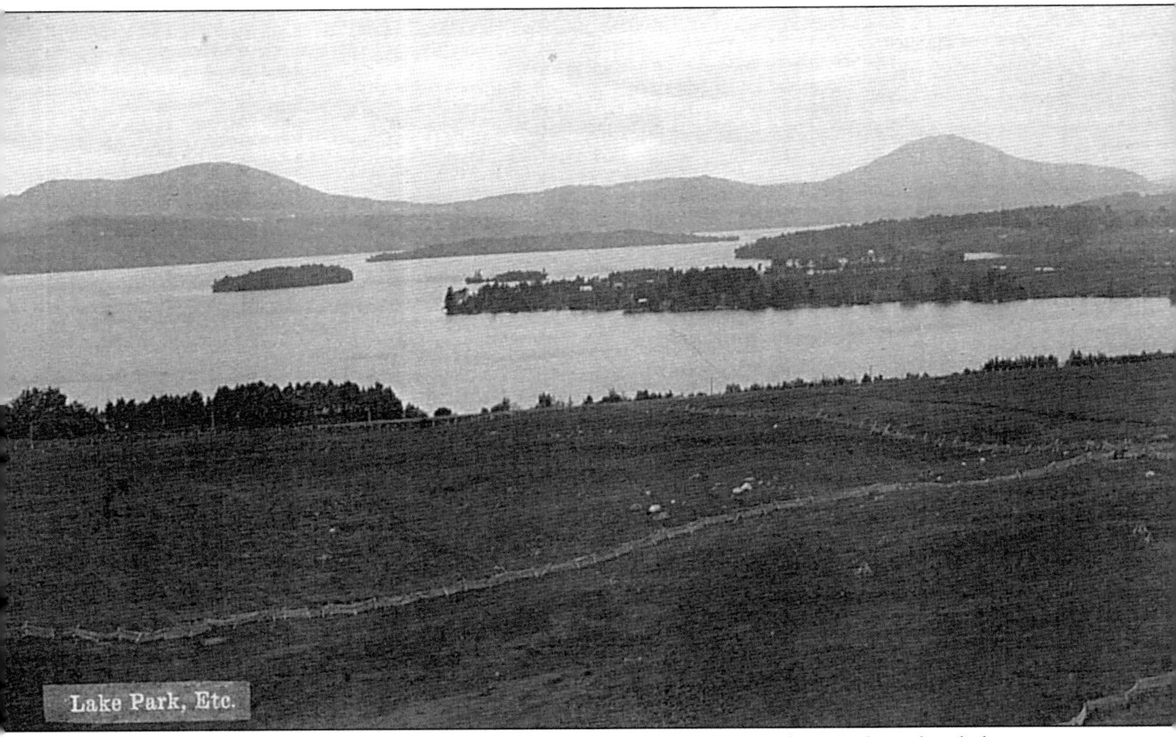

Located in North Derby, Lake Park in the 1880s was Selon Jackson's farm land that was soon to become summer cottages on its shores. Frederick D. Butterfield and Riley Caswell signed the first lease with Jackson on July 22, 1886. Lake Park on Lake Memphremagog was named by Dr. Myron L. Baxter's son, the Honorable Portus Baxter, who retired to his old home in Derby Line. Baxter often occupied one of the Butterfield's bedroom cottages when cartpaths lead to summer cottages in the late 1800s.

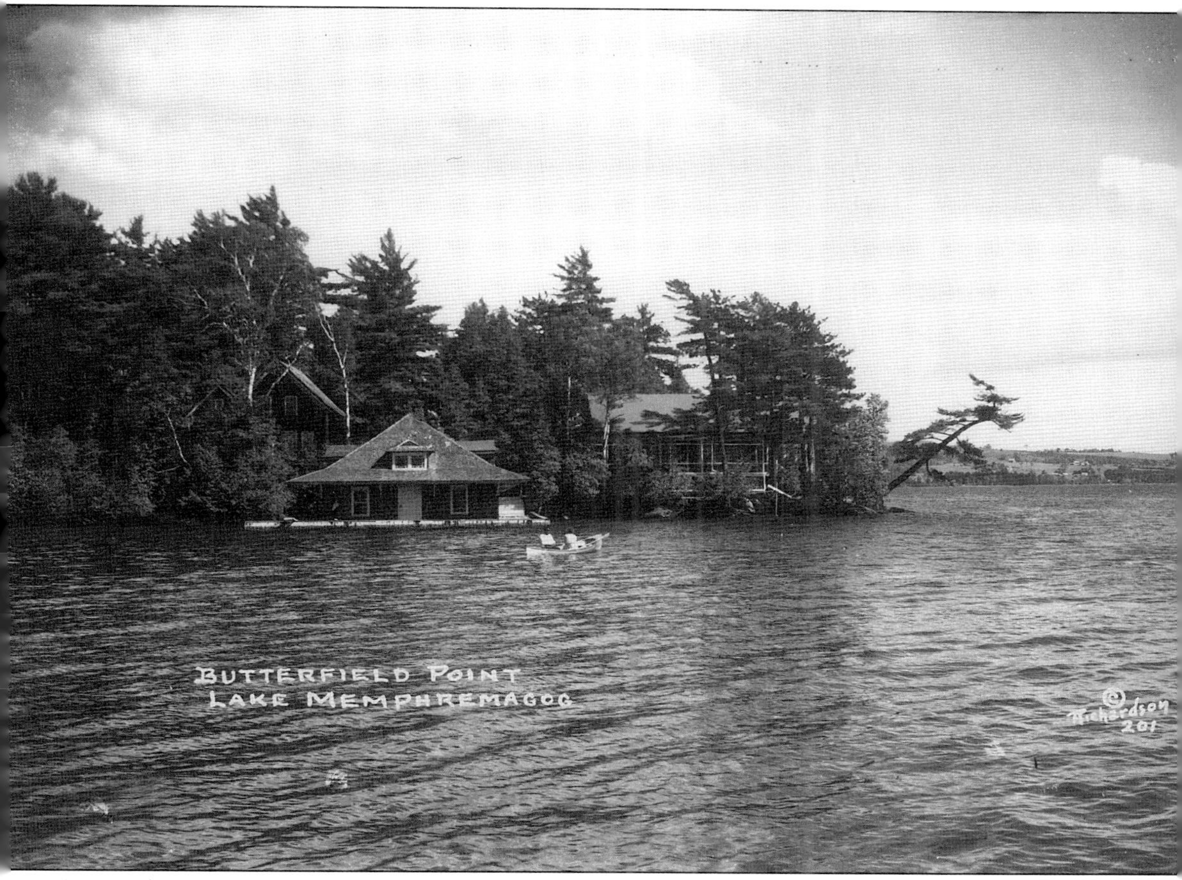

At North Derby's Lake Park with views of Province Island was Butterfield Point, owned by Col. Frederick D. Butterfield, who played a prominent part in the development. Butterfield and his wife Ellen (Morrill) had three children, Ellen, Charlotte, and Benjamin, and built several bedroom cabins. They renamed the point Kittemaug. Here they entertained guests and friends from Washington, and, on both sides of the border on summer evenings, it was a social center of the region. At the shore line at Kittemaug a century ago one could see the lone pine tree that still projects out over the waters of the lake, even though its days are slowly slipping away. The Butterfields had a launch and a spacious boathouse where they kept the first electric boat on the lake, the *Kittemaug*, that made its maiden voyage on July 9, 1905. Col. F.G. Butterfield built a private electric line at a cost of $1,000 to Lake Park, just to recharge the batteries in his launch. (Courtesy of Richardson Cartee Collection.)

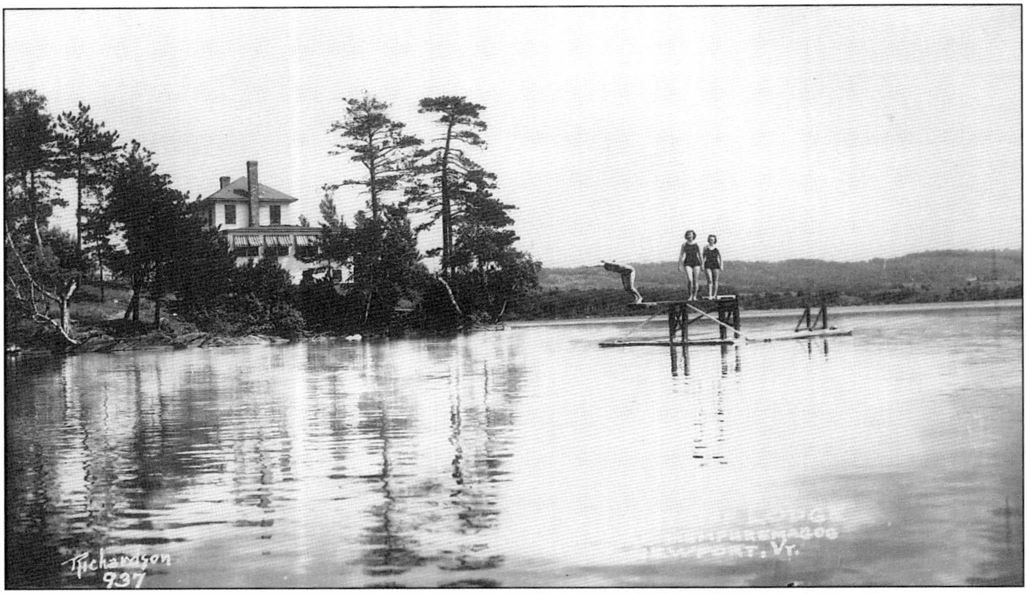

At North Derby on Lake Memphremagog stood Pine Bluff Lodge. In the early part of the century it was a popular summer resort, before the 1960s when the lodge was renovated into a private home. During the summer months in the late 1800s, local Native Americans would come around the lake in canoes to sell baskets of sweet grass, which were always popular with the ladies. (Courtesy of Richardson Cartee Collection.)

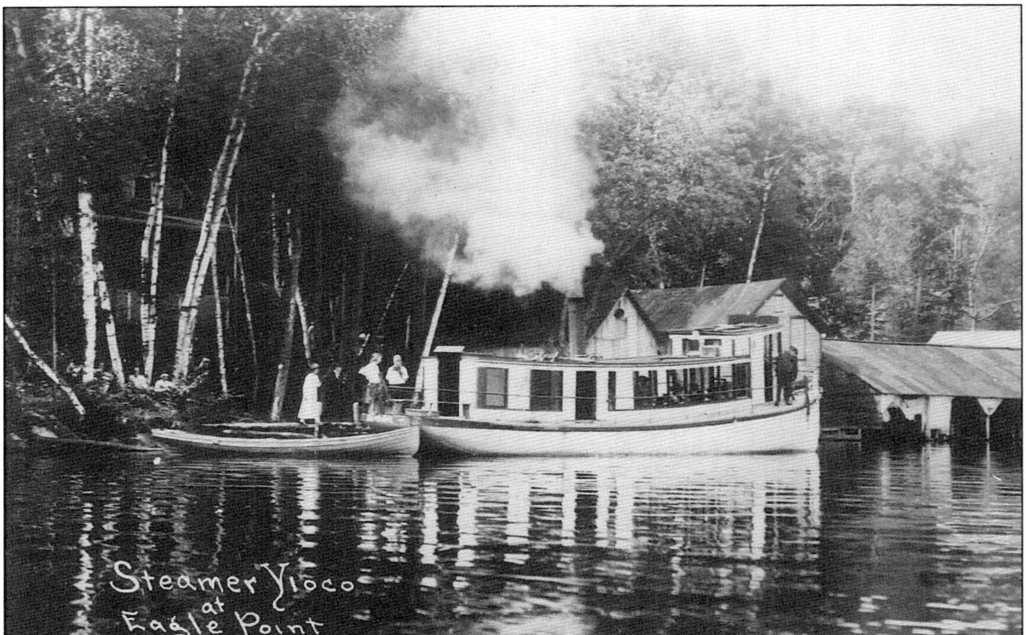

Captain Samuel H. Holbrook's 30-foot steamboat *Yioco* was launched in July of 1903, with headquarters at Lake Park for many years. The boat was very much in demand for Sunday school picnics and private parties, until the death of Holbrook in 1919. (Courtesy of Richardson Cartee Collection.)

Four

Owl's Head Mountain

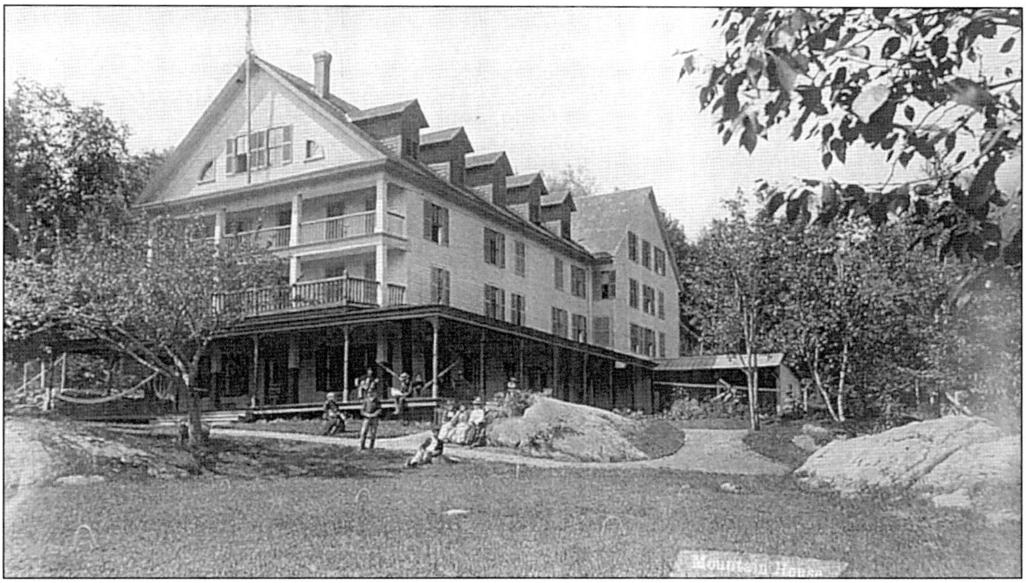

The first Mountain House Hotel was erected in 1858 at the foot of Owl's Head Mountain, Quebec, on the western shore of Lake Memphremagog. It was destroyed by a fire. In 1881, Emmons Raymond of Newport and president of the Passumpsic Railroad bought the property and engaged in the remodeling of this once popular summer resort for those on both sides of the Vermont/Canadian border.

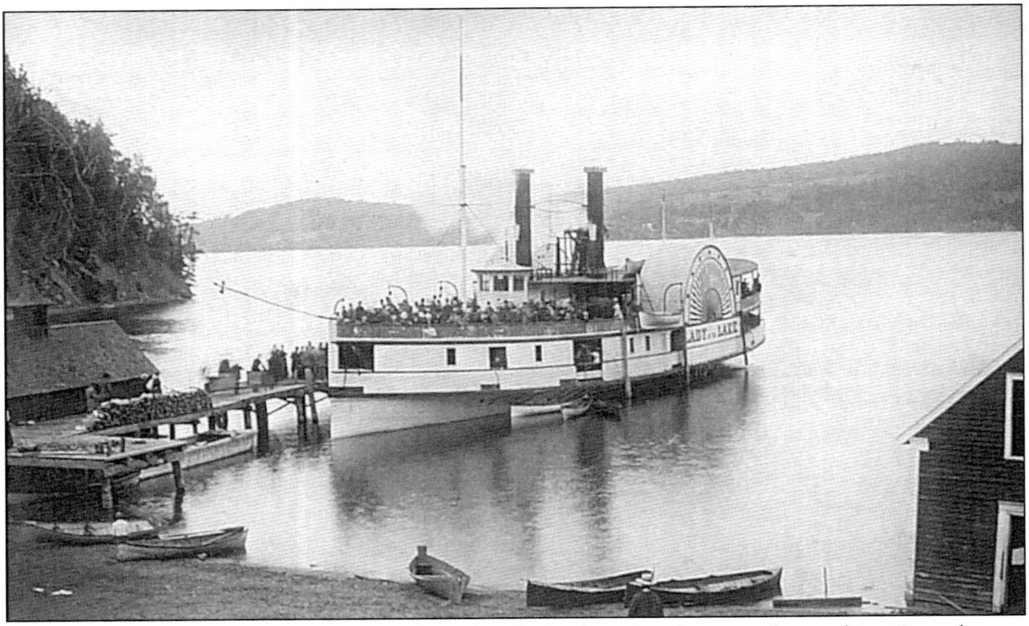

Emmons Raymond used the *Lady of the Lake*, docked at the shore, to house his 40 workmen. They also brought running water to the hotel, a walkway to the new boat wharf, and a path to the summit, a most desirable romantic spot on Lake Memphremagog.

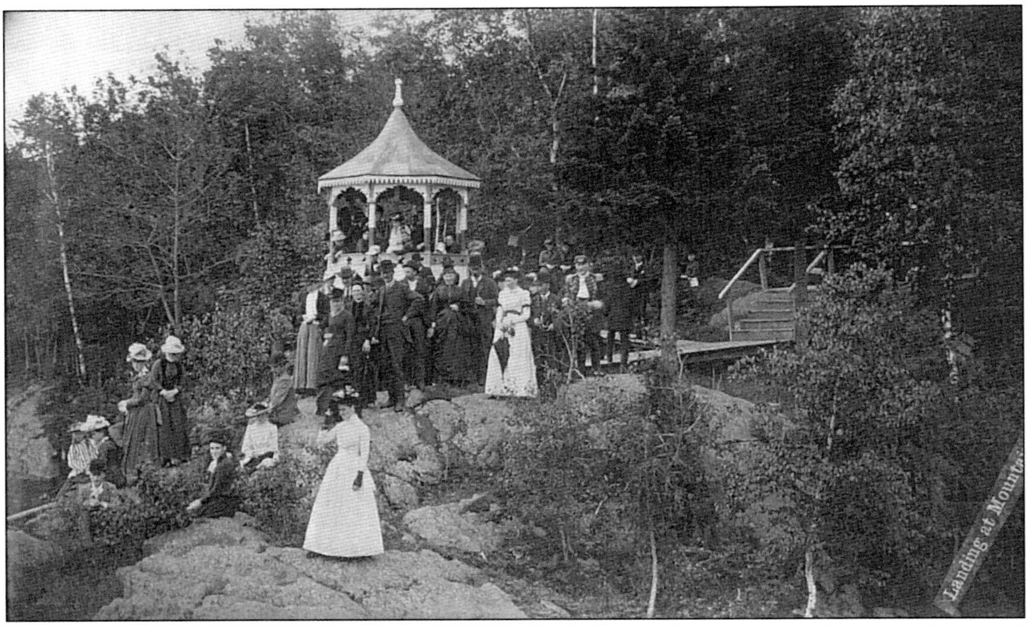

A gathering occurred on the steps of Owl's Head Landing, where paths dodge in and out and around huge boulders, and where Owl Head Mountain reaches 2,484 feet above sea level or about 1,800 feet above the lake. Picturesque in shape, the mountain rising directly from the water and dominating the whole region, always holds one under the fascination of its beauty.

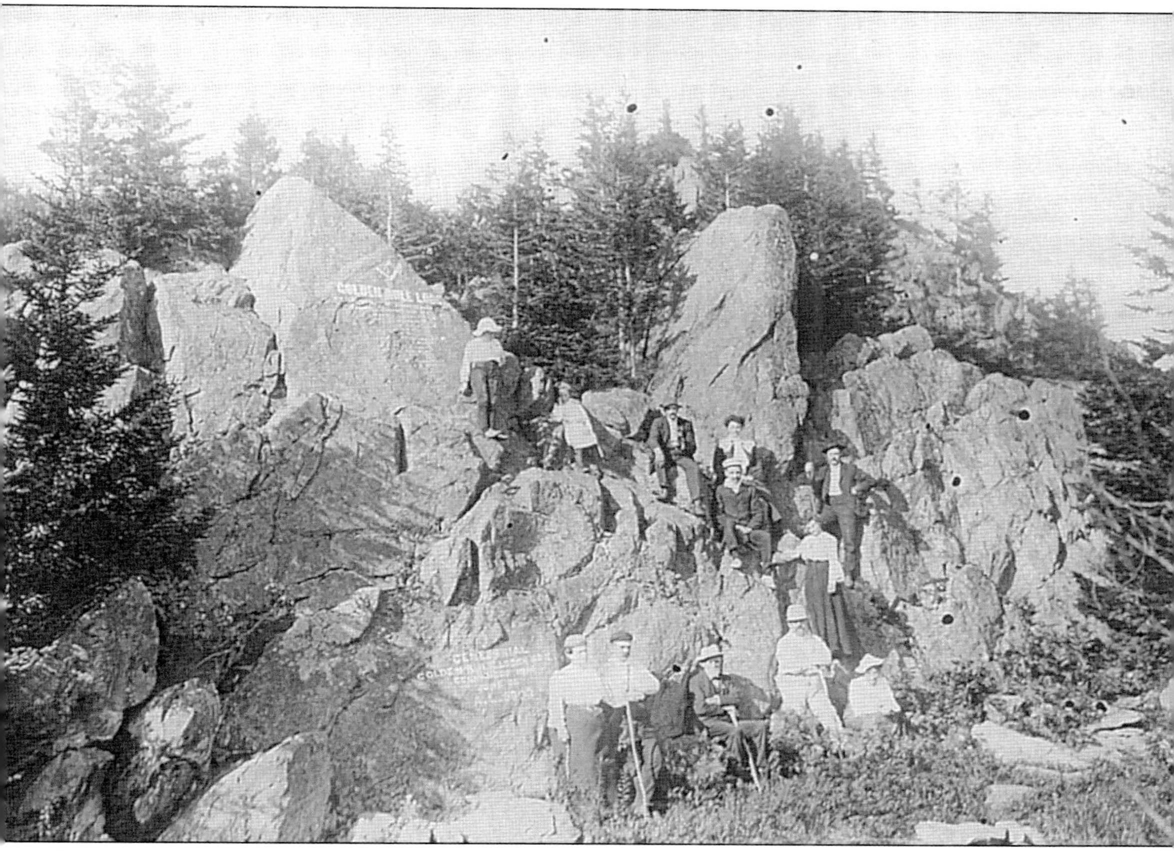

On September 10, 1857, for the first time in the history of the Craft (Free Masonry) in America, a lodge was opened on top of a high hill that was a "Natural Lodge Room" at Owl's Head Mountain in the Province of Quebec.

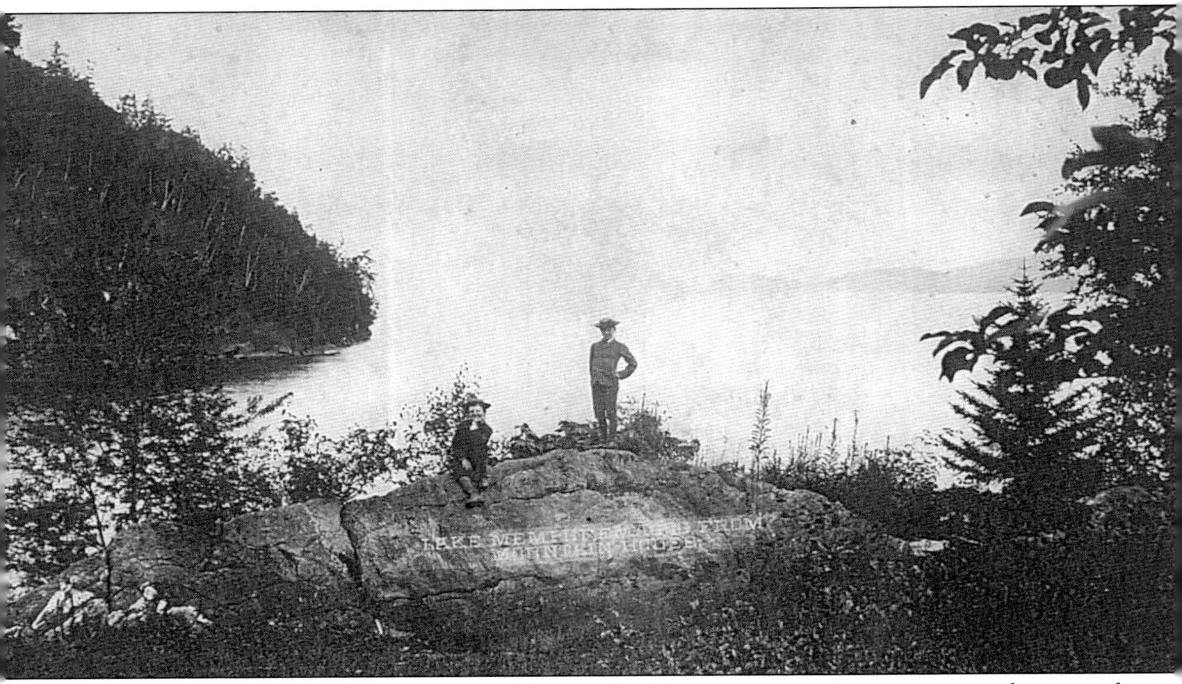

Once every year on June 24, Free Masonry holds an open Lodge meeting under special dispensation given by the Master of the Grand Lodge of Canada to Golden Rule Lodge of Stanstead, Quebec, Canada. The cabalistic signs of the order are cut on the walls of this mountain known as Owl's Head.